AF606640

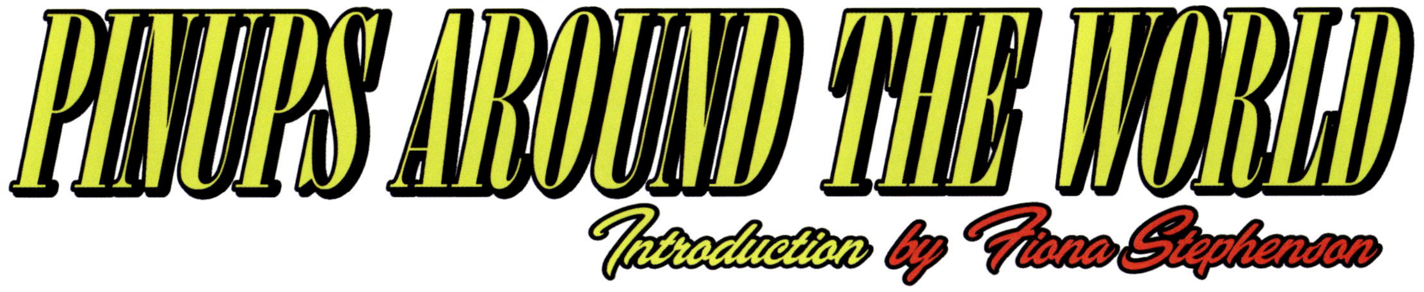
PINUPS AROUND THE WORLD
Introduction by Fiona Stephenson

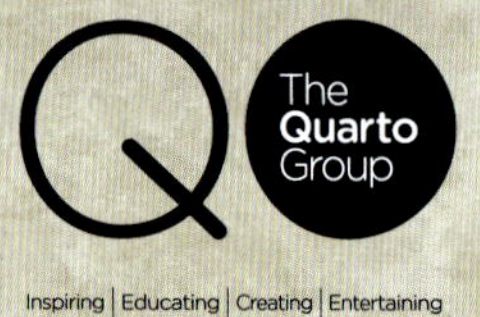

Brimming with creative inspiration, how-to projects, and useful information to enrich your everyday life, quarto.com is a favorite destination for those pursuing their interests and passions.

This edition published in the United States in 2022 by Chartwell Books,
an imprint of The Quarto Group,
142 West 36th Street, 4th Floor, New York, NY 10018, USA
T (212) 779-4972 F (212) 779-6058
www.Quarto.com

Published under license from Graffito Books Ltd, London 2020
www.graffitobooks.com

Chartwell Books titles are also available at discount for retail, wholesale, promotional, and bulk purchase.
For details, contact the Special Sales Manager by email at specialsales@quarto.com or by mail at The Quarto Group, Attn: Special Sales Manager, 100 Cummings Center Suite, 265D, Beverly, MA 01915, USA.

10 9 8 7 6 5 4 3 2 1

ISBN: 978-0-7858-3796-1

Library of Congress Cataloging-in-Publication Data
Names: Stephenson, Fiona (Comic book artist), writer of introduction.
Title: Pinups around the world / introduction by Fiona Stephenson ;
general editor, Lucy Radford-Earle.
Description: New York : Chartwell Books, 2020. | Includes index. | Summary:
"Pinups Around the World features 200+ new images from the greatest
pinup artists of today with a vintage look at developments throughout
the history of pinup design"-- Provided by publisher.
Identifiers: LCCN 2020007129 | ISBN 9780785837961 (hardcover)
Subjects: LCSH: Pinup art--Themes, motives.
Classification: LCC NC778 .P57 2020 | DDC 741.5/6--dc23
LC record available at https://lccn.loc.gov/2020007129

General Editor: Lucy Radford-Earle
Art Director: Karen Wilks

Printed in China

PINUPS AROUND THE WORLD

Introduction by Fiona Stephenson

Lucy Radford-Earle

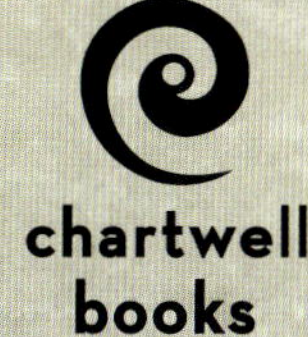

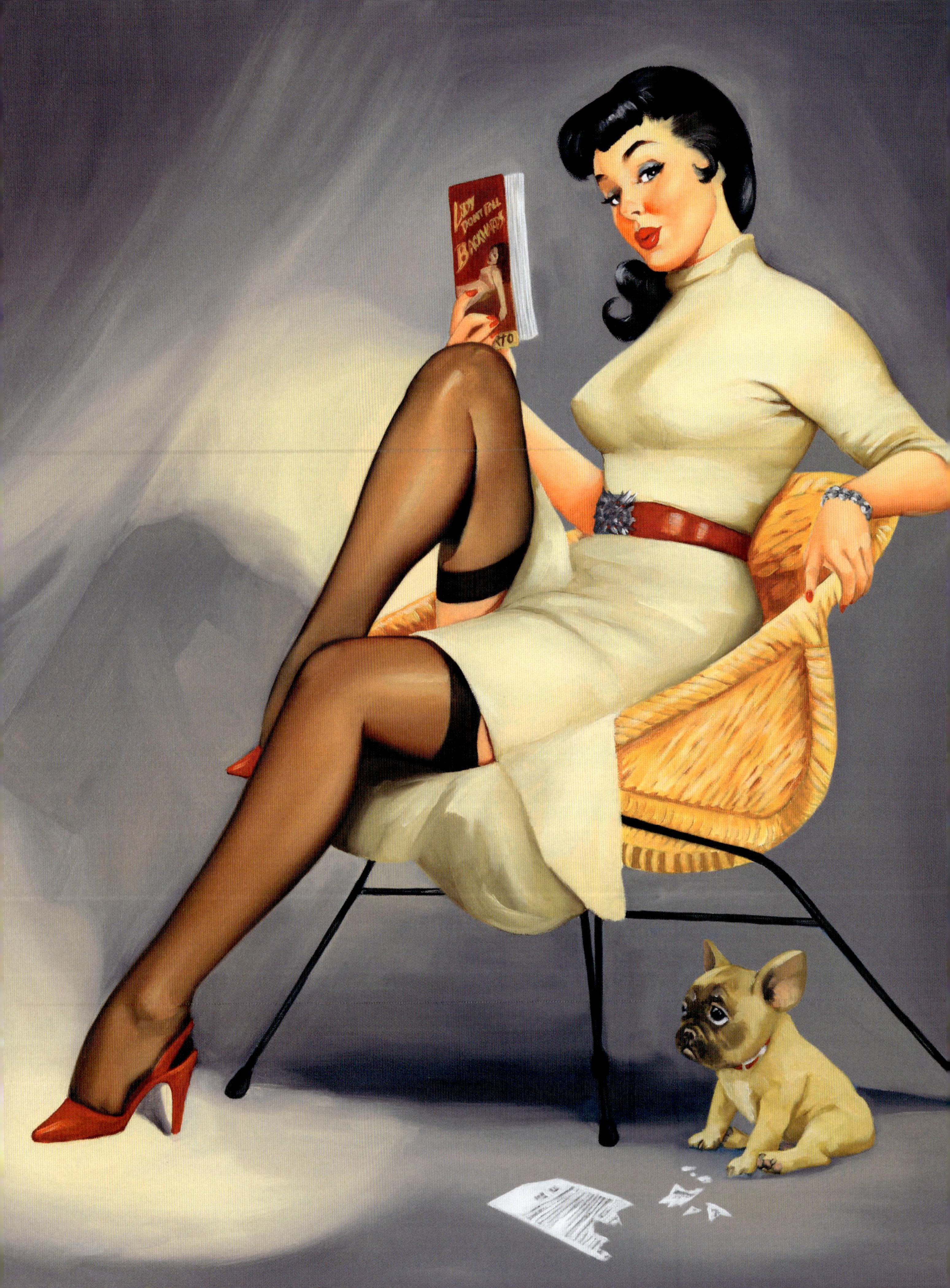

Contents

LEFT: ***Unsolved Miss-Tery***
Fiona Stephenson

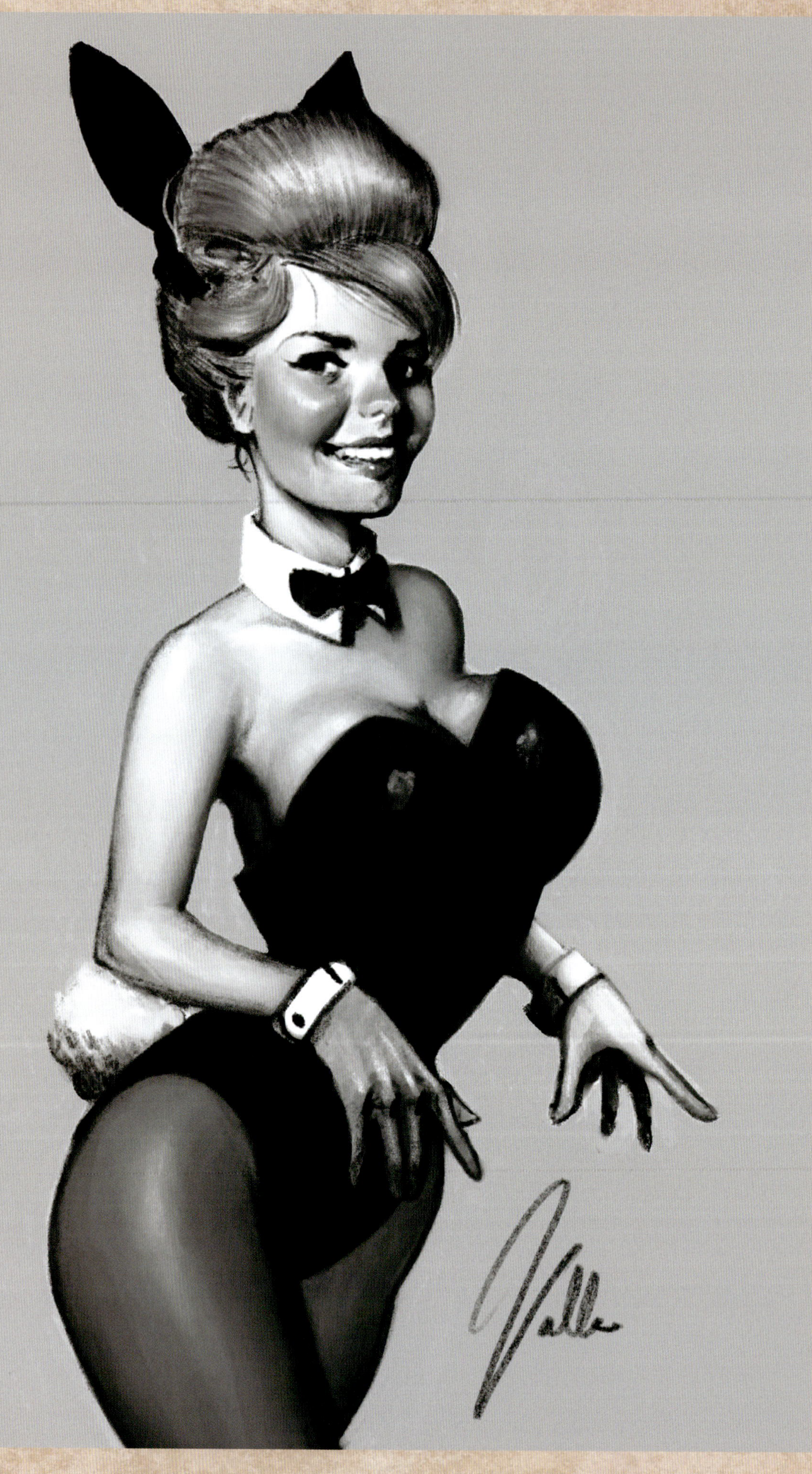

Introduction

I fell in love with pinup art the moment I saw the work of Gil Elvgren. I was working as a comic letterer at the time and was perusing the stalls at the comic convention in San Diego when I came across a booth selling prints of his work. The second I got home I set myself the challenge of copying Elvgren's wonderful 'Quick Change,' a fabulous painting of a pouting, stocking-clad blonde changing a car tire. A couple of friends bought the painting and it hangs in their kitchen to this day. I haven't looked back since that first foray into painting and soon imitation was no longer enough for me; I just had to create my own originals.

For me, when it comes to painting it always starts with an idea. If I feel like drawing a burlesque dancer I begin by trawling the internet for outfits and poses that fit for the dream girl in my mind's eye. The girls you see in my paintings are an amalgamation of several images – I'll take a graceful hand from one picture, a gorgeous hairstyle from another. She is concocted piece by piece, detail by detail. Many artists use models or just one photographic source but in general I find this makes it tricky to stay true to that initial image in my head. One model who did epitomize the pinup genre is Bettie Page, whose success was built upon her spunky personality and bodacious sense of fun which set her apart from stylish, well-groomed peers like Marilyn Monroe and Jane Russell. Page was very risqué at the time but not so much as to alienate her fans. A contemporary model who comprises some of the same rare qualities as Bettie Page is Bernie Dexter, whose sexy, exuberant style has informed some of my paintings over my career.

Today, pinup art has maintained its vitality because what it stands for is timeless. We are, thankfully, no longer tied by the societal constraints of the 40s and 50s. Yet many artists, including myself, find inspiration within those classic boundaries, discovering something empowering about an image that manages to be sexy, not sleazy. Brimming with personality and charm, these women exist far beyond simple titillation. Yet, the future has also provided some welcome improvements too. When pinup began, the vast majority of famed artists were men but the past few decades have seen a surge of women artists creating, and receiving renown for, pinup art alongside some great new male artists. Everything shifts and develops with time; the variety of styles featured in *Pinups Around the World* is no different, serving as a testament to how the genre has grown and diversified over a century.

My tip for aspiring artists is an oldie but a goodie–practice makes perfect. Another thing I have learned over my career is that a commission you don't love and don't get excited about is not worth doing–your heart won't be in it and neither you nor the client will be happy. Keep creating; there are no shortcuts. My only regret is that I didn't start sooner!

Fiona Stephenson

LEFT: ***Bunny***
Ivan Valle

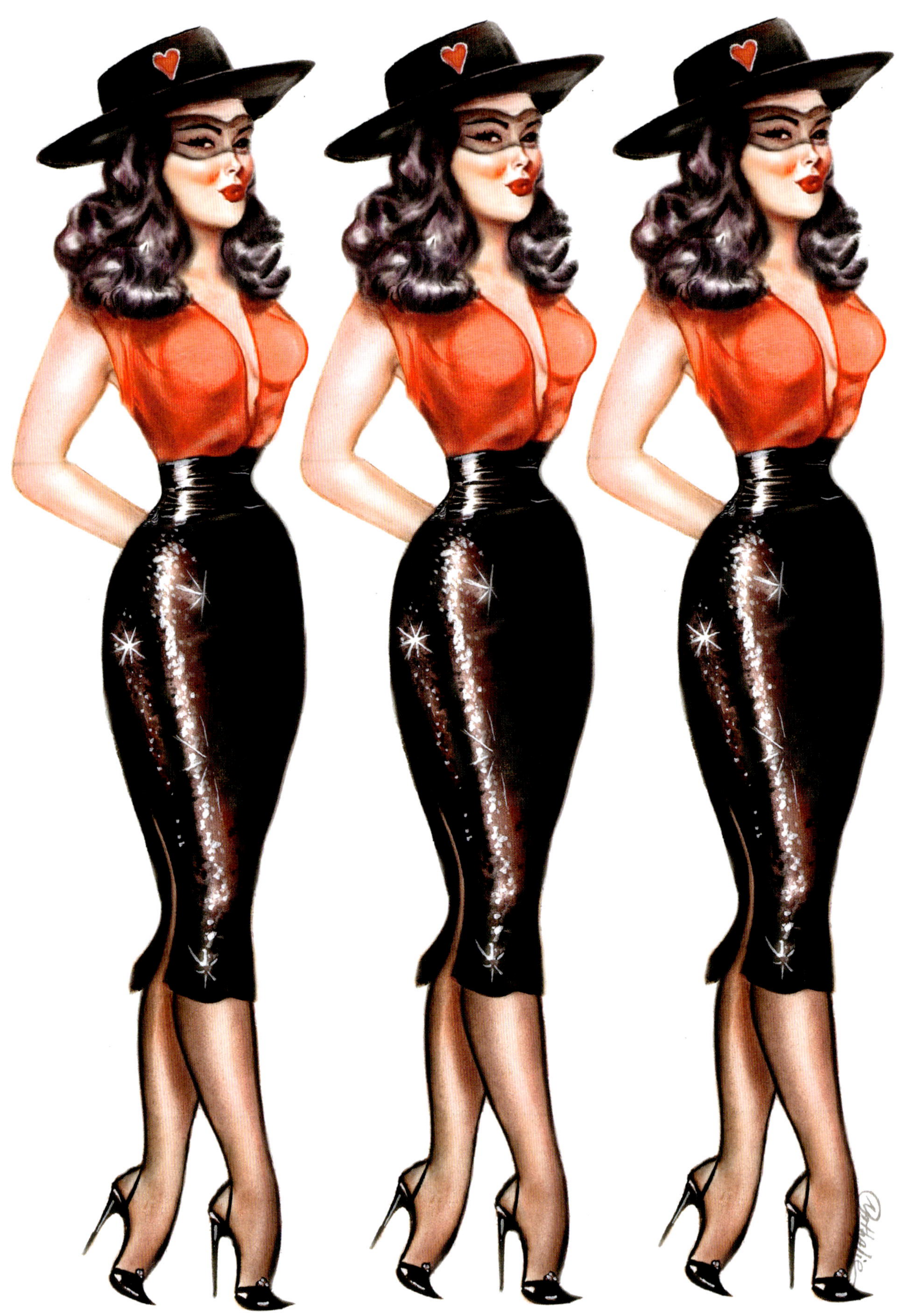

Classic American

The classic American pinup is bound to conjure a fond mental image of WWII era buxom babes, classy and sophisticated with a friendly, approachable and often ditzy persona. This imagery saw an explosion of popularity in the 1940s, with pictures often included for free in gentlemen's magazines to soldiers overseas looking for a comforting glimpse of what might be waiting for them at home. However, the concept was born much earlier; as far back as the late 1800s. Charles Dana Gibson, an illustrator for US Life magazine, drew inspiration for his fashion pieces from his wife and her family and drew sensuous, dark haired women with hourglass figures. This modern ideal of the female was dubbed 'The Gibson Girl'; America's first sweetheart, known for her independence and appeal. In 1903, Thomas Murphy and Edmond Osborne had the idea to feature illustrations of beautiful and fashionable women in their first ever girl calendar, 'Cosette'. These calendars proved much more popular than their predecessors which boasted images of George Washington - it seems he was not quite as alluring! Other publications soon jumped on the bandwagon and Harrison Fisher's "Fisher Girl" took over the pages of Puck Magazine and Cosmopolitan from 1912 until 1932, while Howard Chandler Christy made the "Christy Girl" for The Century. The pinup image was becoming a popular and useful propaganda tool in the First World War, with President Woodrow Wilson having posters made showing attractive women in playful military garb with slogans such as 'Gee, I Wish I Were a Man, I'd Join the Navy!' After the war, men returned to women who had developed a sense of sass and independence (and shorter hemlines)! Enter WWII and that classic pinup girl we all know and love was born. Photos of all-American dream girls were spread across barrack walls and inside submarines as a way to boost morale. Artists such as Gil Elvgren and Alberto Vargas made paintings of flawless, comely women in playful situations which only continued to gain favour after the war and was a style used extensively in advertising into the 1950s.

Attitude is what sets the classic American pinup apart; she is a well-rounded character who is somehow simultaneously convivially attainable and deliciously elusive. She finds fun in the most mundane of tasks and is never overtly sexual or trashy. She's smart and saucy but always seems to find herself in sticky situations – an innocent walk in the park sees her shapely ankles wrapped up in an over-excited puppy's leash; a culinary foray ends in disaster when her mixer explodes and leaves cake batter absolutely everywhere… what can she do but pout?

LEFT: ***The Love Bandit***
Nathalie Rattner

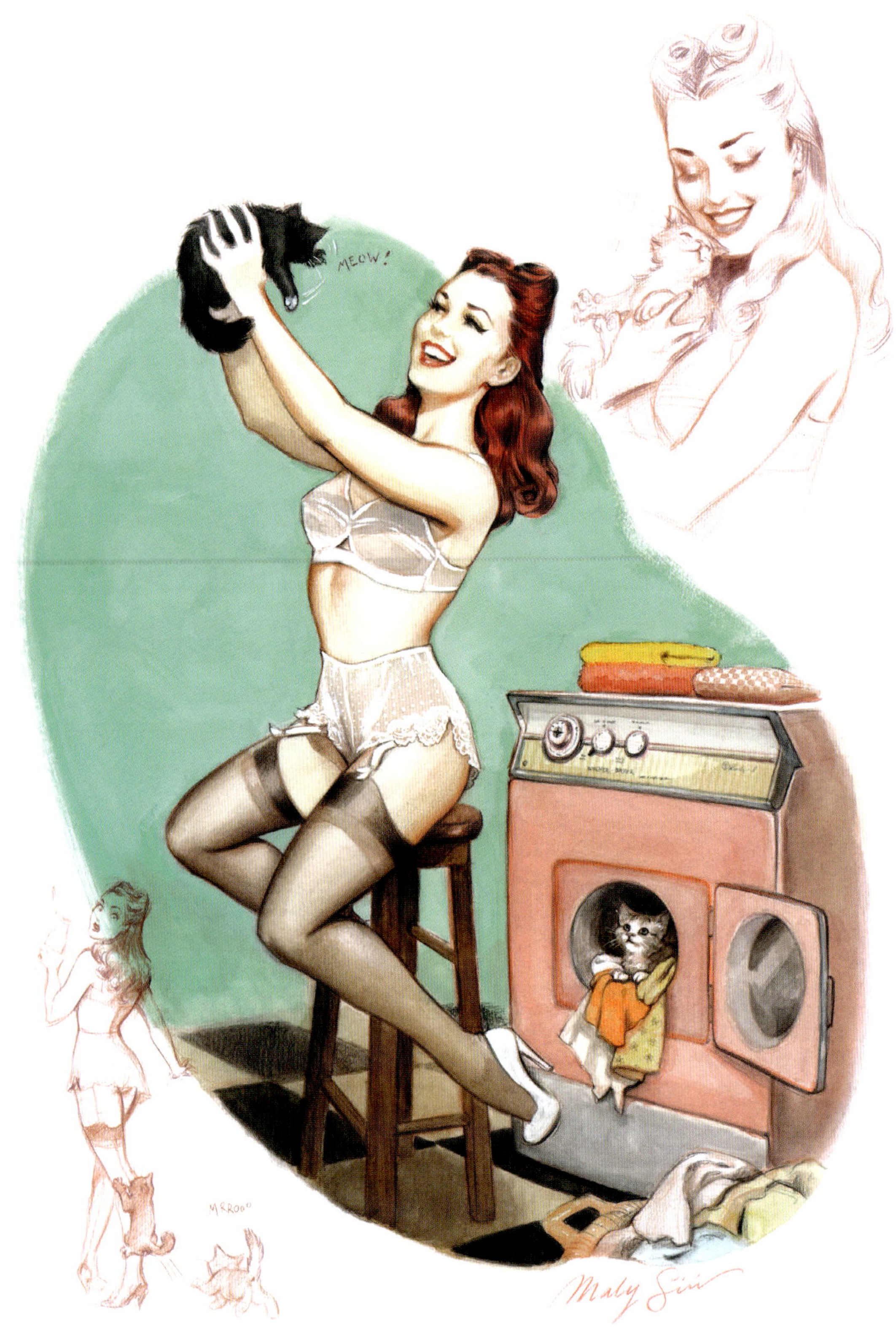

ABOVE: ***Kittens***
Maly Siri

RIGHT: ***Neighbors***
Maly Siri

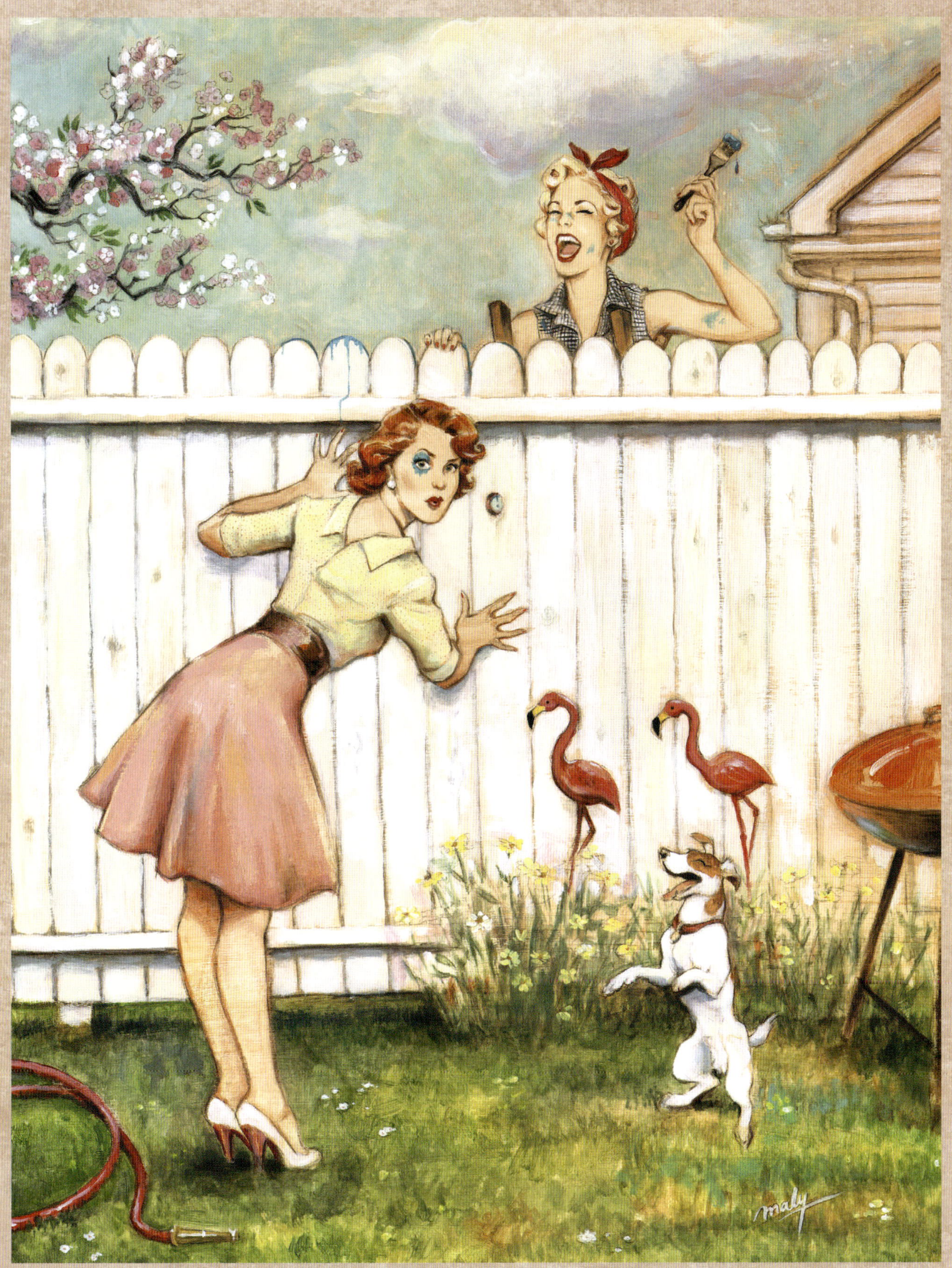
maly

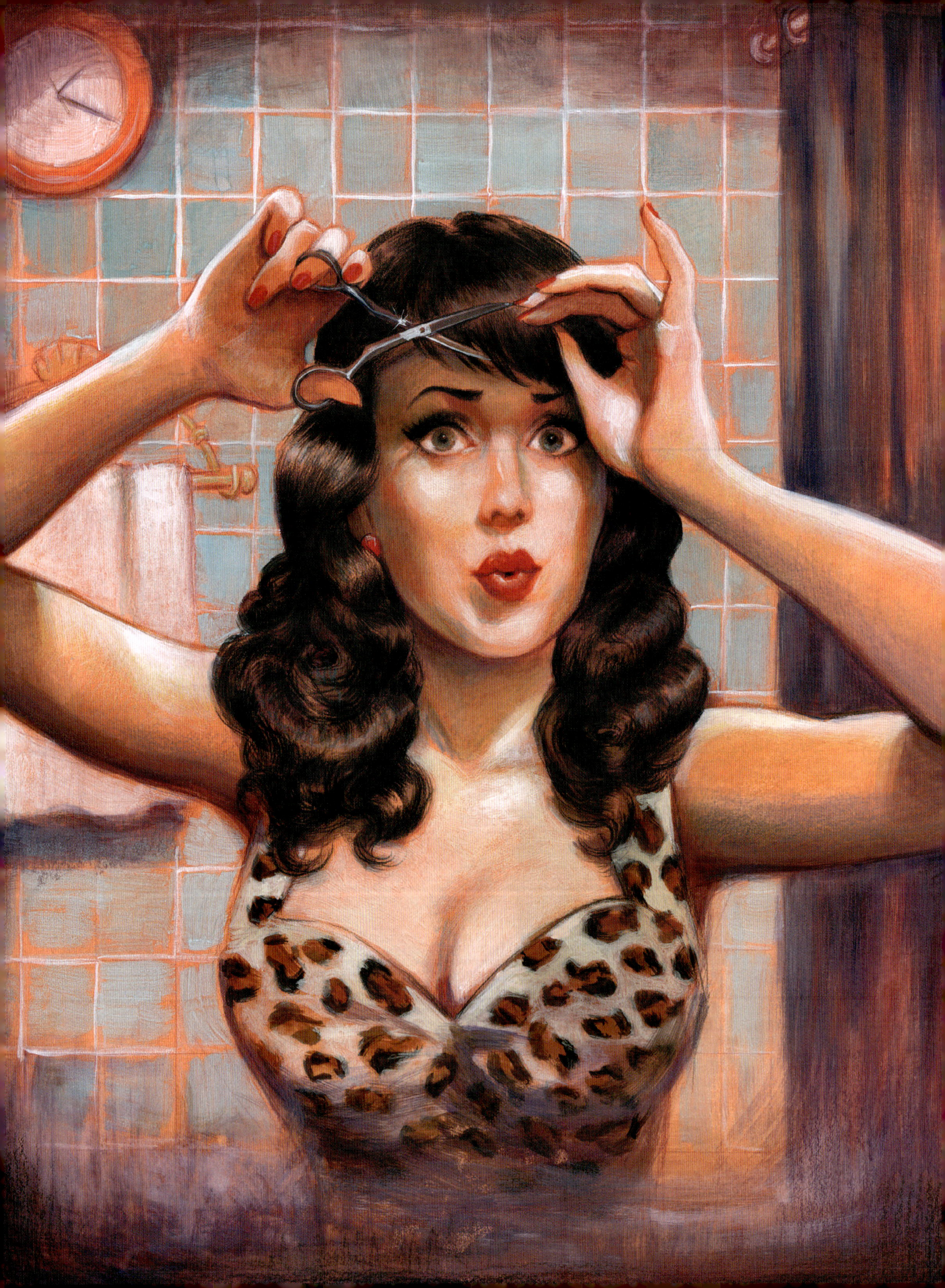

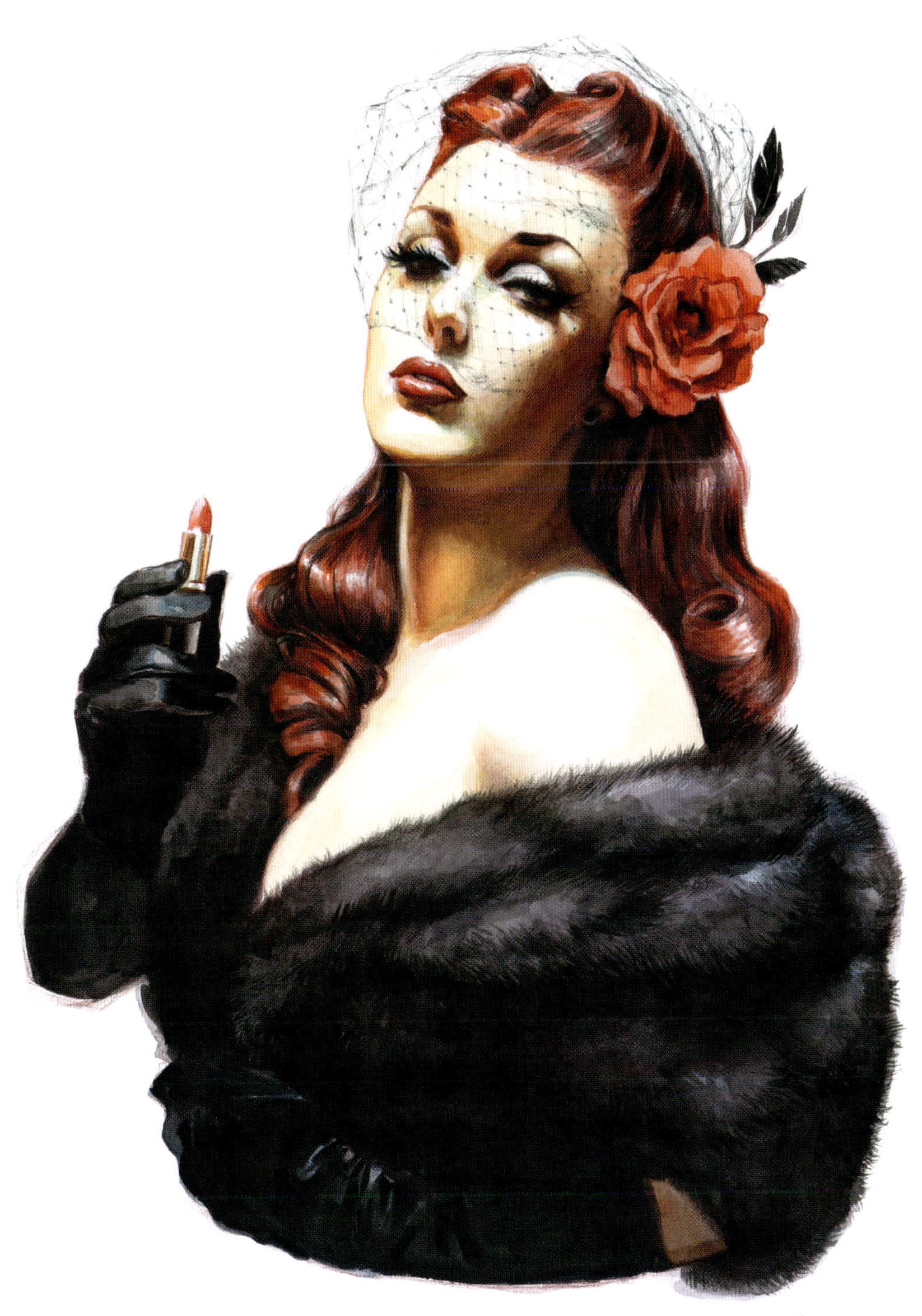

LEFT: ***To Cut or Not to Cut***
Maly Siri

ABOVE: ***Ruby Lips***
Maly Siri

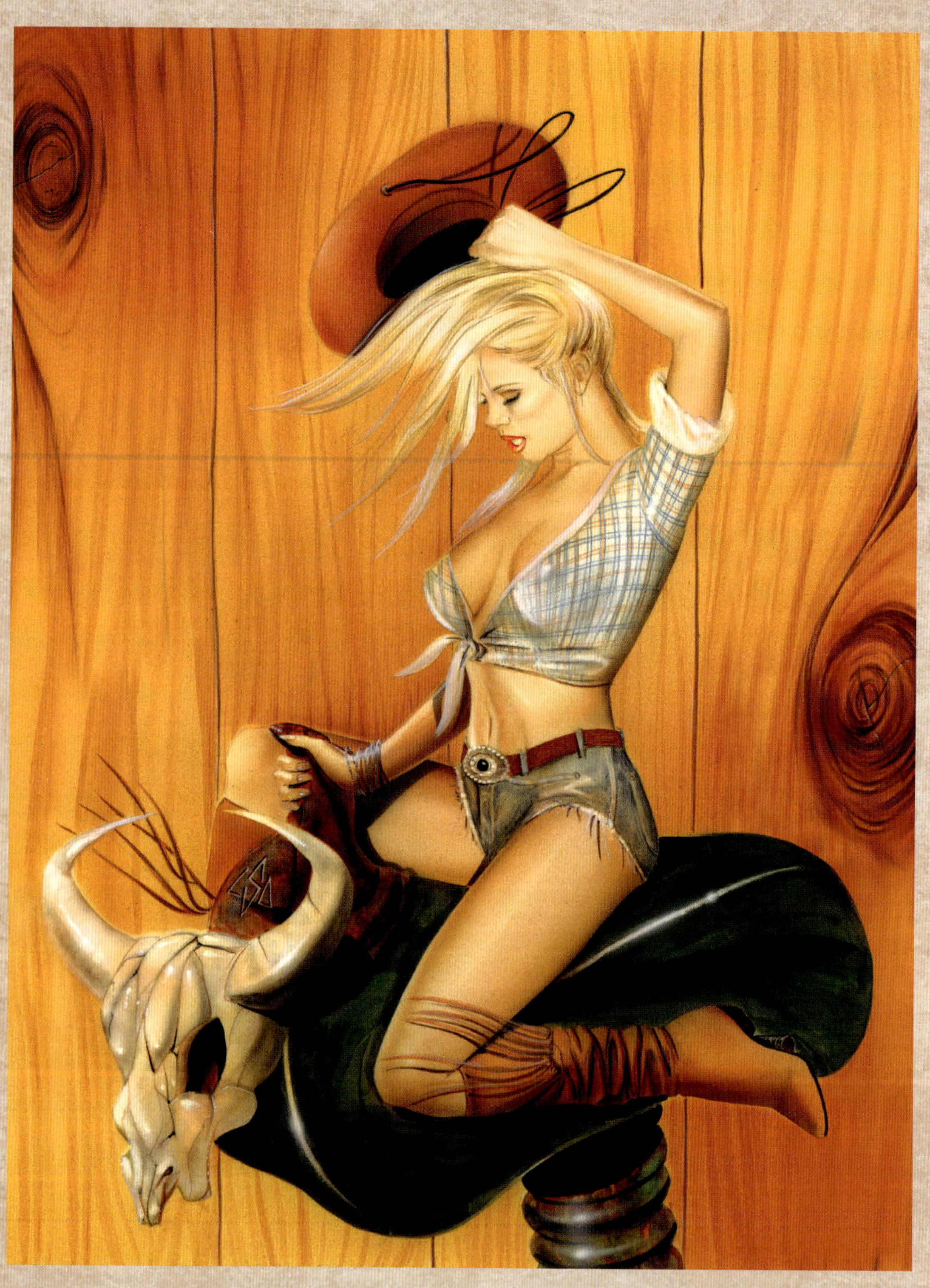

ABOVE: ***Rodeo Girl***
Lorenzo Sperlonga

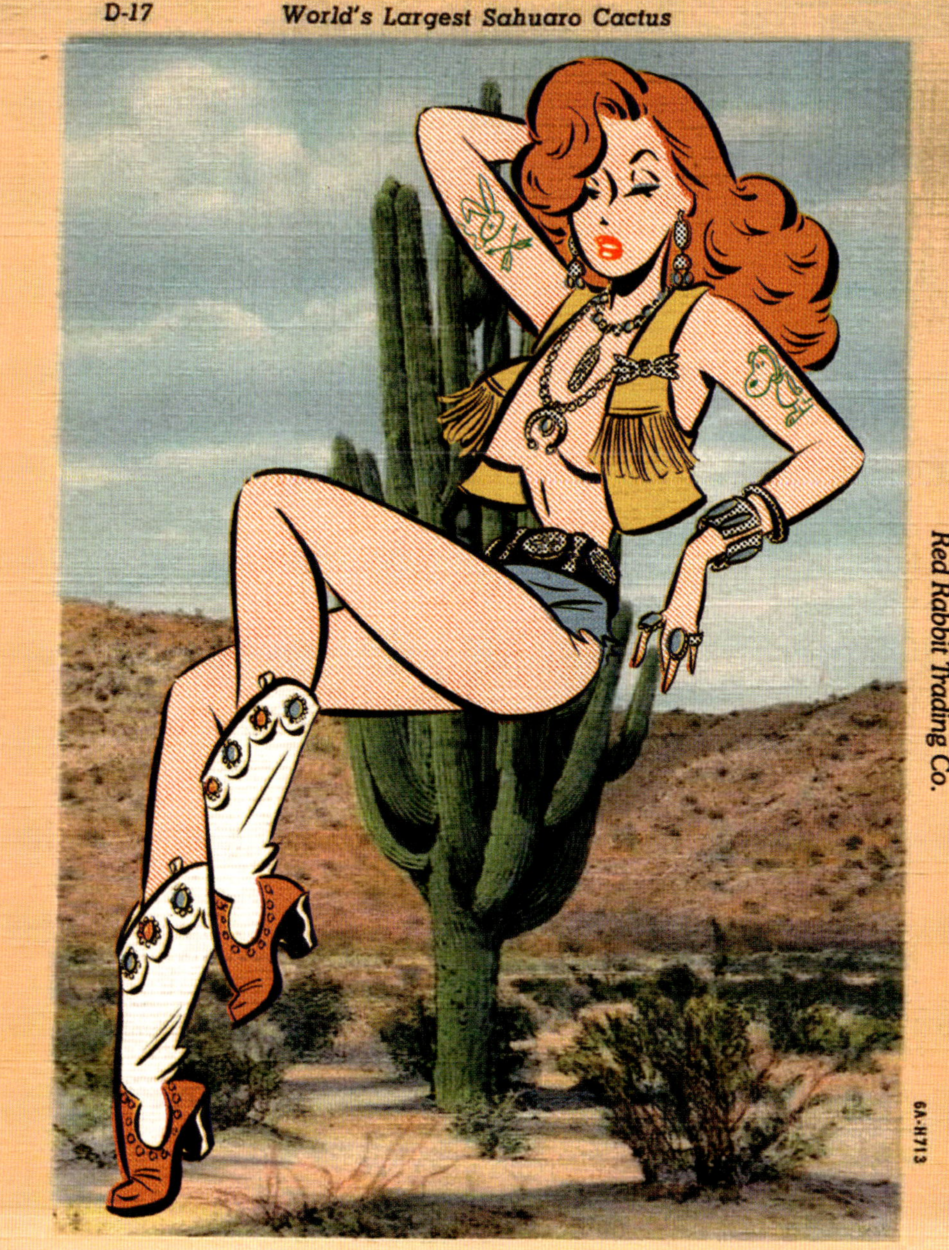

ABOVE: ***Red Rabbit Cactus***
Sveta Shubina

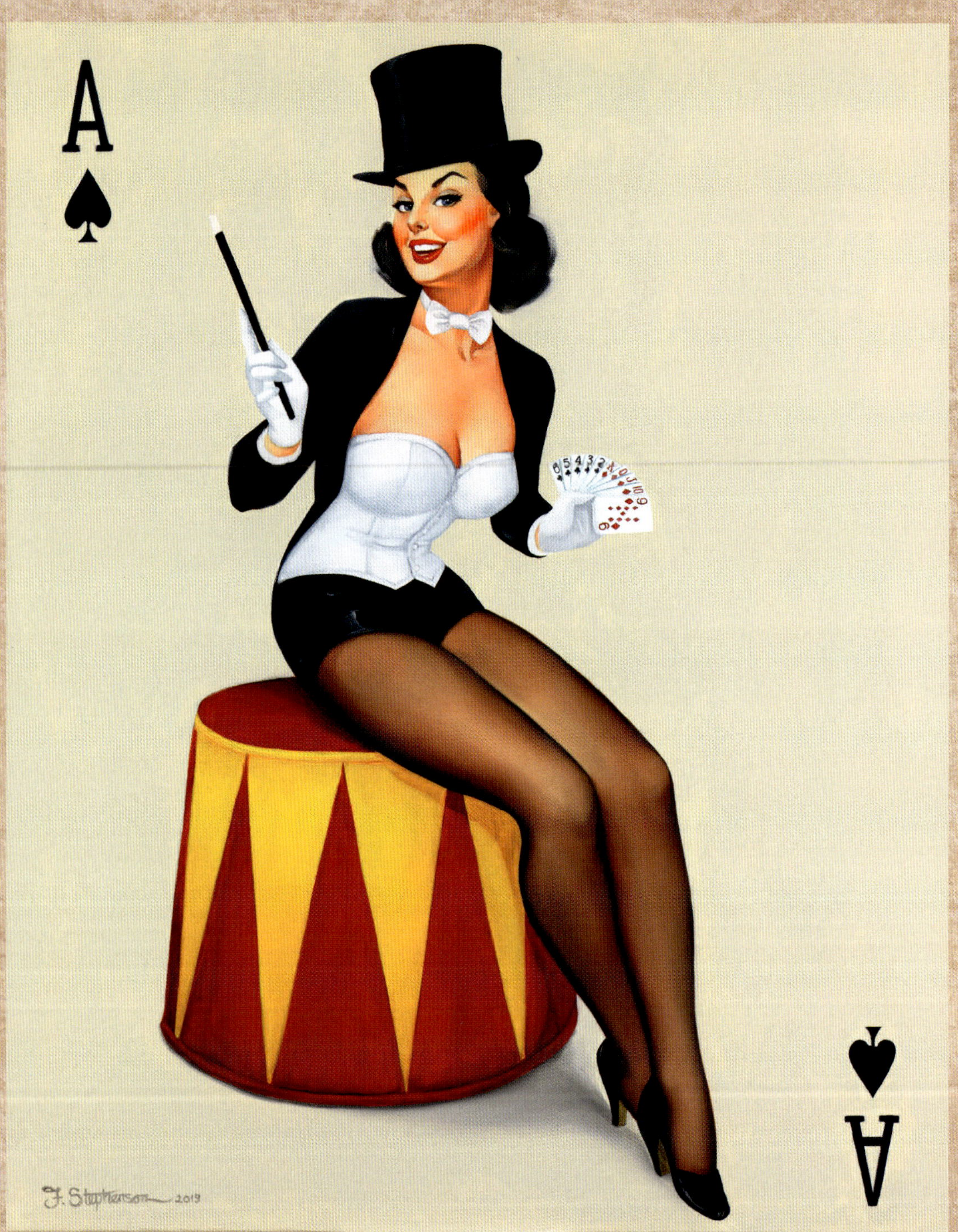

ABOVE: ***Aces High***
Fiona Stephenson

RIGHT: ***Bubble Trouble***
Fiona Stephenson

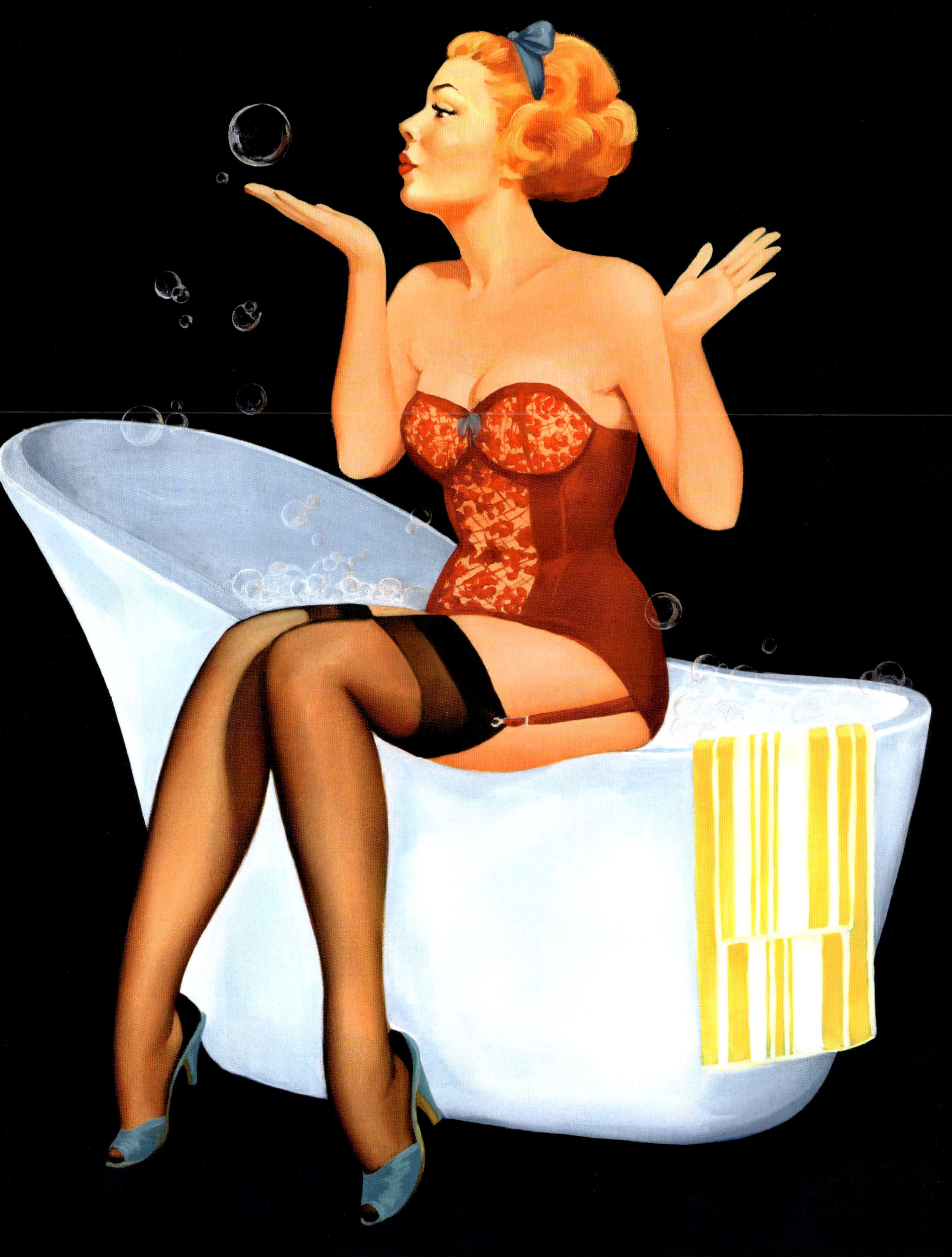

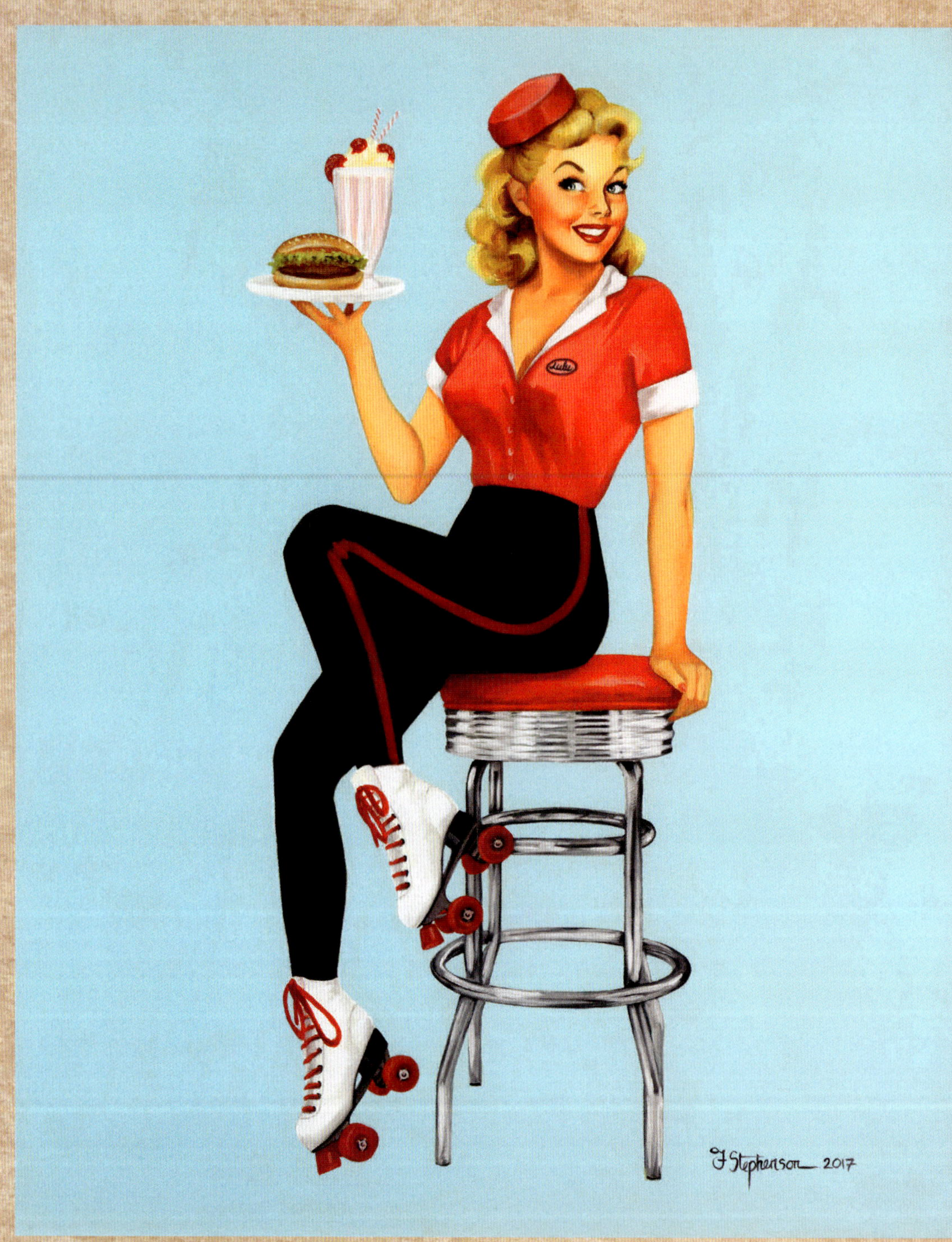

ABOVE: ***Diner Girl***
Fiona Stephenson

RIGHT: ***Party Delights***
Fiona Stephenson

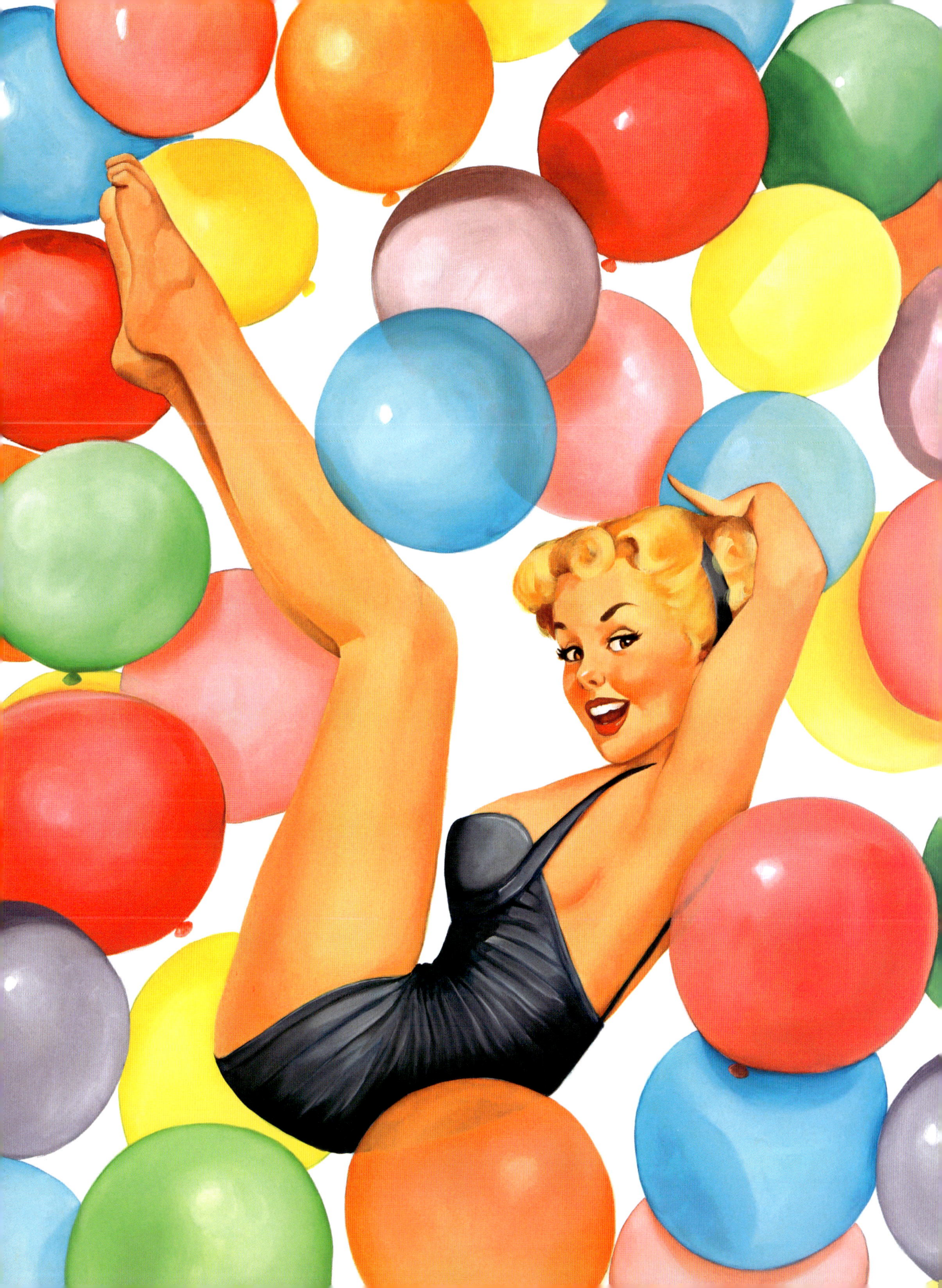

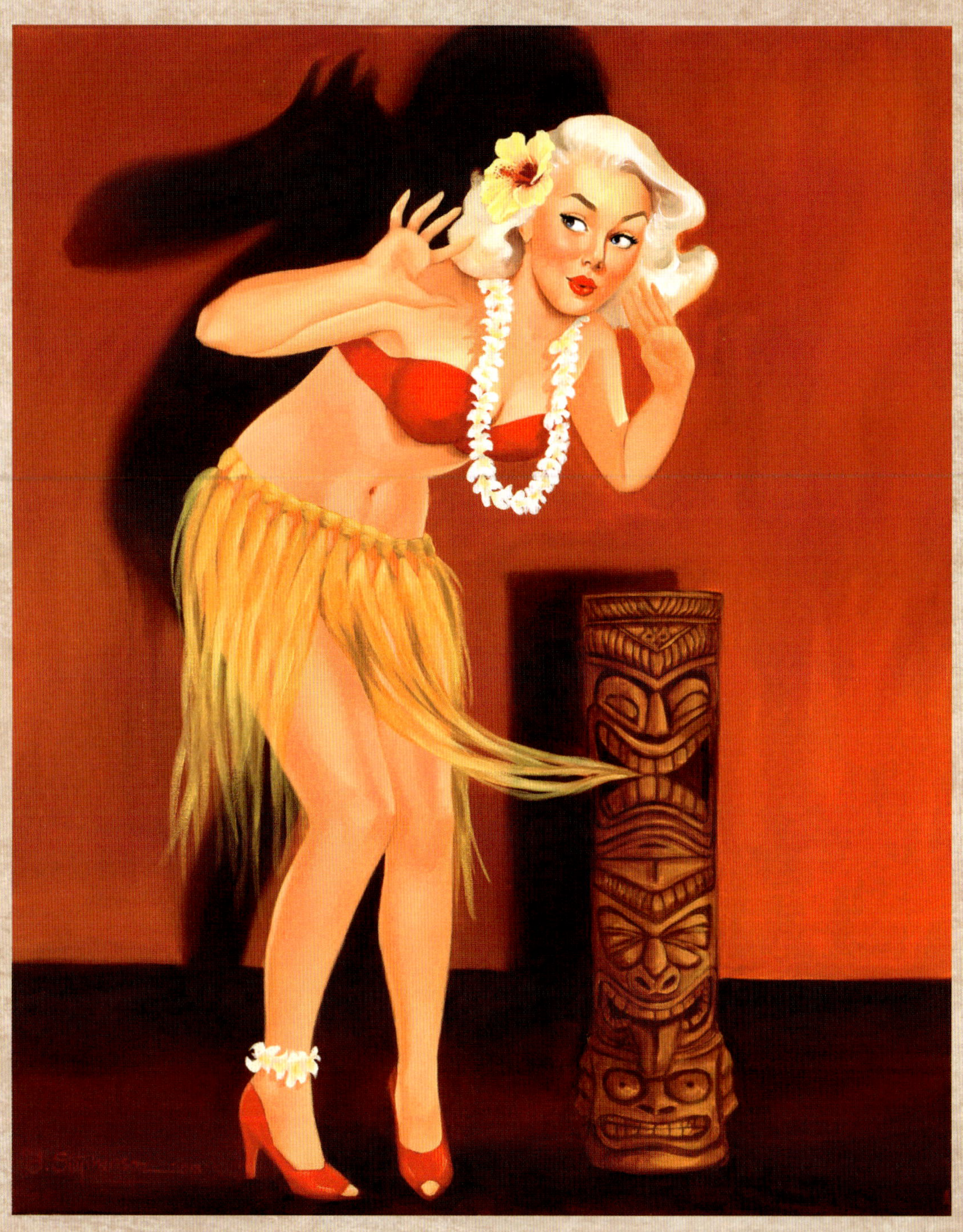

ABOVE: ***Tiki Talk***
Fiona Stephenson

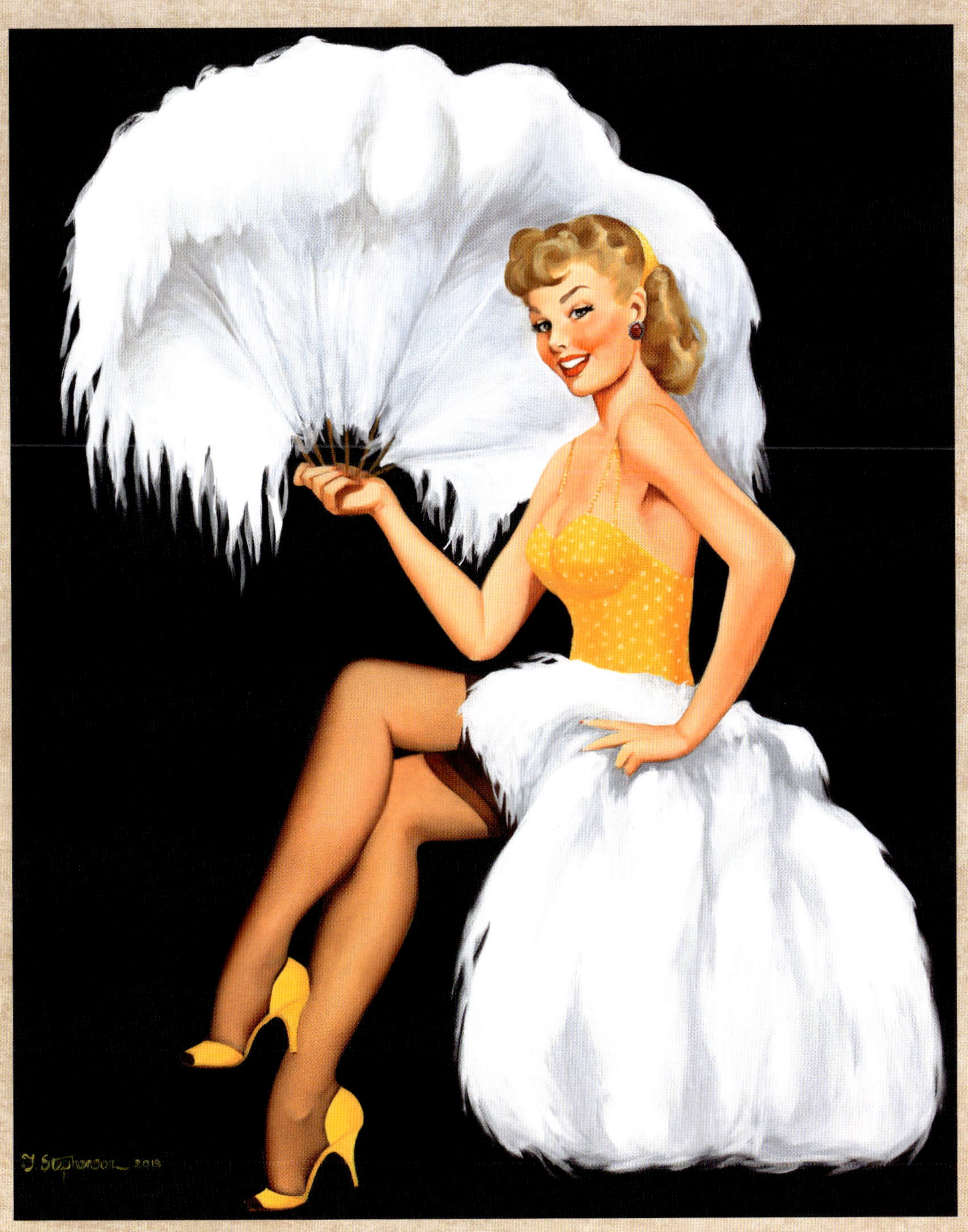

ABOVE: ***Fan-Tastic***
Fiona Stephenson

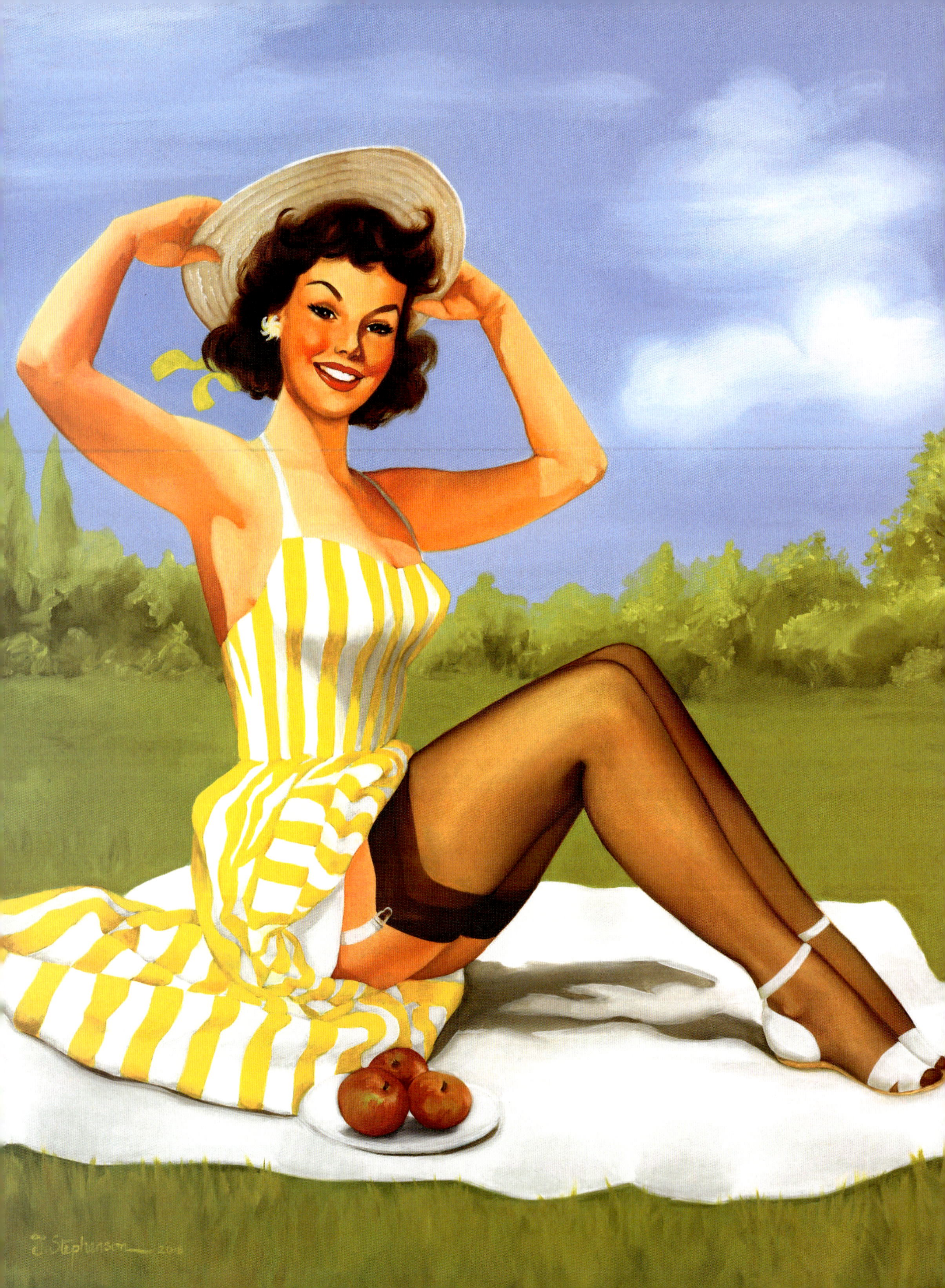
Stephenson

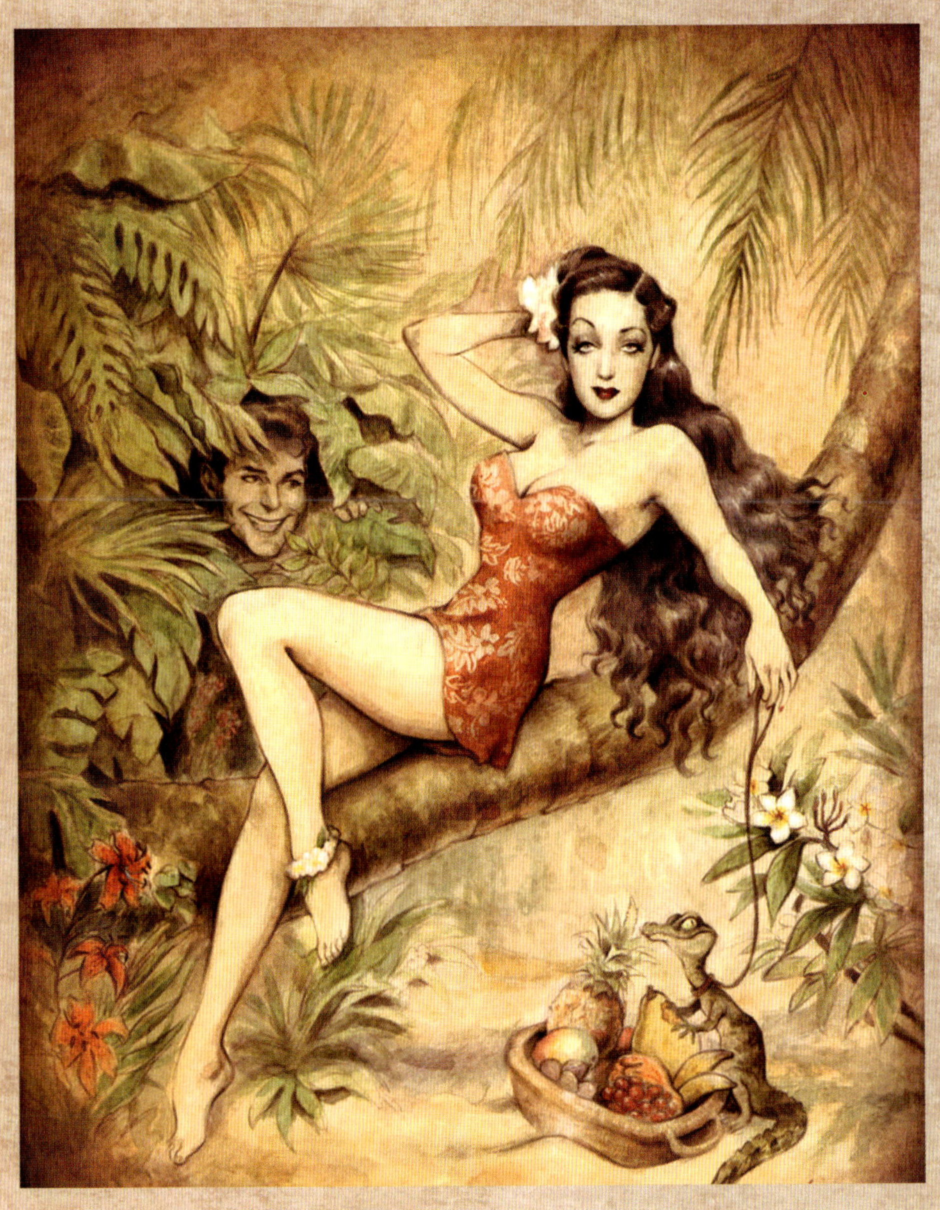

LEFT: ***Sunshine Smile***
Fiona Stephenson

ABOVE: ***Dorothy Lamour***
Maly Siri

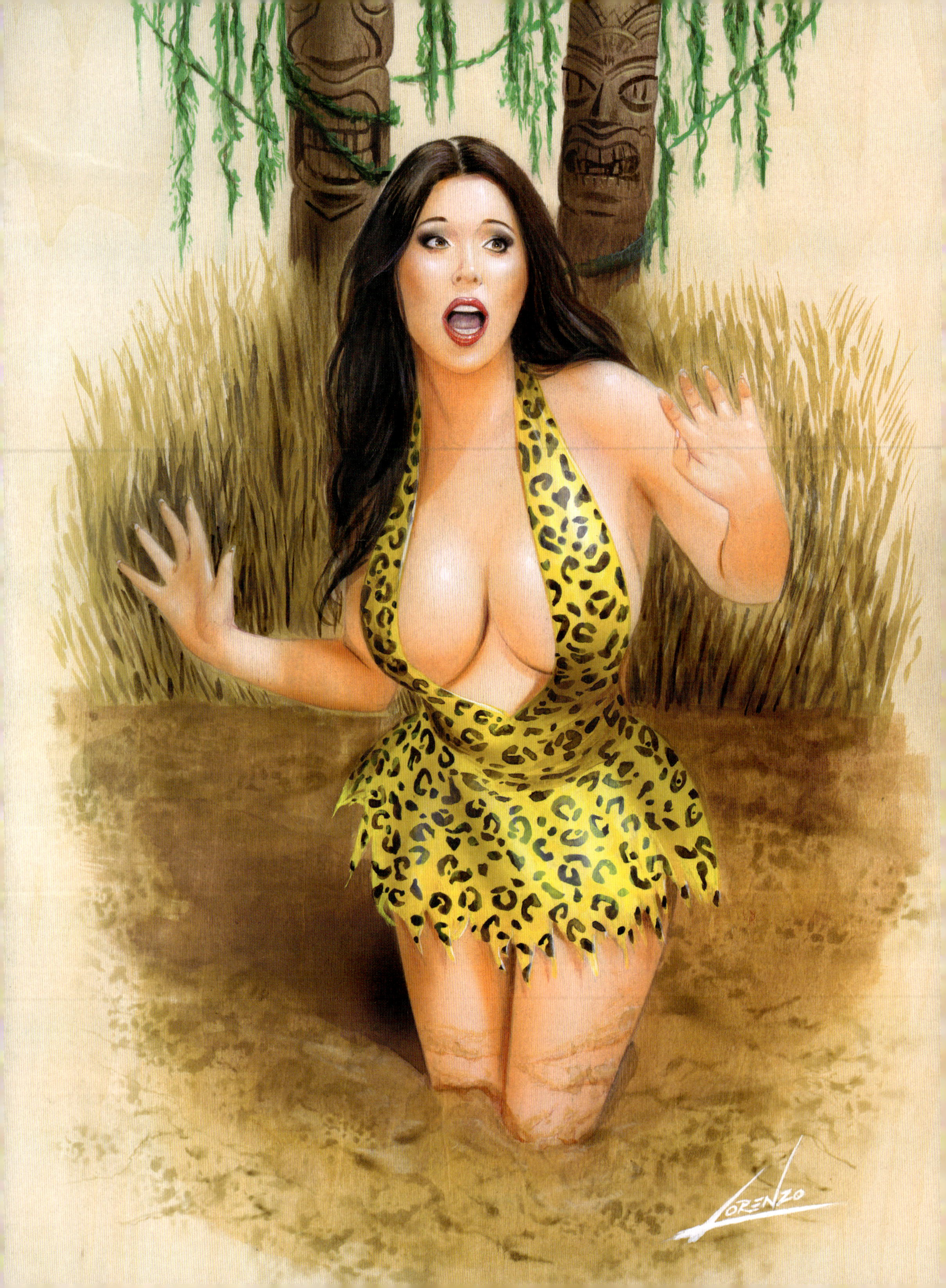
LORENZO

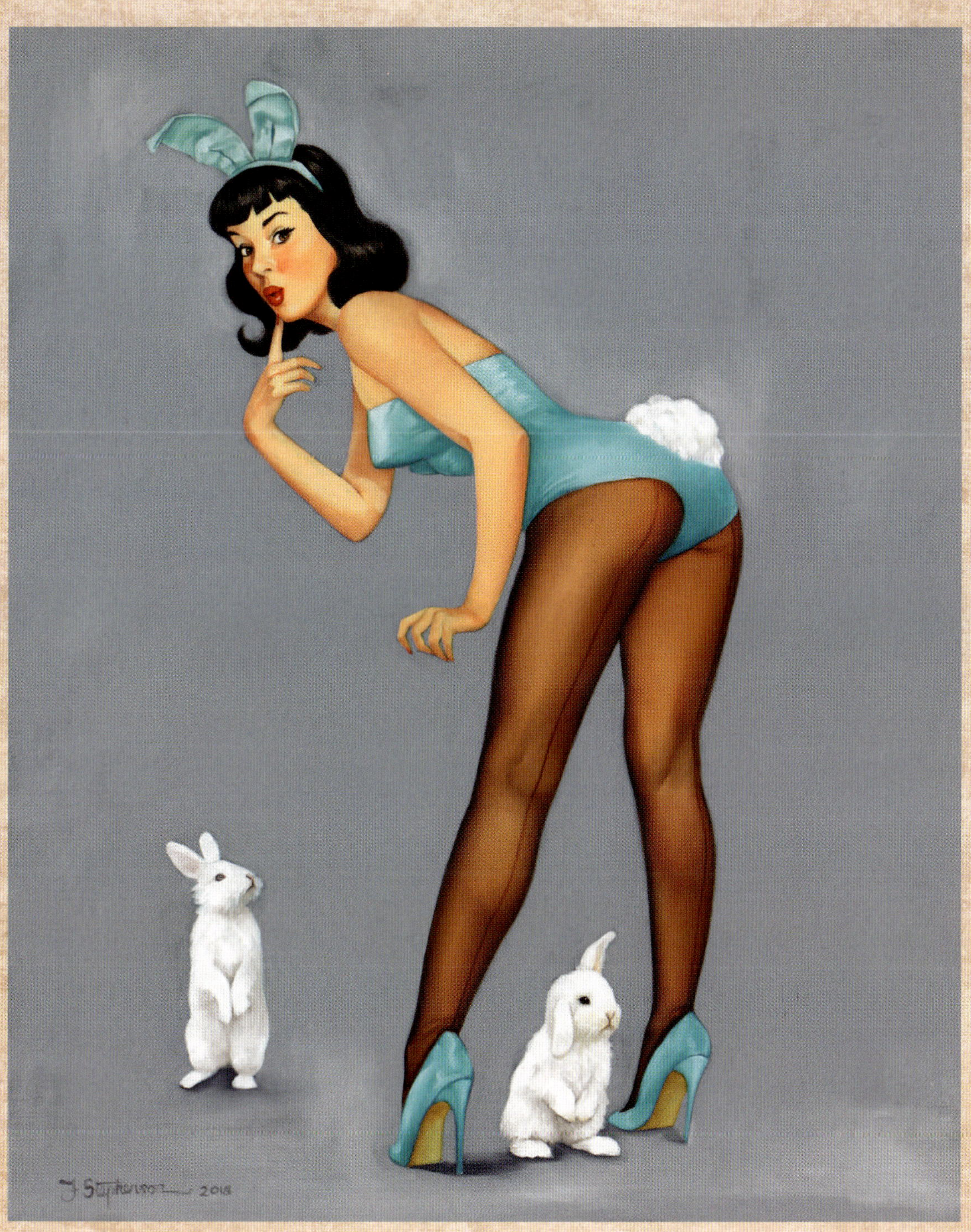

LEFT: ***Jane in the Quicksand***
Lorenzo Sperlonga

ABOVE: ***Some Bunny Loves You***
Fiona Stephenson

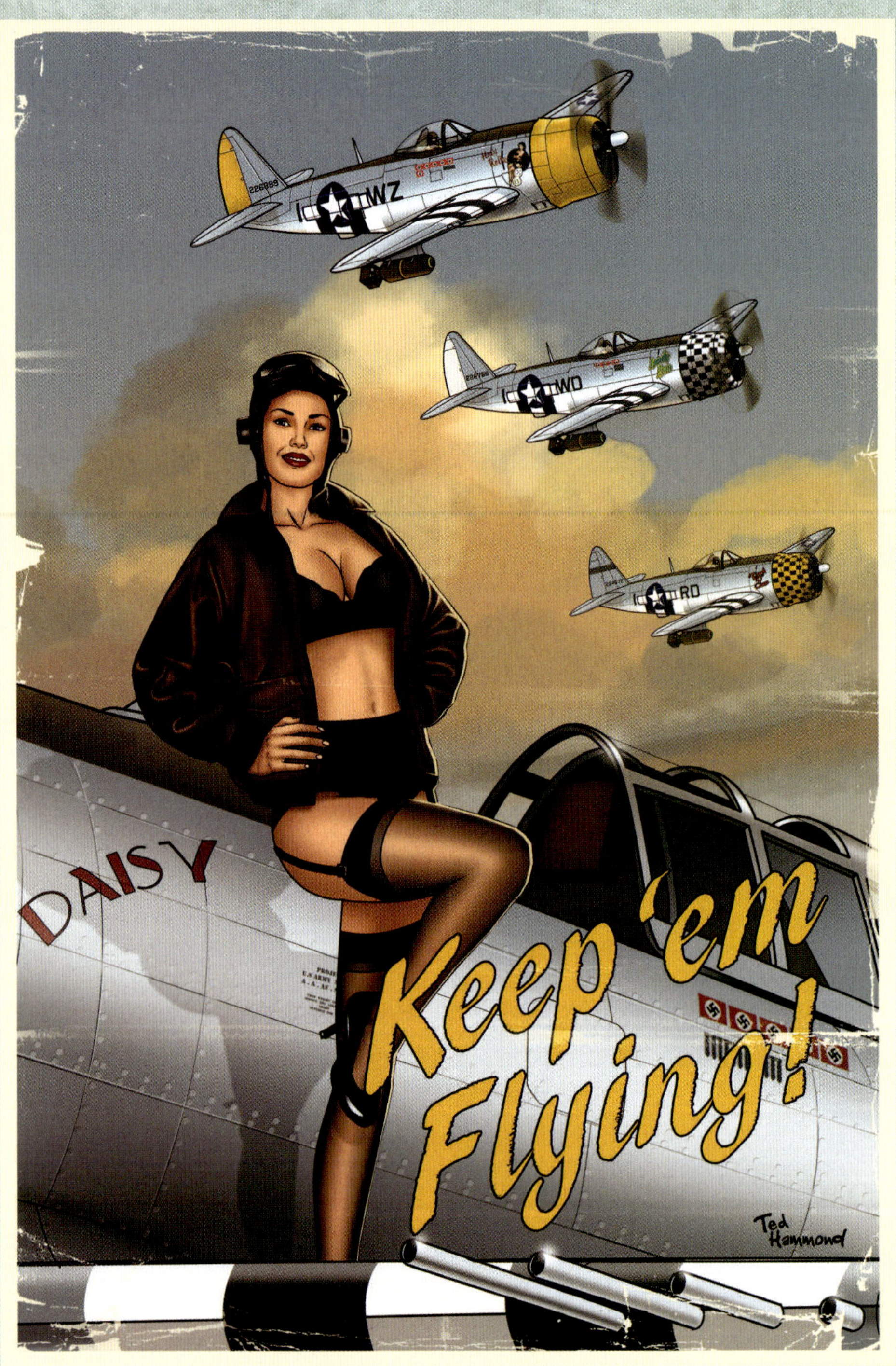

ABOVE: ***Ms Thunderbolt***
Ted Hammond

RIGHT: ***Betty***
Ivan Valle

OVERLEAF: ***Marilyn***
Bern Foster

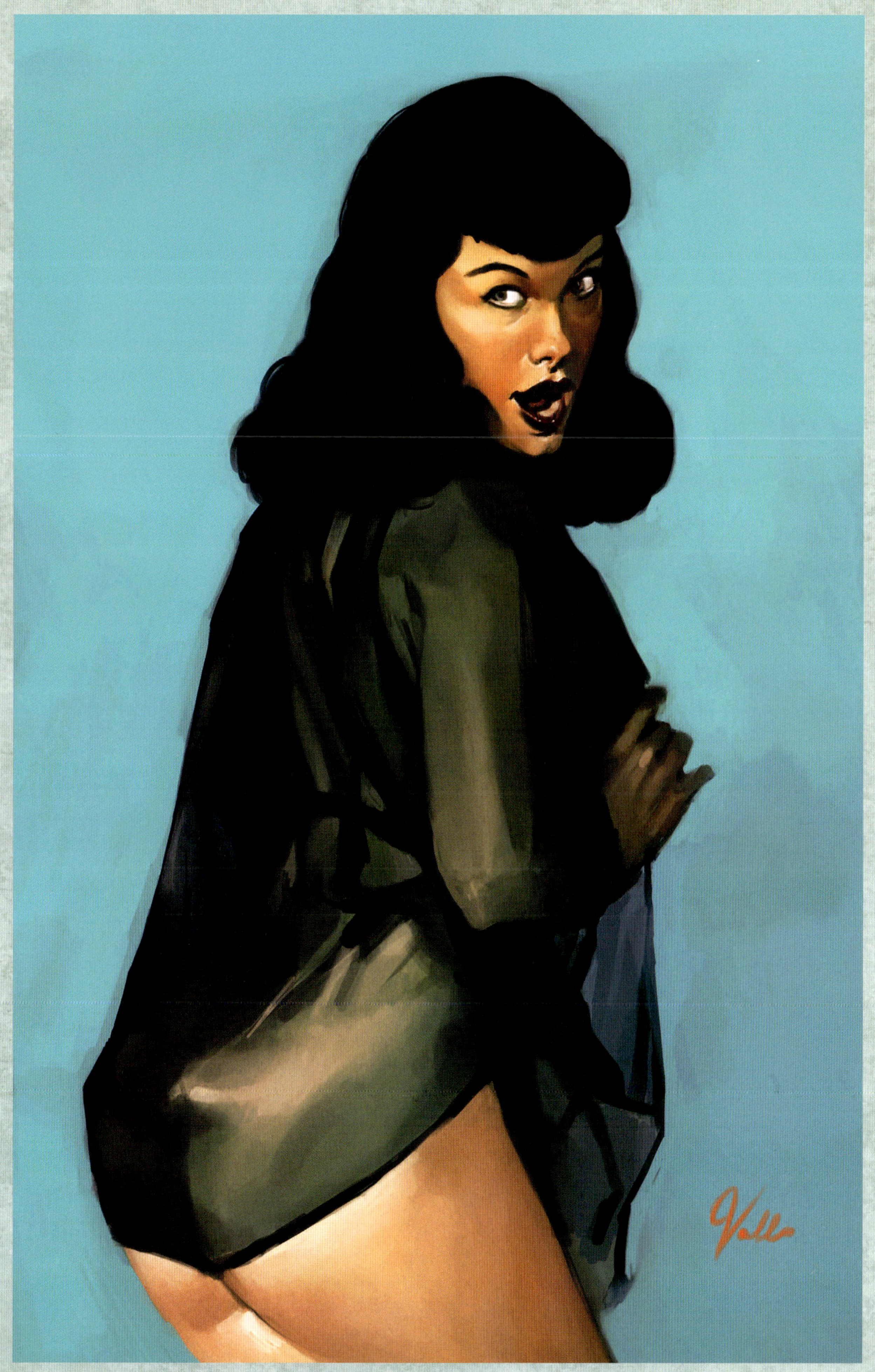

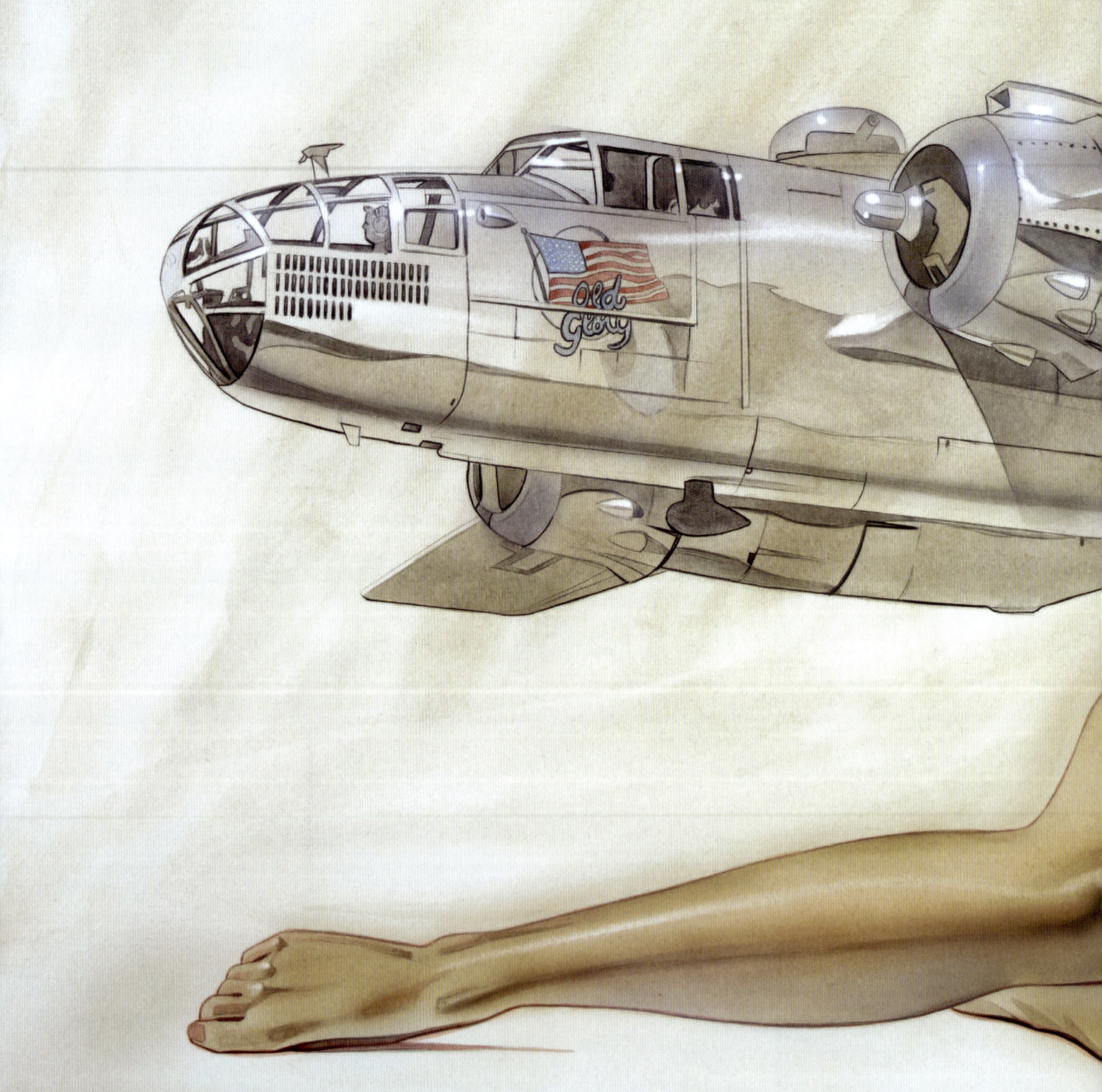
Old Glory

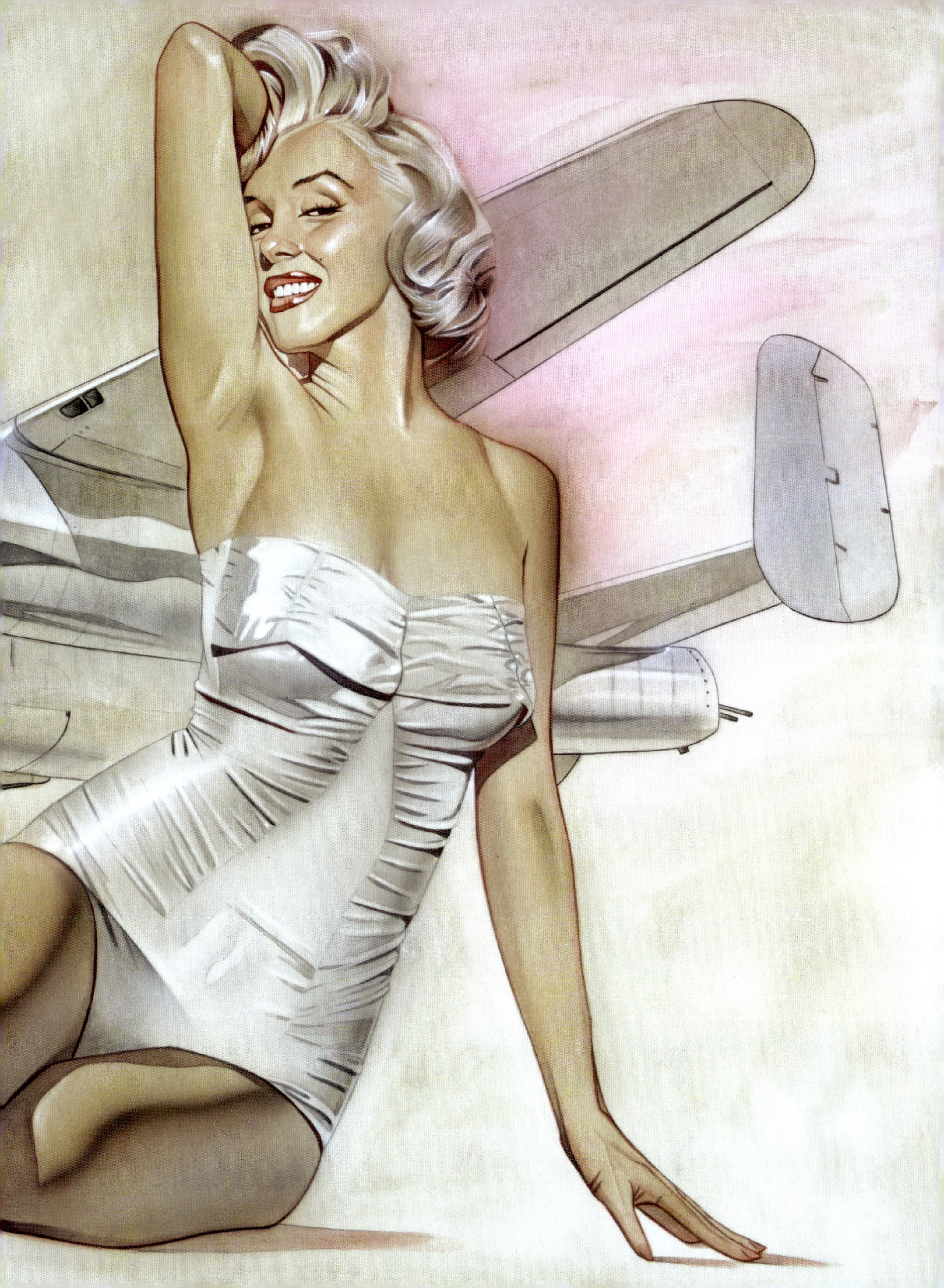

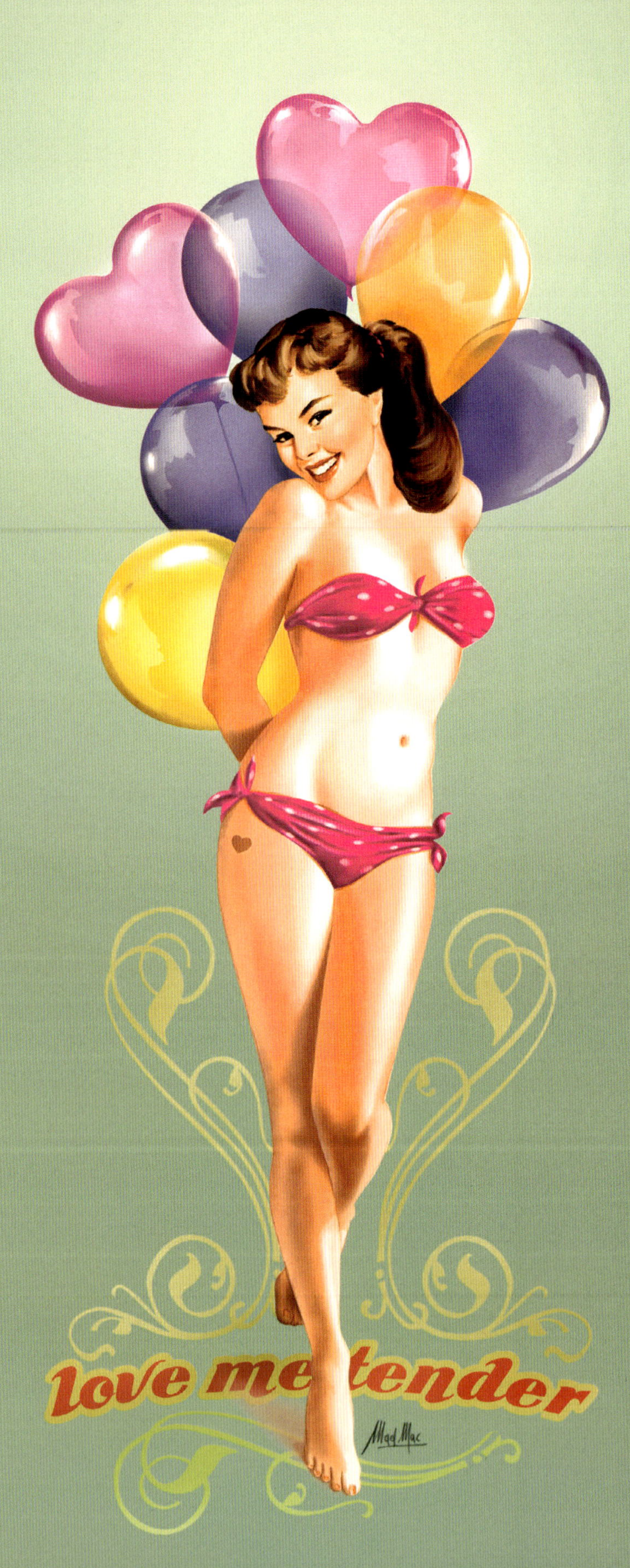
love me tender
Mad Mac

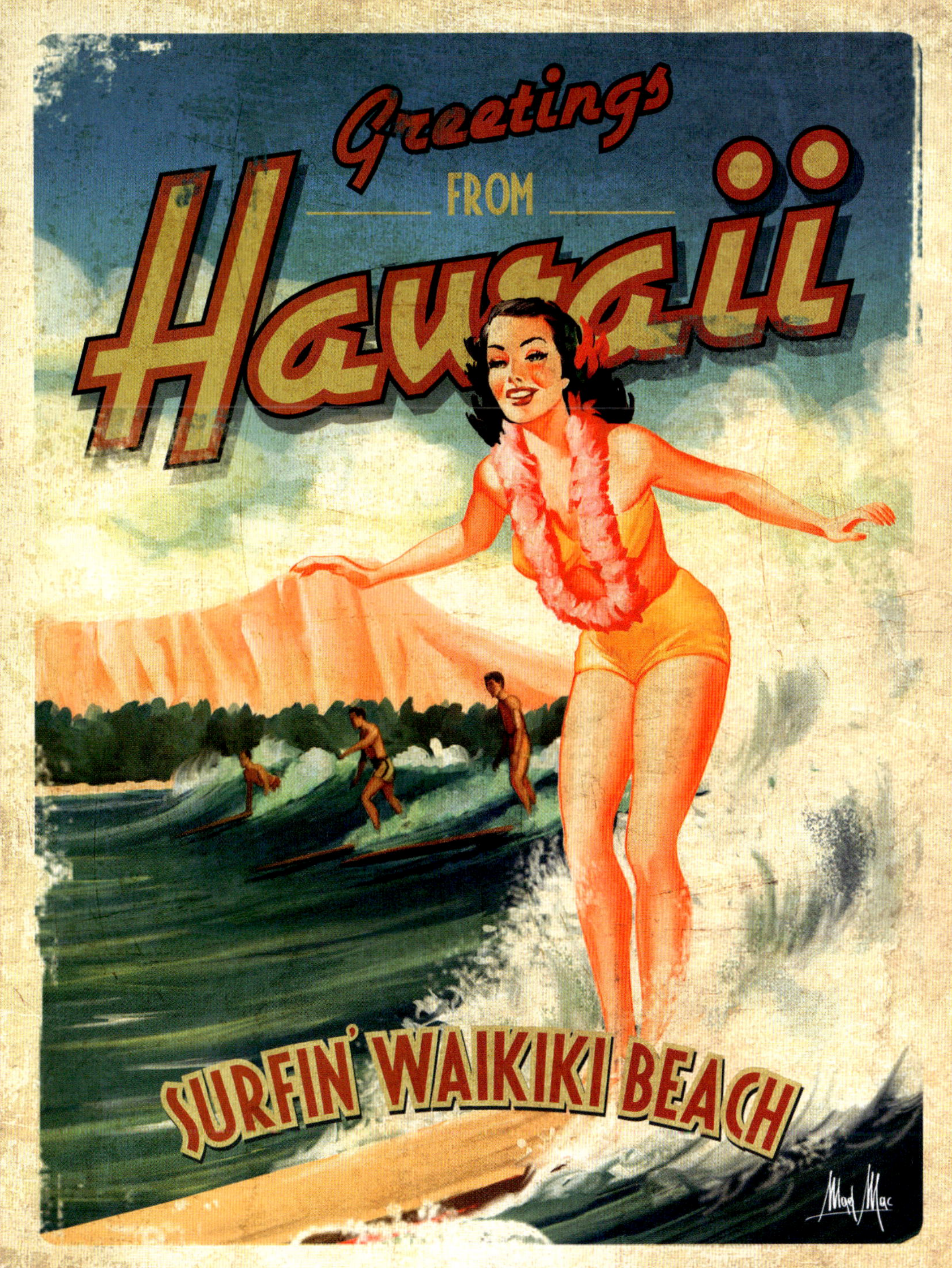

LEFT: ***Love Me Tender***
Mad Mac

ABOVE: ***Hawaii***
Mad Mac

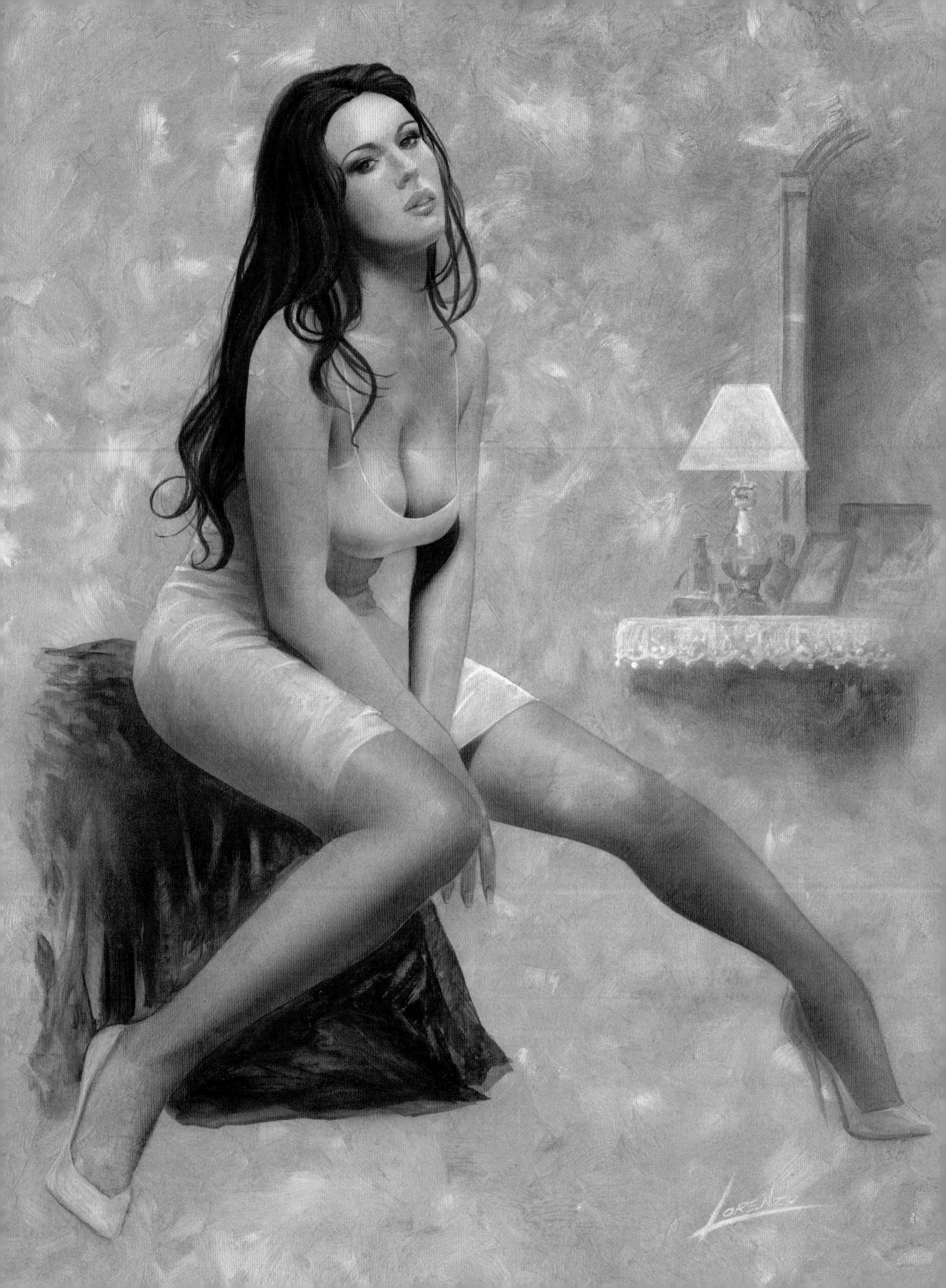
LORENZO

European Classic

The US were not the only ones with a penchant for pinup. More provocative than her American counterpart, the European pinup girl is self-assured and unafraid of her sexuality. She is purposeful and knows she cannot be resisted. She is a youthful beauty and yet her striking countenance stretches back to ancient history; as the Greeks adored their Hellenic figures and the Romans weaved sensuality into their art, culture and even graffiti on their walls. The Renaissance artists championed comely Venus and her strikingly fertile figure in their aspirations to recentre the best of human values and traditions.

So, the European tradition of the beautiful feminine intersects elegantly and excitingly with that of the more contemporary and deliberately exaggerated American pinup. Here there is inspiration and imitation, tradition either respected or subverted in a cornucopia of imagery.

Yet, even amidst all this new, playful and deconstructive turmoil, there is a pleasingly supple and irreverent continuity – the inimitable feminine pinup, she who winks as mysteriously in her guise as the Mona Lisa as her modern counterparts. The pleasure of the form, the essential vitality and richness of the woman portrayed here is one factor that no pinup artist could ever overlook.

The original French master of the form Alain Aslan claimed that 'woman' remains the most beautiful subject ever given to artists because it is inexhaustible and eternal. For eighteen years, Aslan painted a monthly pinup for *Lui* magazine between 1963 and 1981. Inspired by the work of renowned US pinup painter Alberto Vargas, Aslan adopted a similar naturalistic style but left the cheesecake element at the door, painting unapologetically raunchy girls and thus blazing the way for the modern European pinup.

This balance of the artistic, the sophisticated and the worldly with the natural, the sensual and the physical furnishes European pinup with a rich tradition of its own, a refined continental 'je ne sais quoi' and brazen confidence which enhances the female beauty it celebrates. Timelessly, the female and feminine remain the subject at the heart of an opulent and knowing European tradition of sensuality and sexual confidence.

LEFT: ***The Italian Wife***
Lorenzo Sperlonga

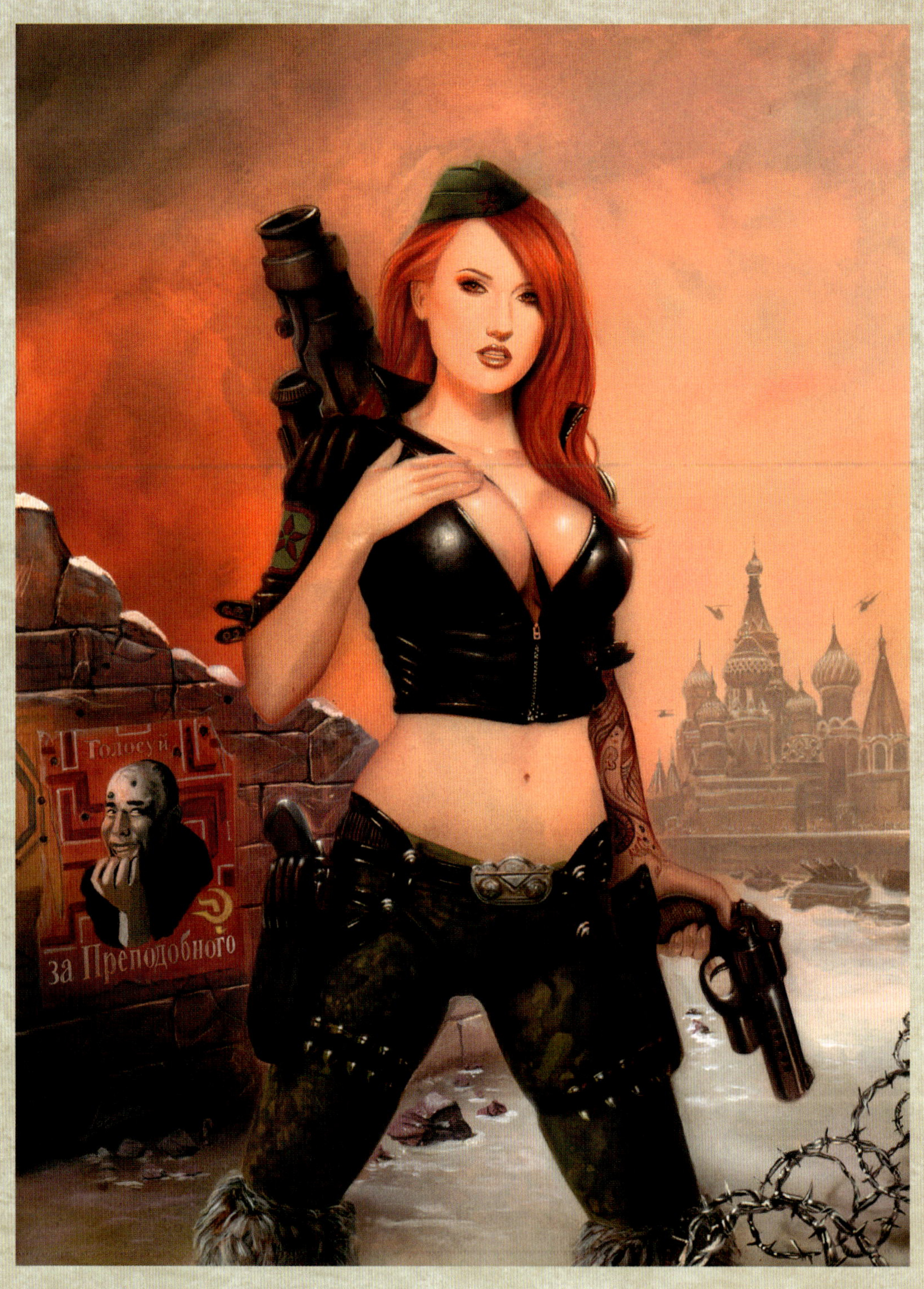

ABOVE: ***Red Square***
Lorenzo Sperlonga

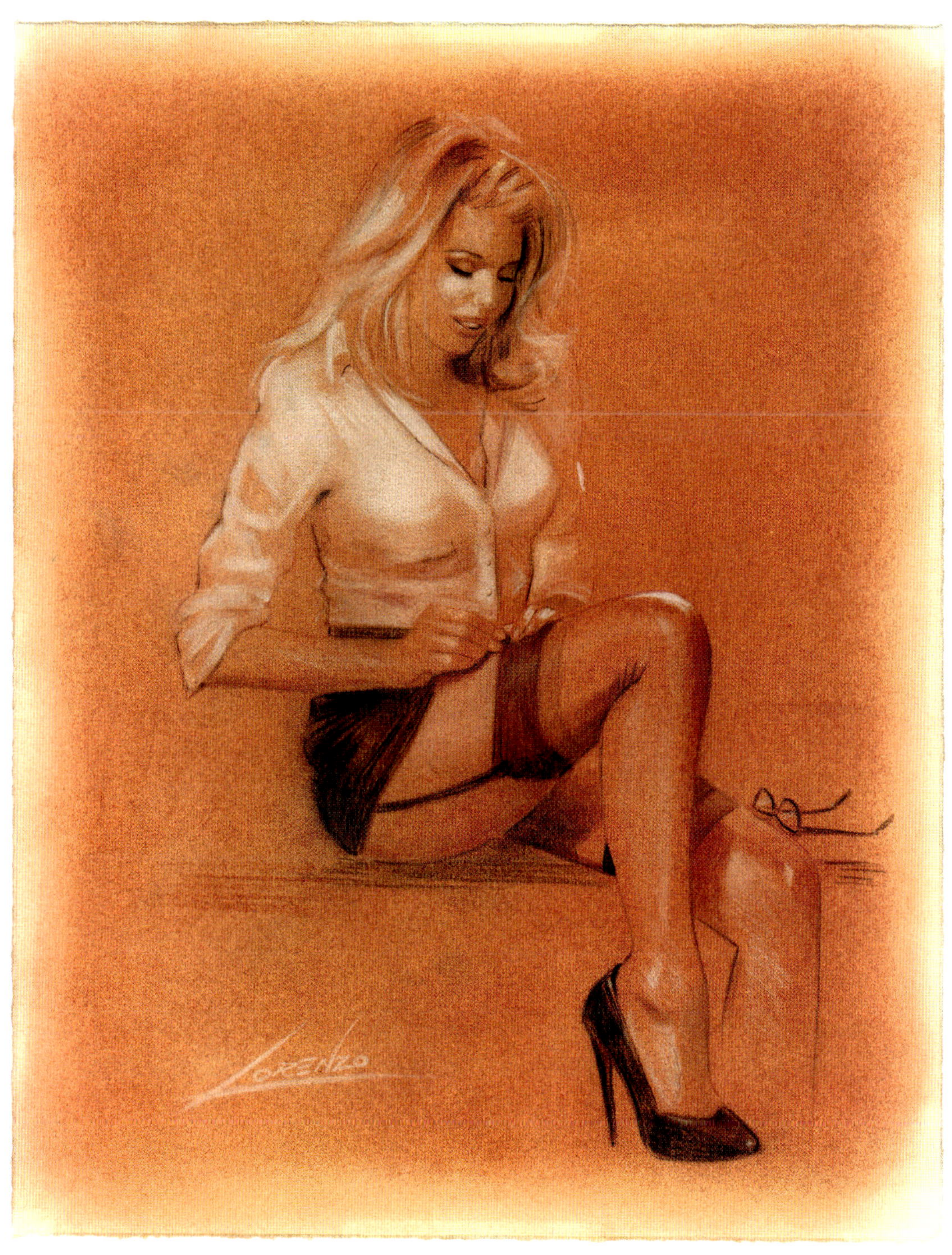

ABOVE: ***The Substitute***
Lorenzo Sperlonga

OVERLEAF: ***A Bed of Roses***
Lorenzo Sperlonga

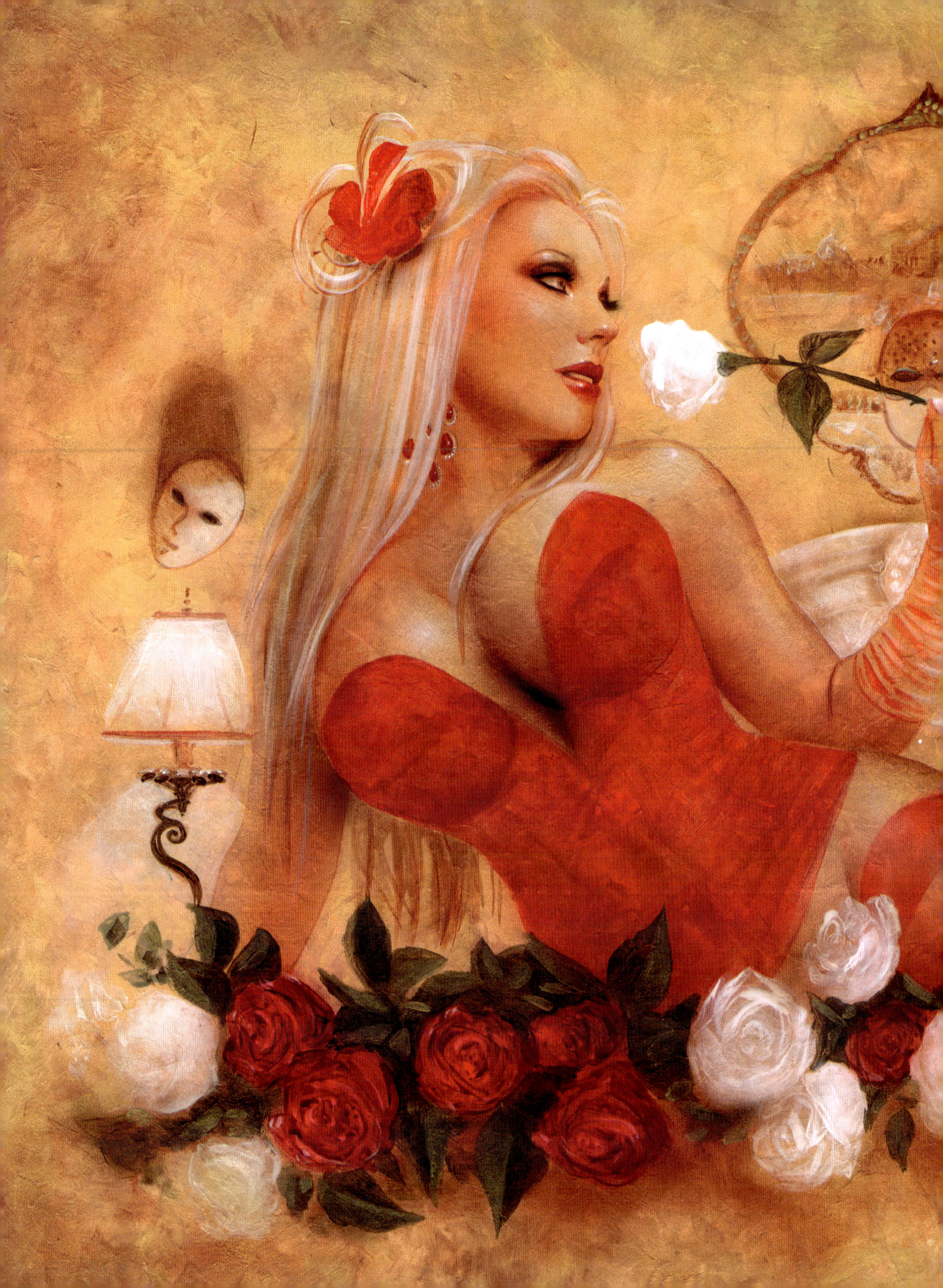

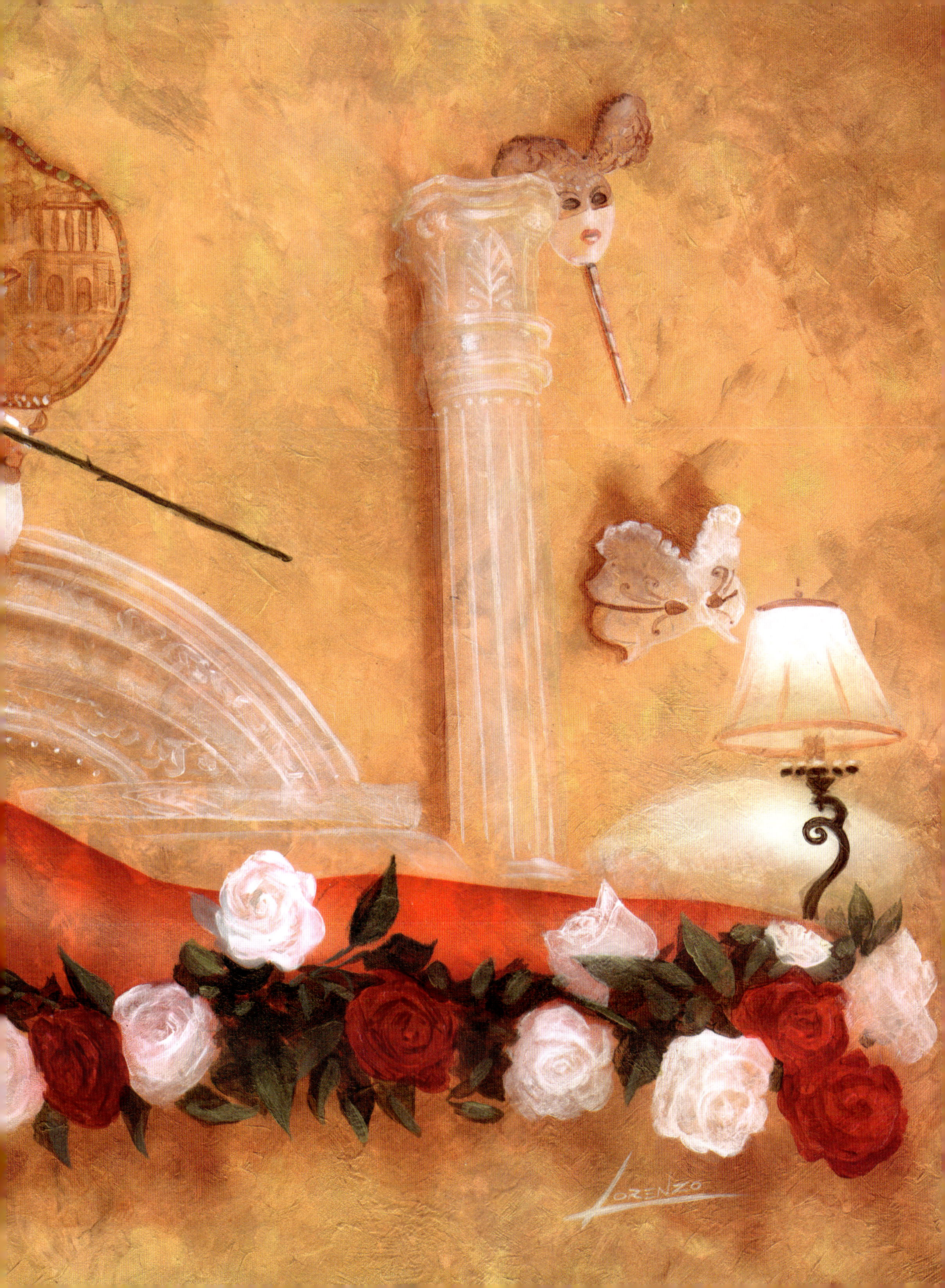
LORENZO

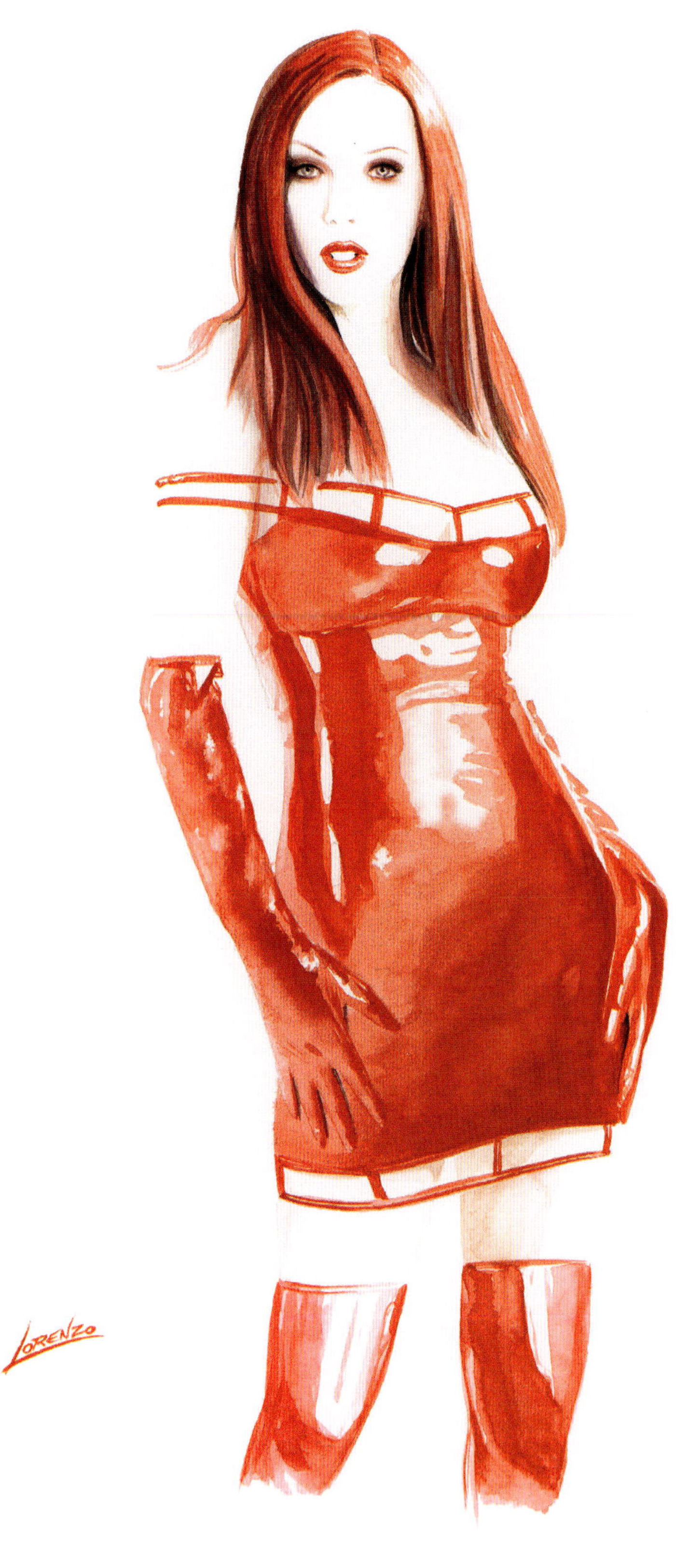

ABOVE: ***Emily***
Lorenzo Sperlonga

RIGHT: ***Venetian Rendezvous***
Lorenzo Sperlonga

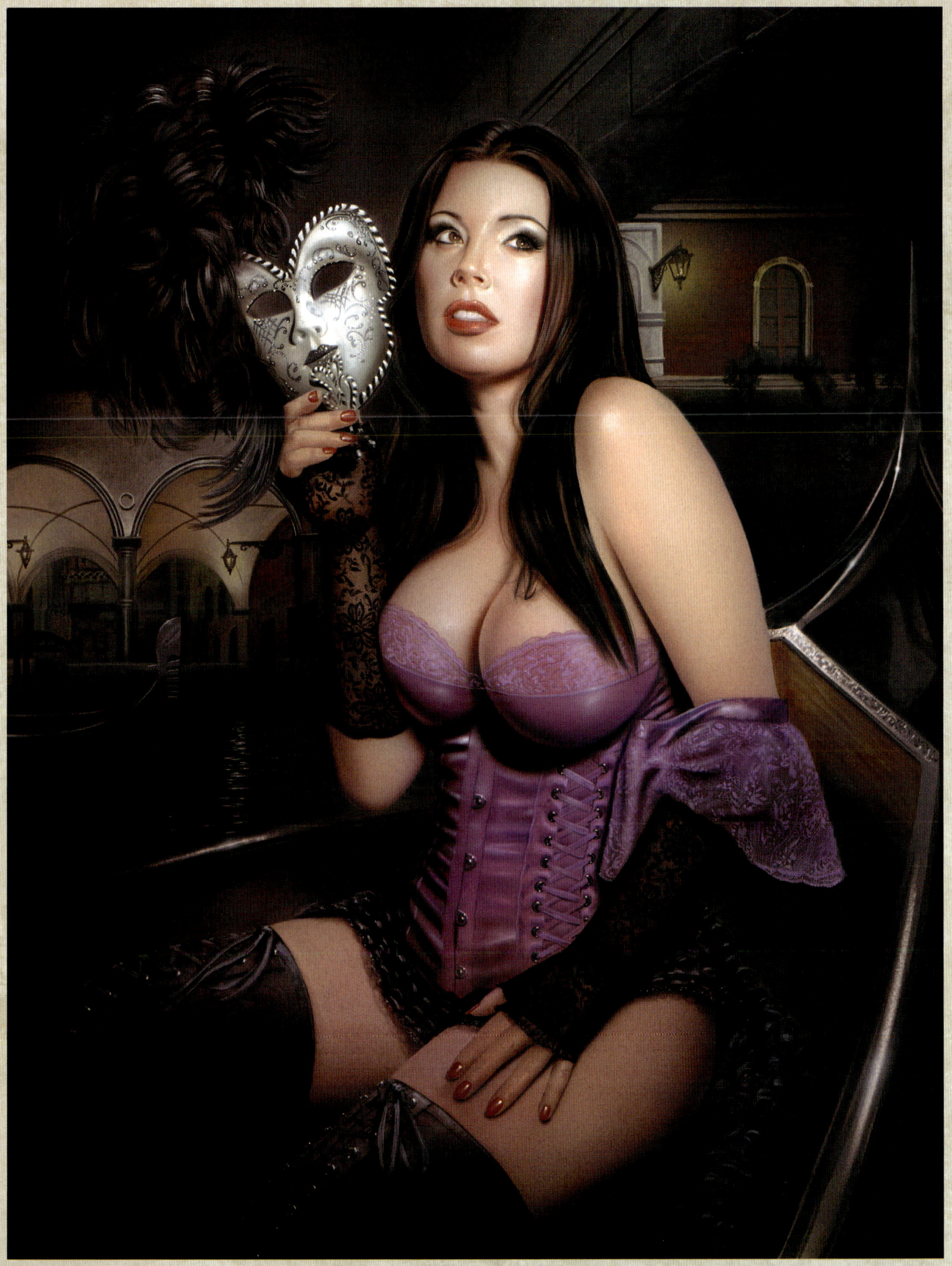

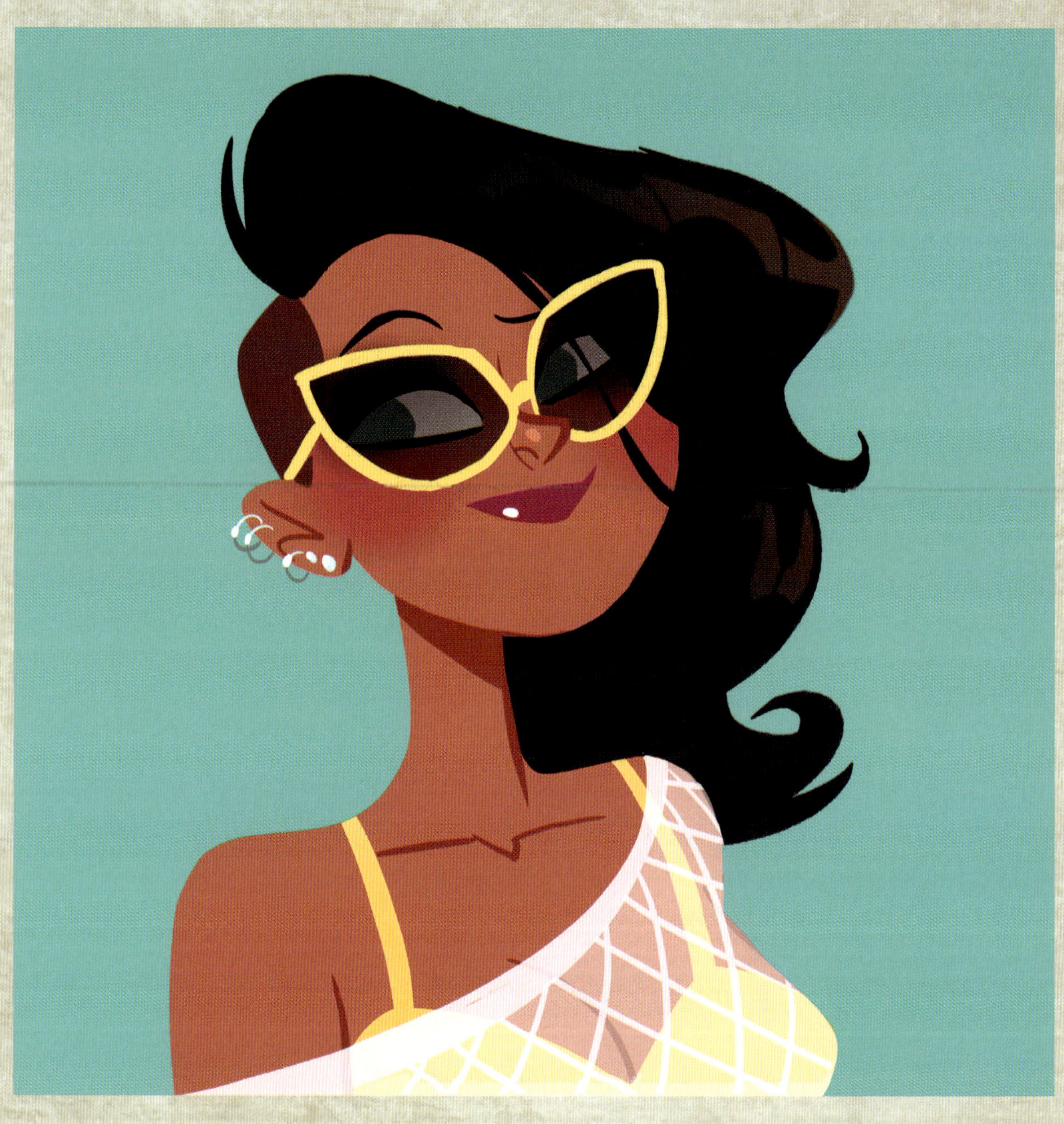

ABOVE: ***Barcelona Girl No. 4***
Guillaume Poux

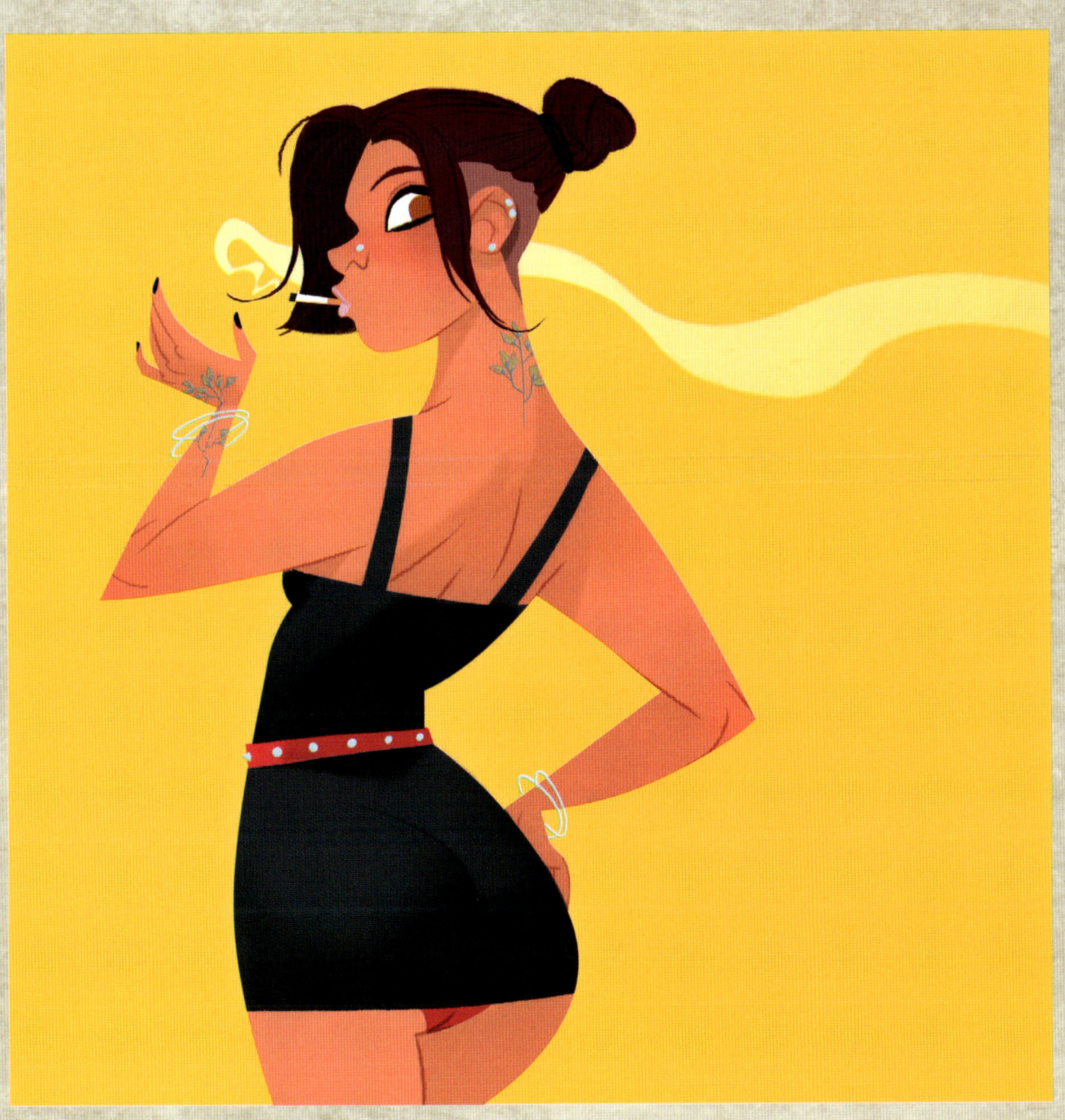

ABOVE: ***Barcelona Girl No. 2***
Guillaume Poux

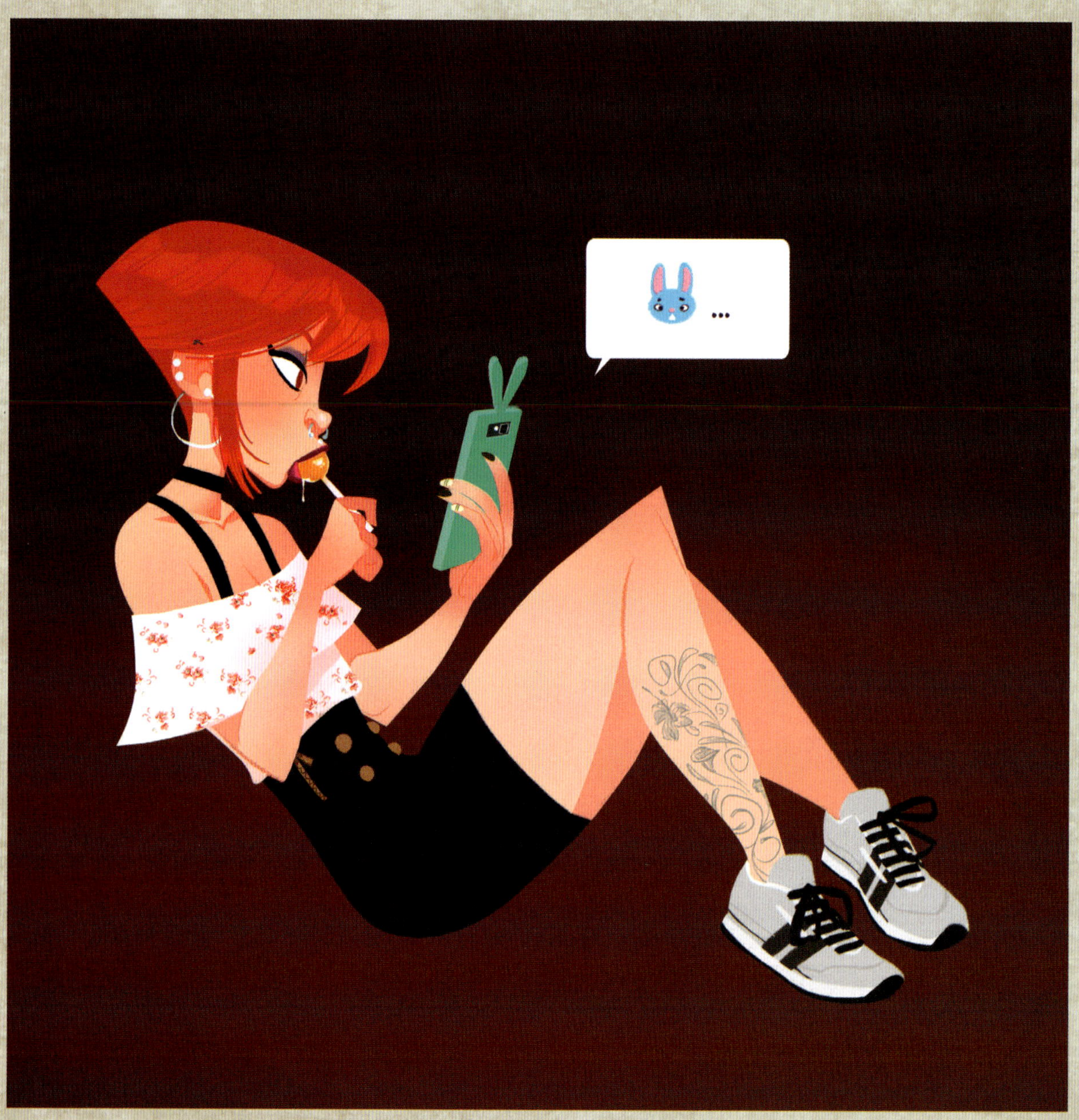

ABOVE: ***Barcelona Girl No. 5***
Guillaume Poux

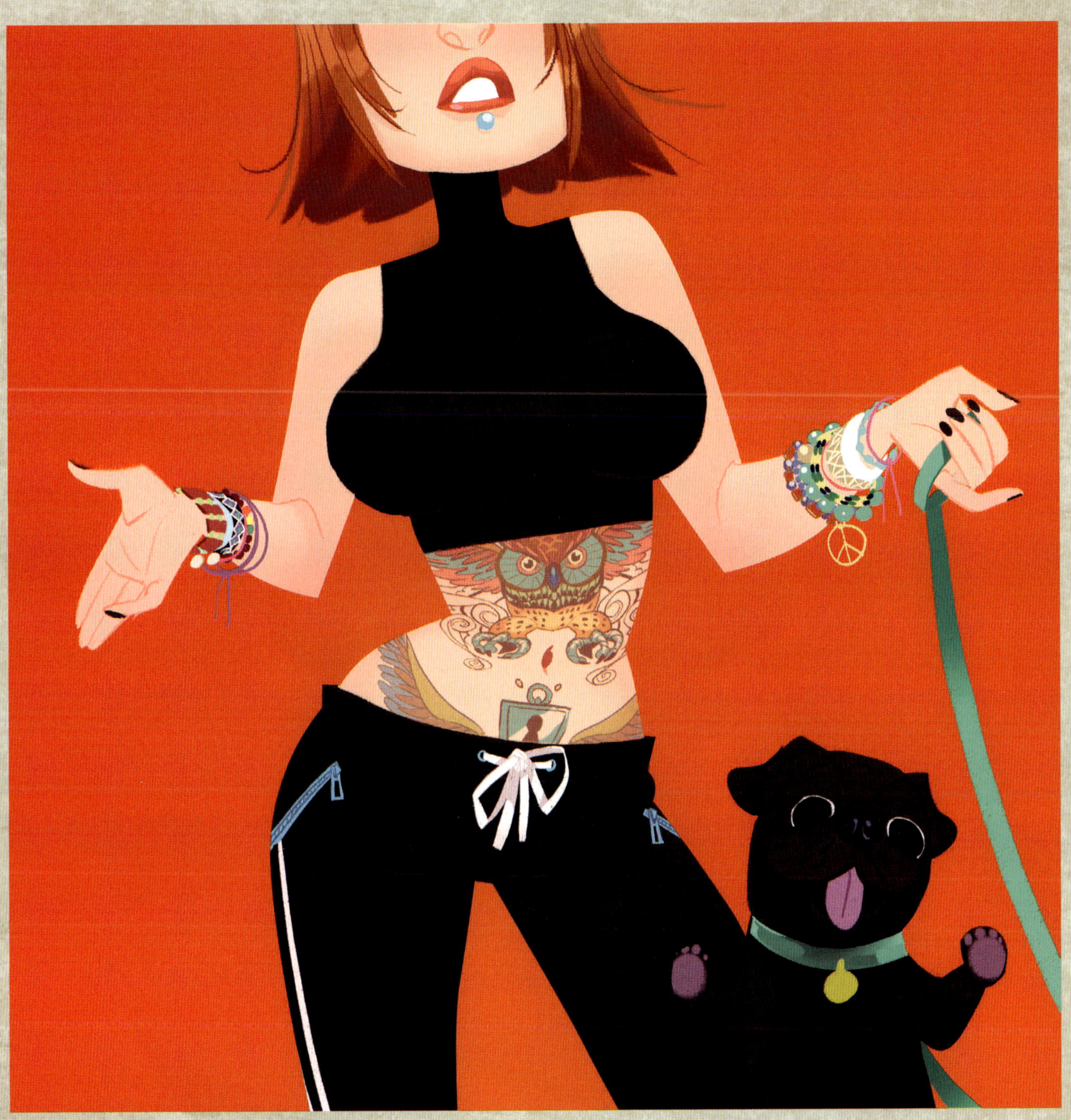

ABOVE: ***Barcelona Girl No. 9***
Guillaume Poux

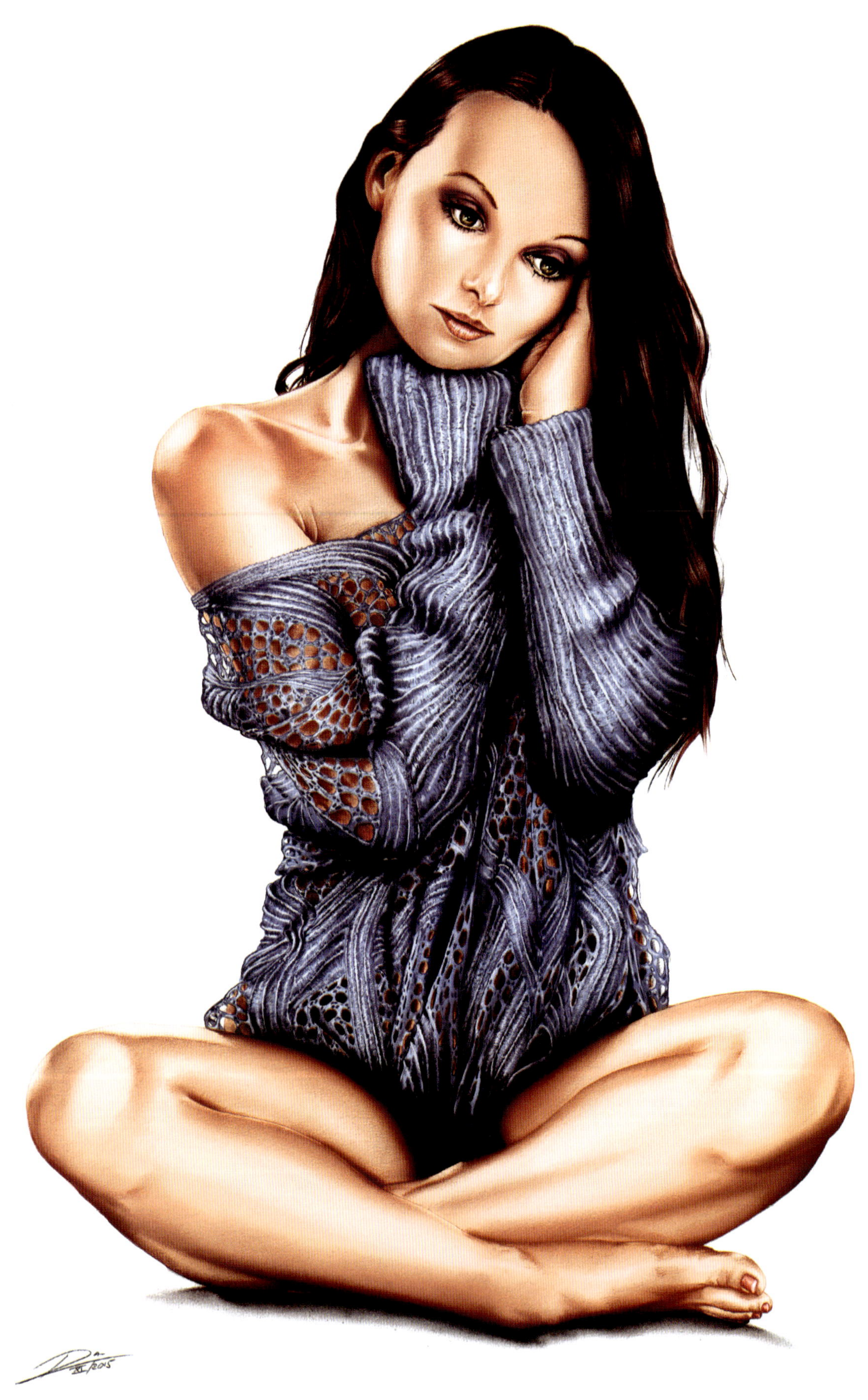

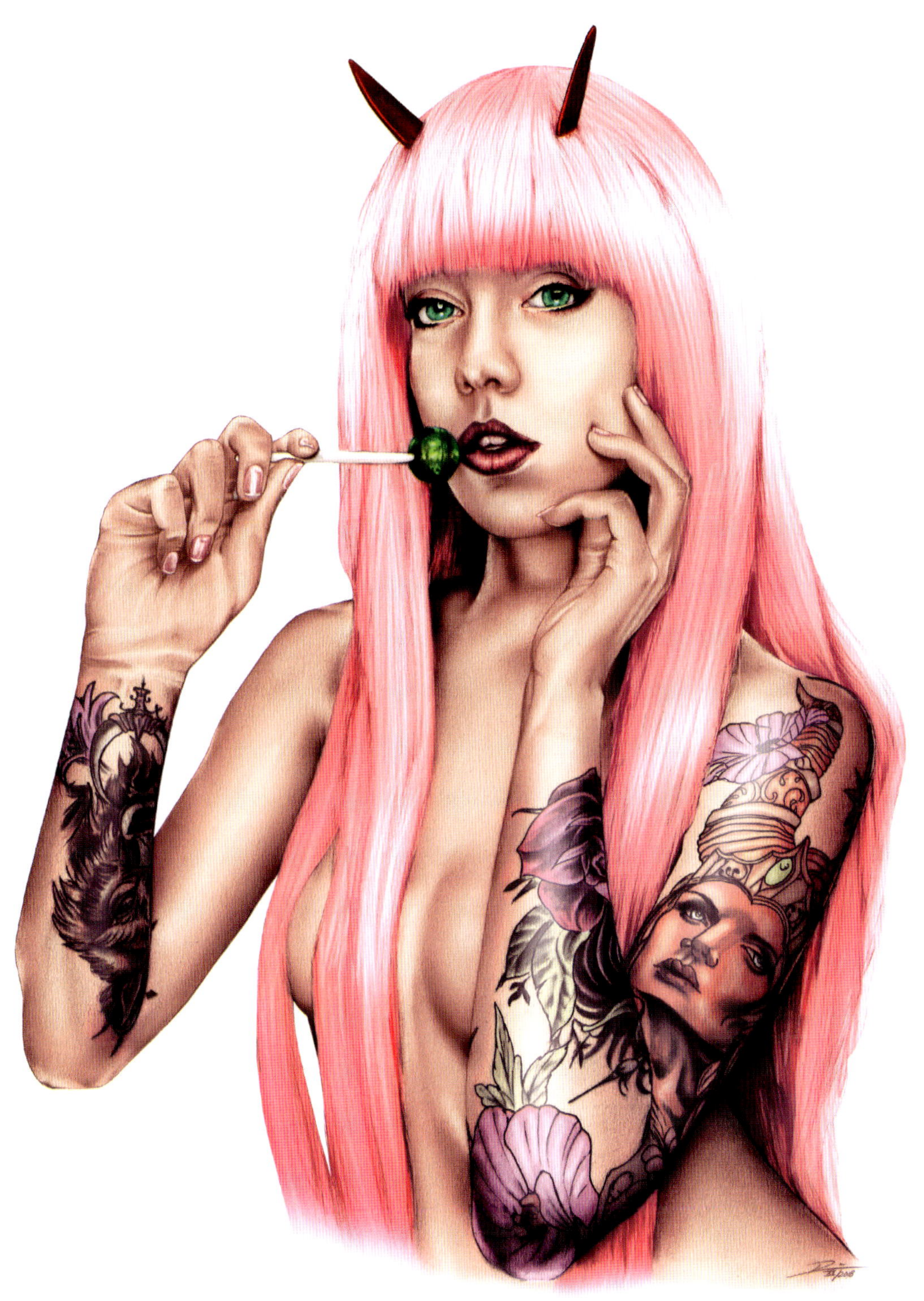

LEFT: ***Desire***
Dirk Richter

ABOVE: ***Zero Two***
Dirk Richter

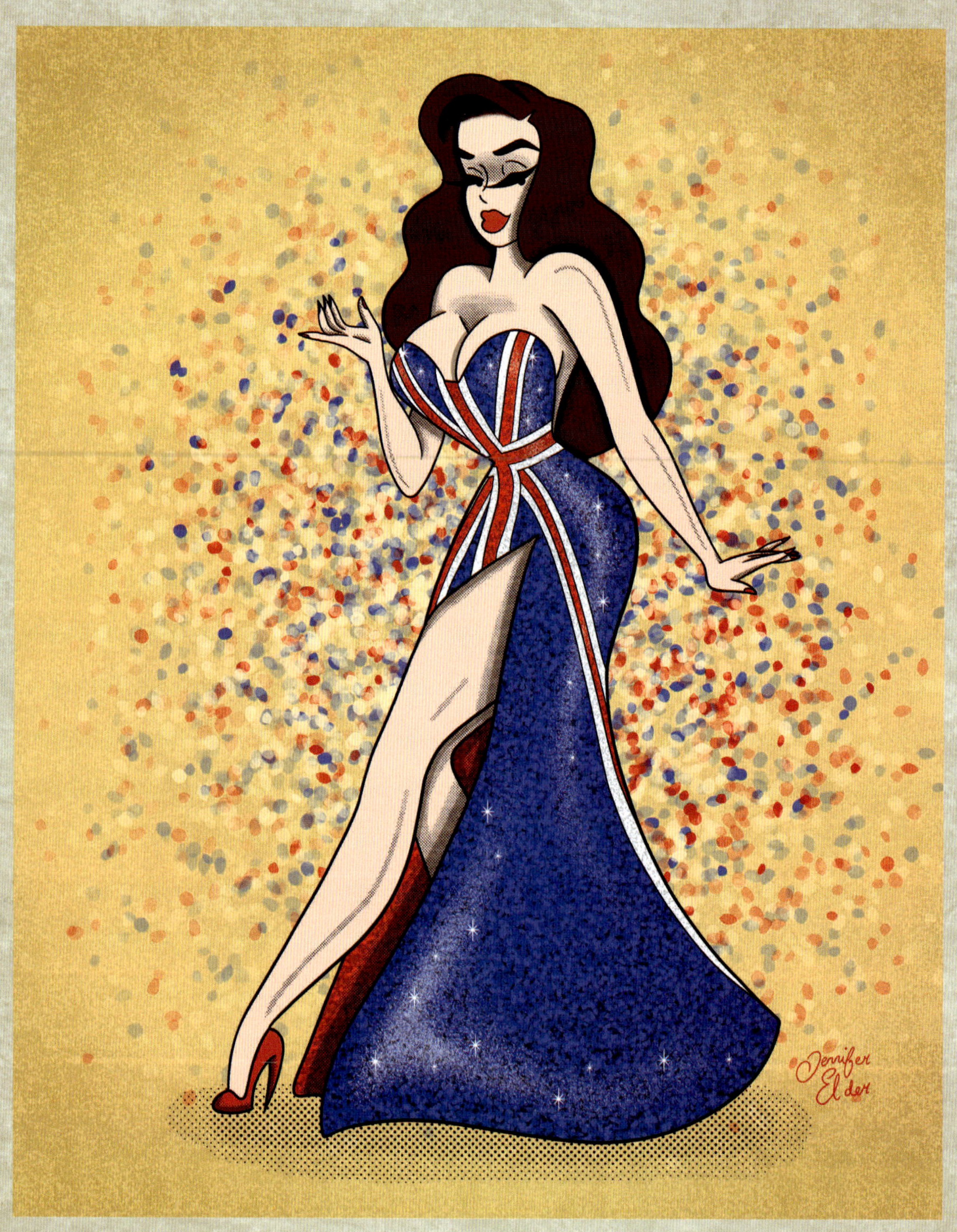

ABOVE: ***Miss Aston Martini***
Jennifer Elder

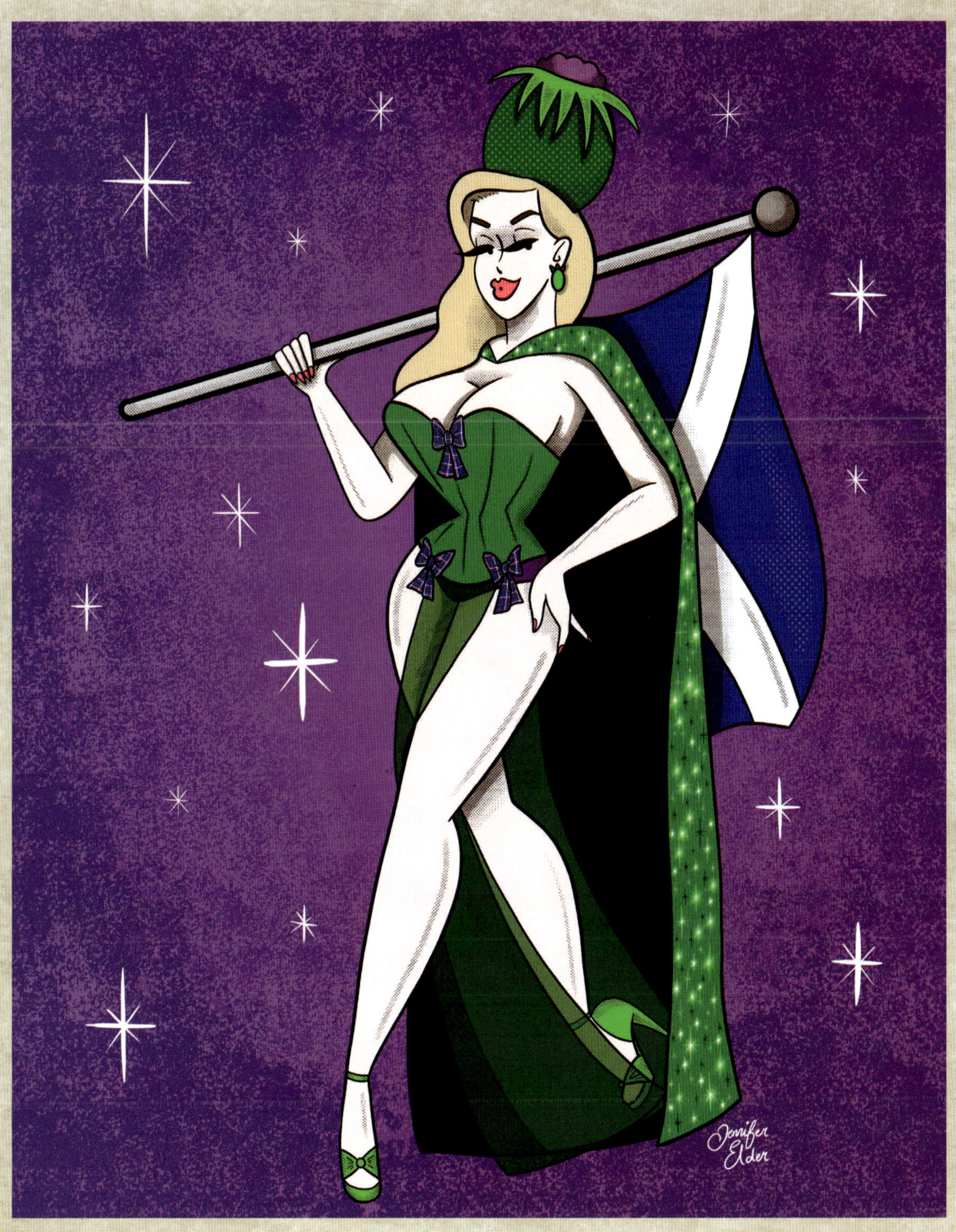

ABOVE: ***Pride of Scotland***
Jennifer Elder

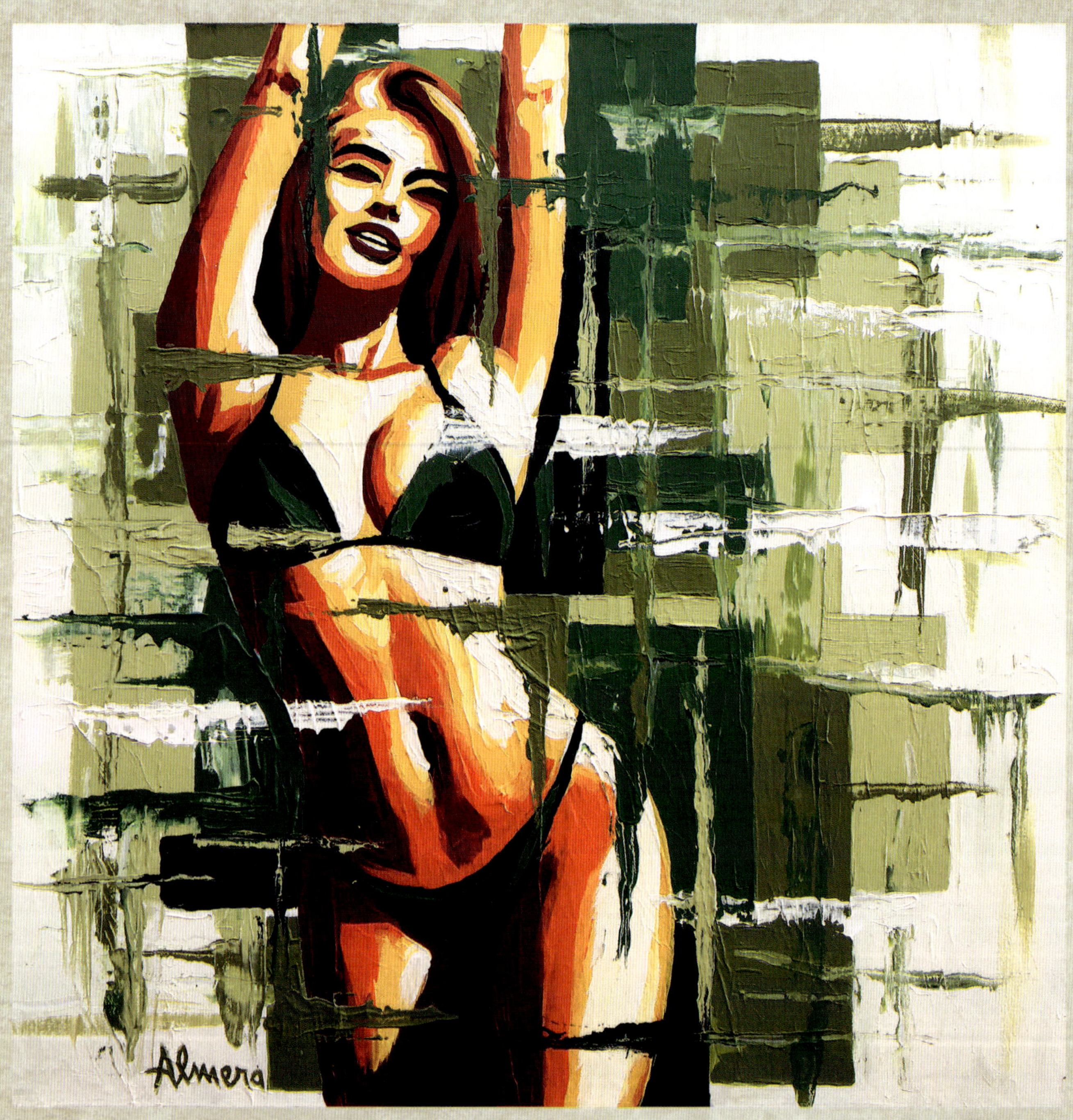

ABOVE: ***Adriana***
Marco Almera

RIGHT: ***Red***
Ivan Valle

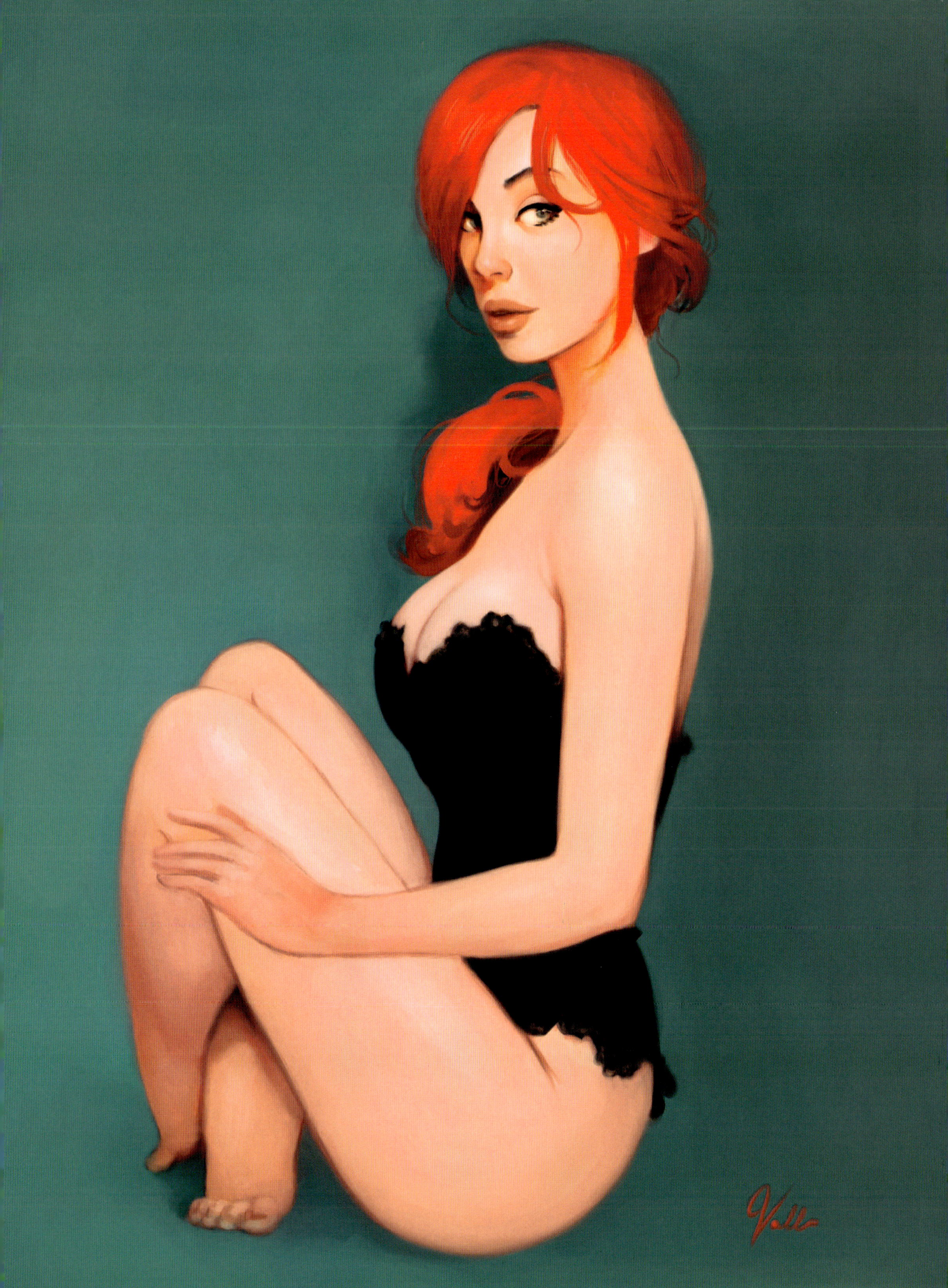

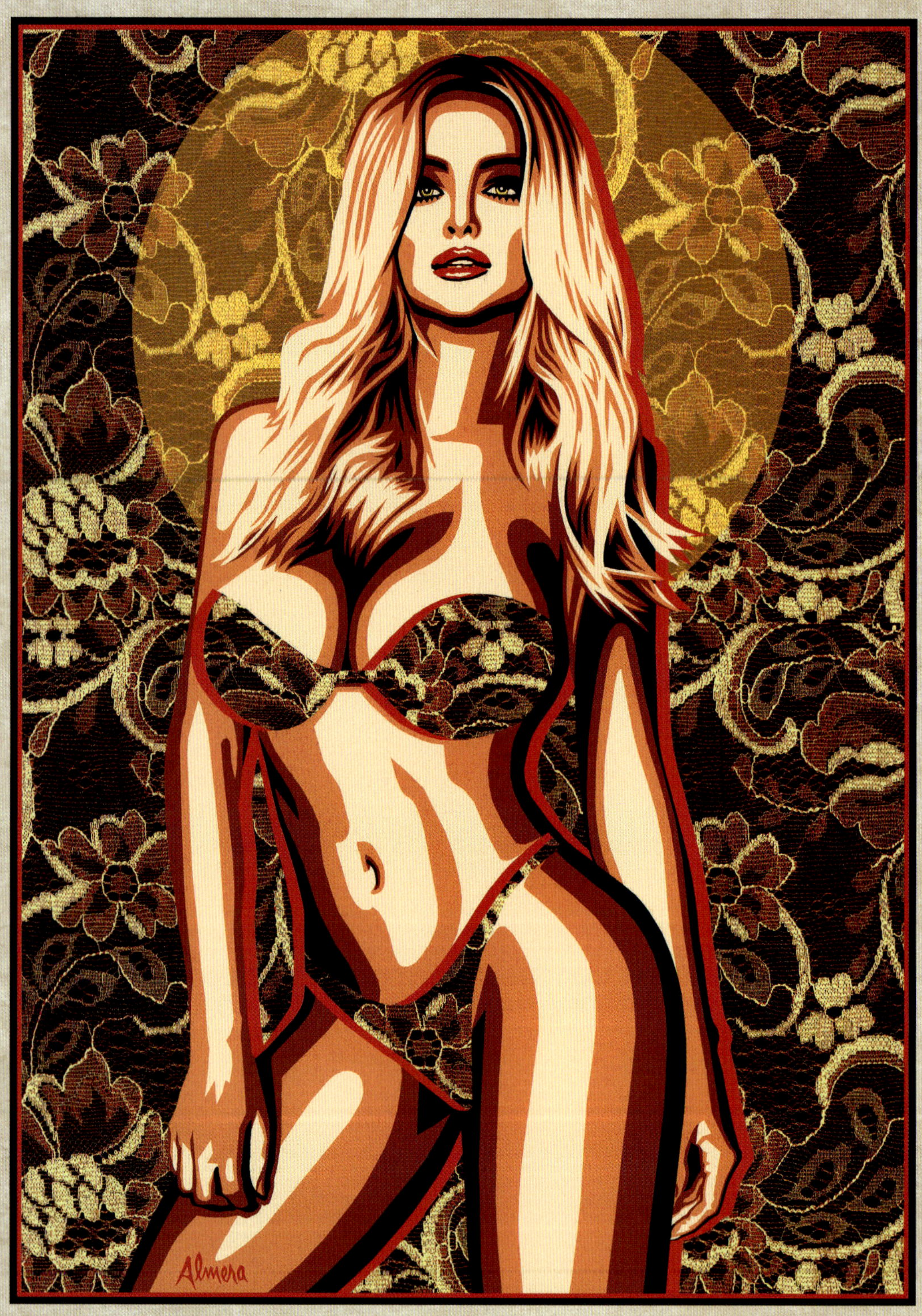

ABOVE: ***Uplifted***
Marco Almera

RIGHT: ***Pure Gold***
Marco Almera

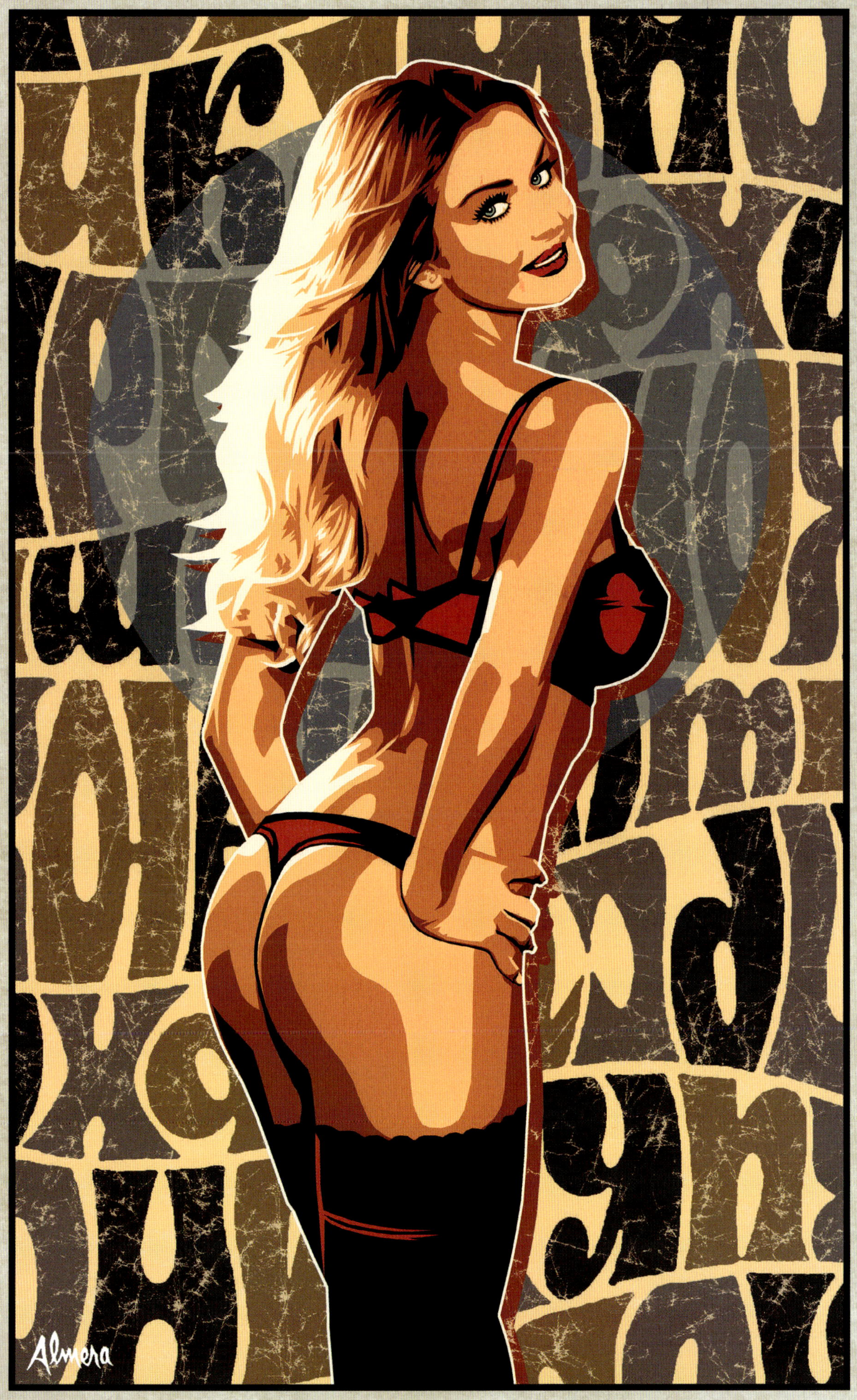
Almera

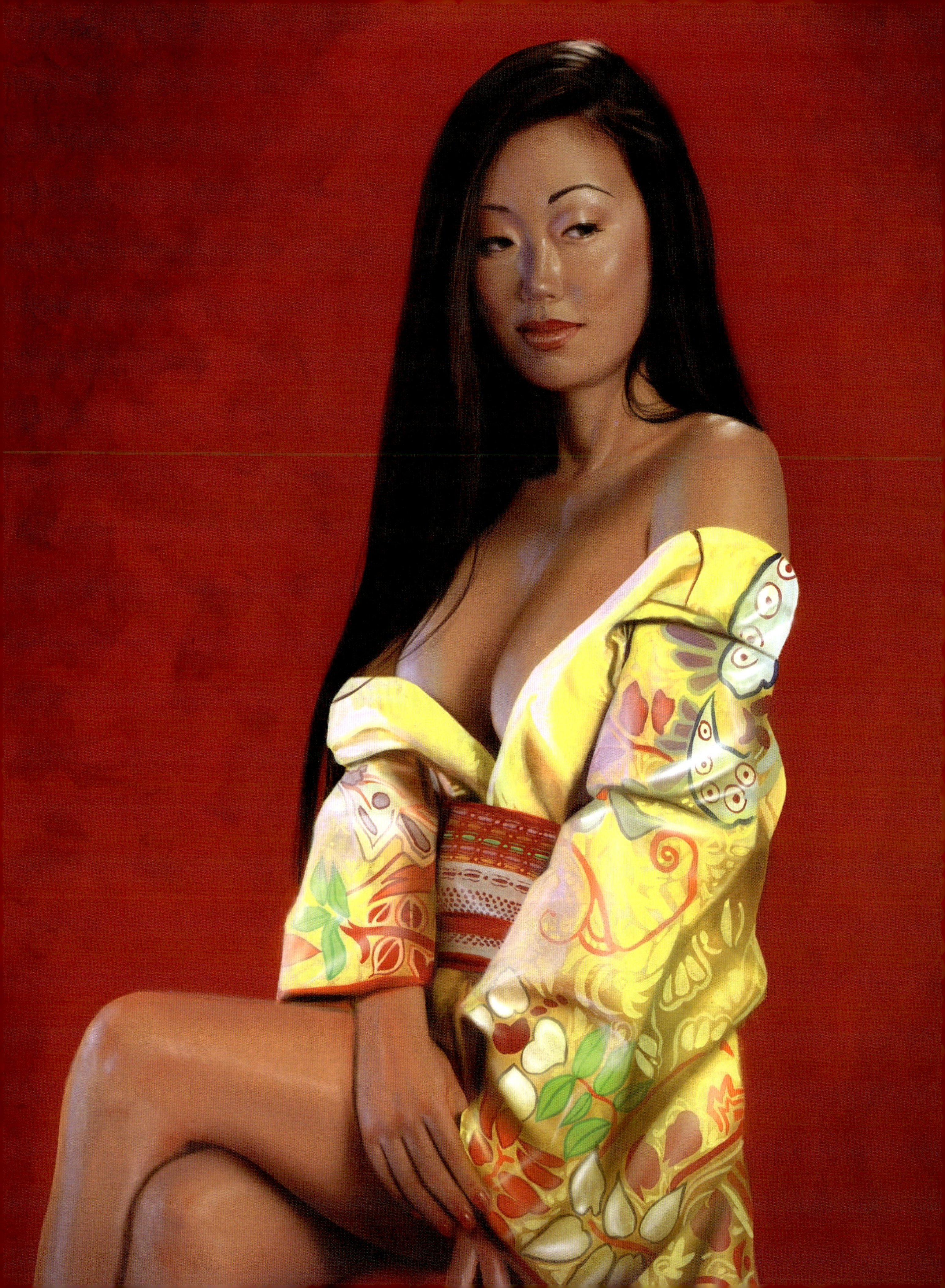

International

Recalling the gauzy, veiled artistry of its ancestors, the heritage of the pinup girl is clearly defined; American influences in mid-20th century art reflected back with a cultural twist and the infusion of other graphic traditions. Whether from Japan, Brazil or Egypt, the women in these images tantalize with an unconcerned glance away from the viewer or a flirtatiously direct peek over provocatively lowered sunglasses. Yet there is something different here, a line that diverges from those famed pinups decorating the temporary billets of GIs in war torn Europe.

The recreation of the unassuming sexuality and empowered confidence of the glossily glowing pinup of the 40s and 50s finds an altered mirror in playful, often surreal moments suspended in ink or a digital brush. The coy playfulness with costume and dress of that former pin up era is transformed into a recreation of history, a geisha surreally dipped in ramen noodles as if enjoying a traditional Japanese bath house, a Brazilian carnival queen with jet black hair topped with a fanning, opulent headdress – drenched in samba sensualism through her pose and curvaceous figure, yet still sparkling and wholesome.

There is a vitality and richness to these women, so closely linked to their surroundings, aware of our gaze and yet not held captive by it; they are performers of their own show, for themselves – how lucky we are to see them! The cultural backgrounds from which they stem, a curious fusion of the American and the international, are both a backdrop to their looks – often standing in front of temples, reclining in a place of local interest or draped in front of the symbolism of the flag – and an inversion of the classic Americana from which they stem. The playful toying with nostalgia through style and symbolism is reflected in the varying aesthetics – diaphanous and light, graphic and rounded – in which these contemporary international pin ups are delivered.

The sensuality of the pinup and a nation's sexual conventions (often riotously at odds) are brought together with a knowing wink, subverting culture and history through a well proportioned leg or a confident, steady gaze. Beds of roses, a seductively open fan or the animal companion that calls attention to our primal instincts, the lens of our interest is always tastefully tinted in the contemporary style of a nation, artfully flirting with a shared heritage as they enrich the potential directions of the inimitable (but endlessly adaptive) pinup.

LEFT: *Geisha*
Lorenzo Sperlonga

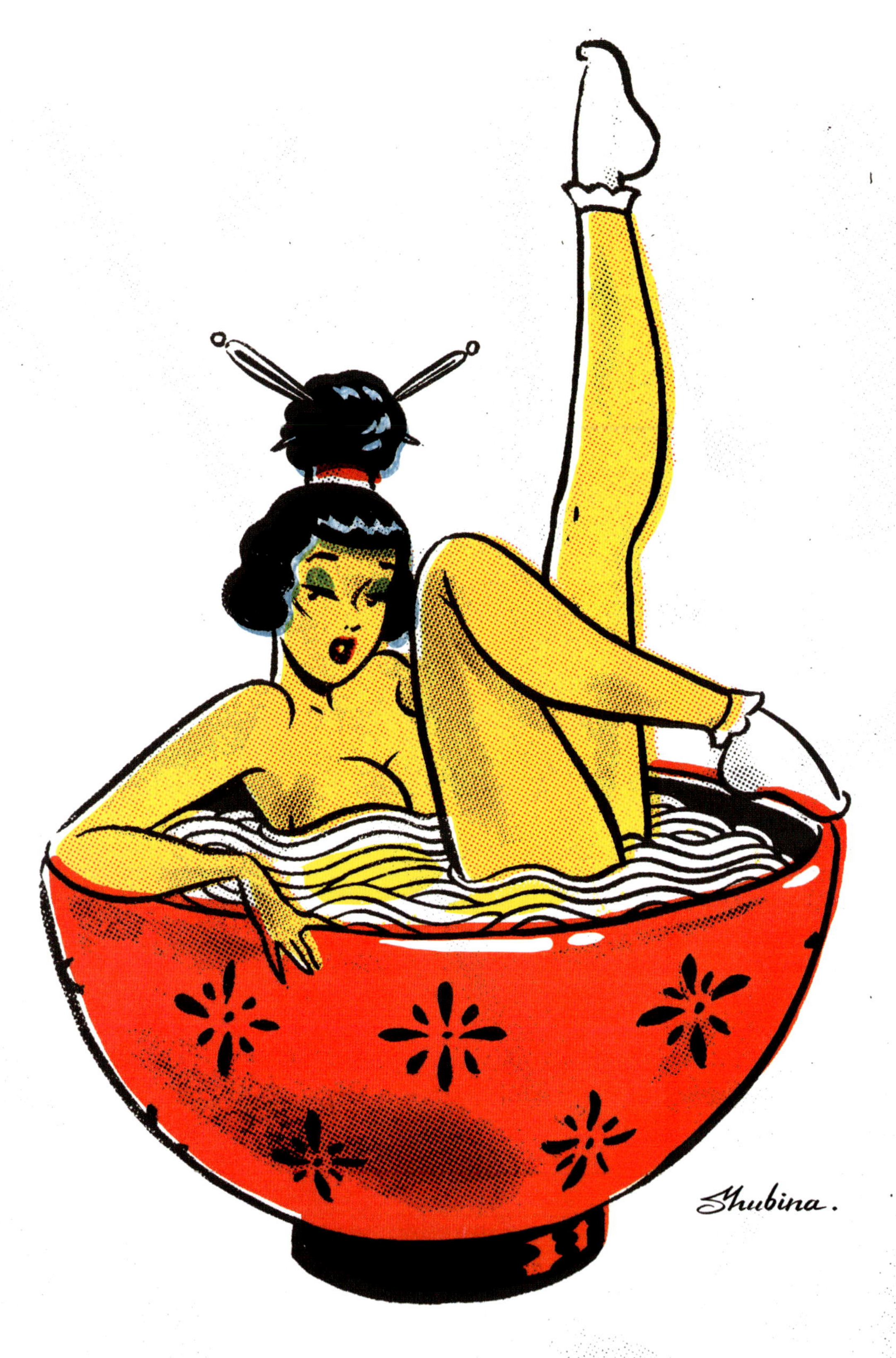
Shubina.

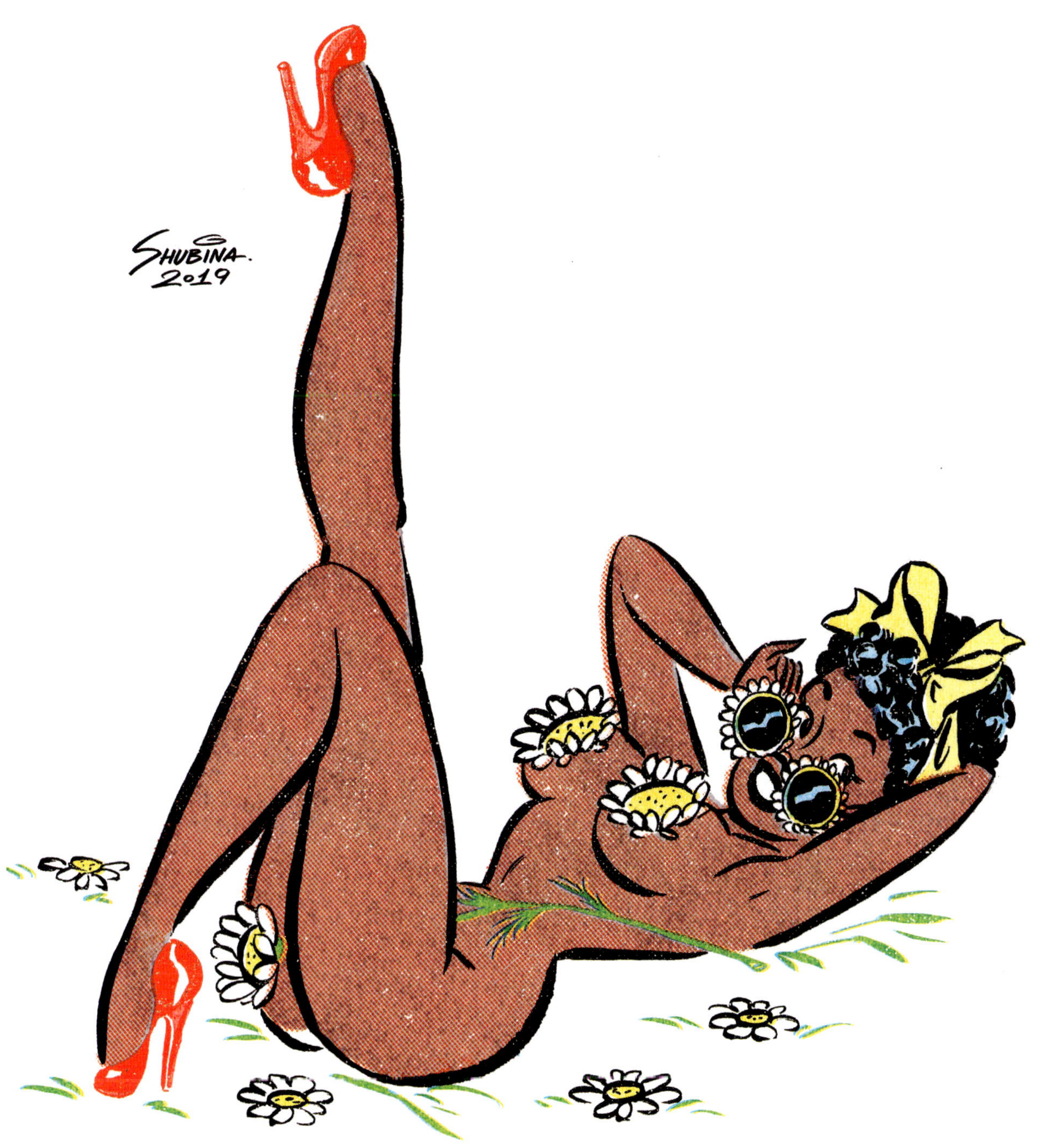

LEFT: ***Noodle***
Sveta Shubina

ABOVE: ***Flowers***
Sveta Shubina

OVERLEAF: ***Venus and the Moon***
Lorenzo Sperlonga

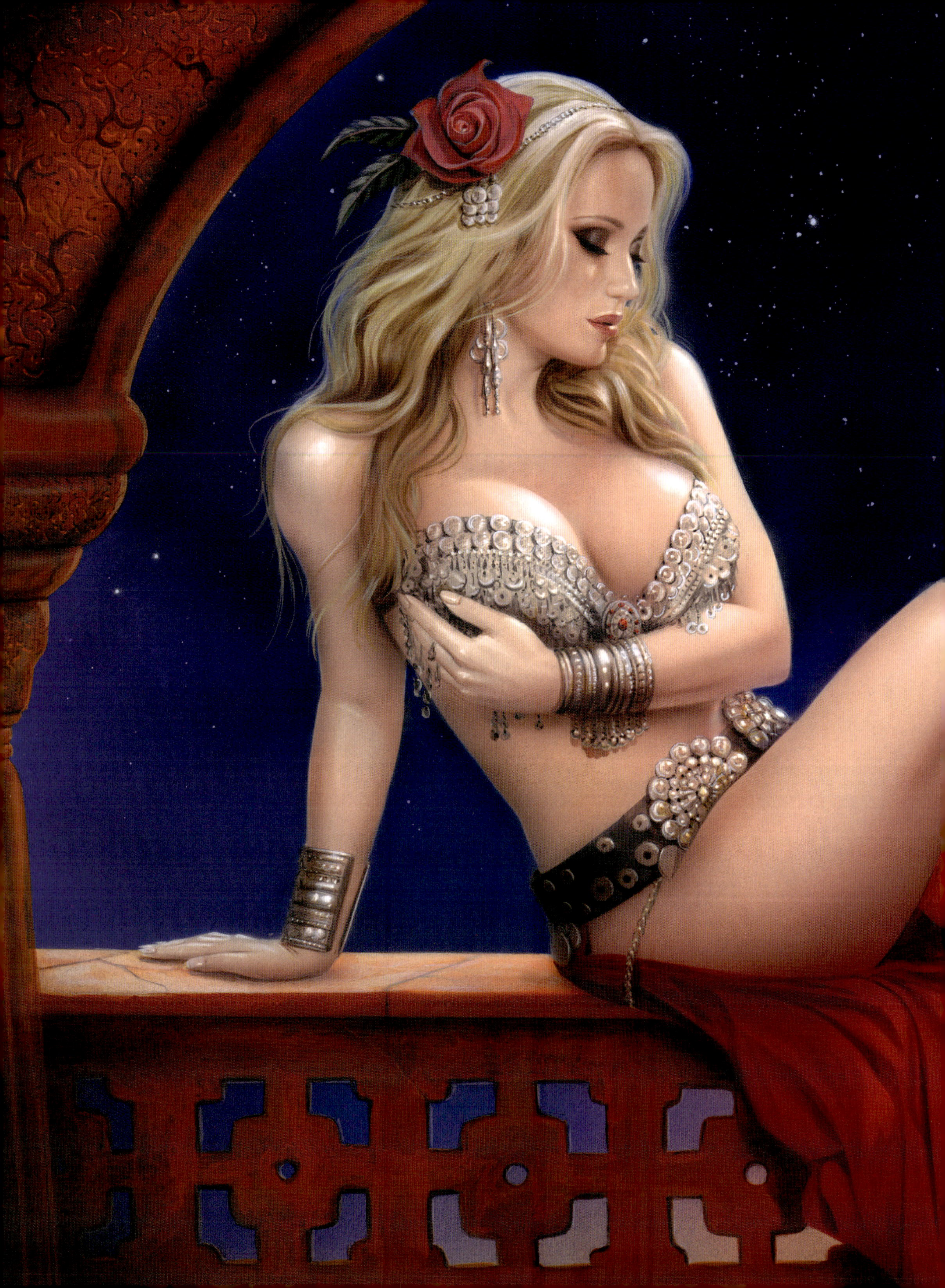

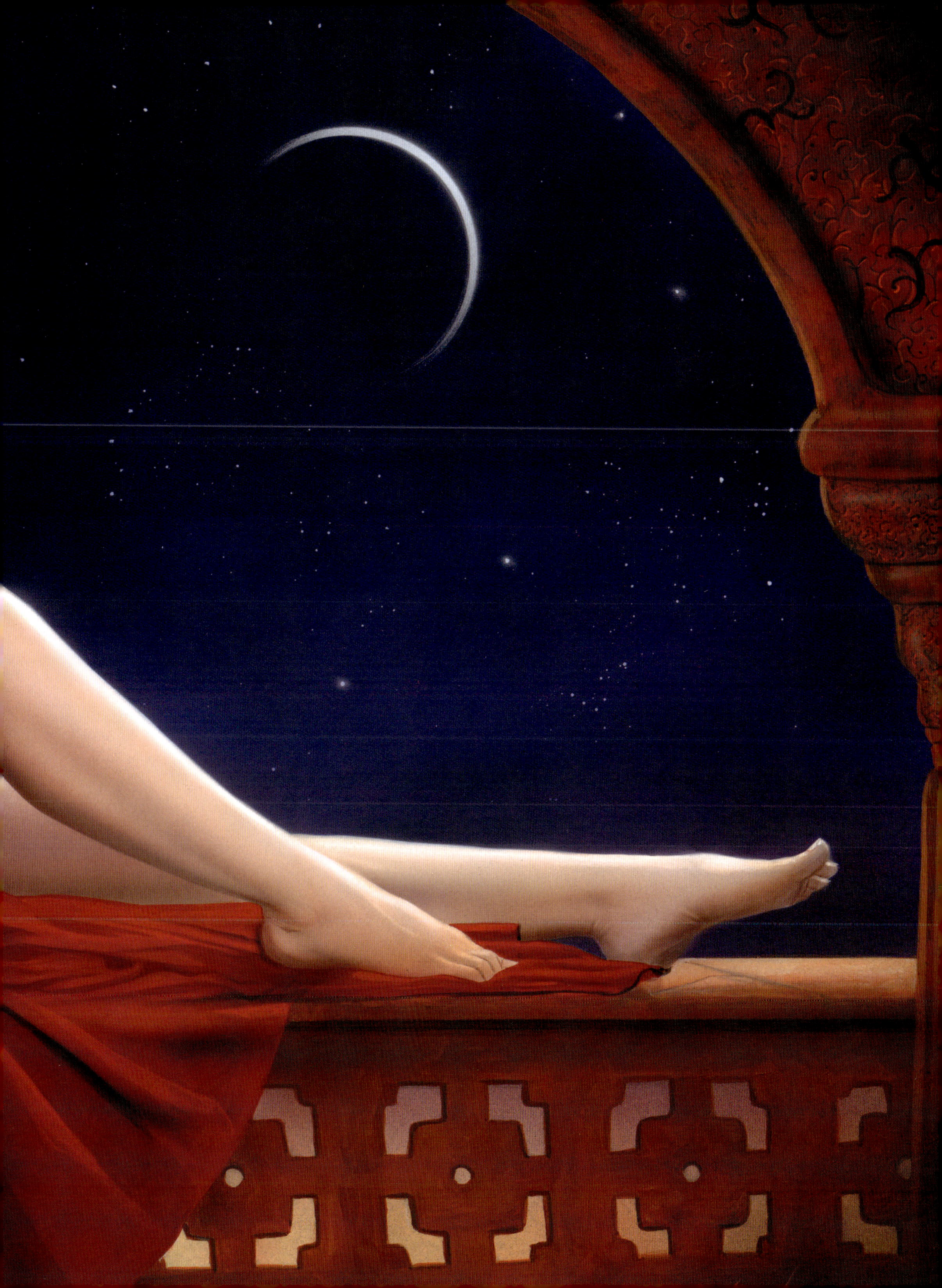

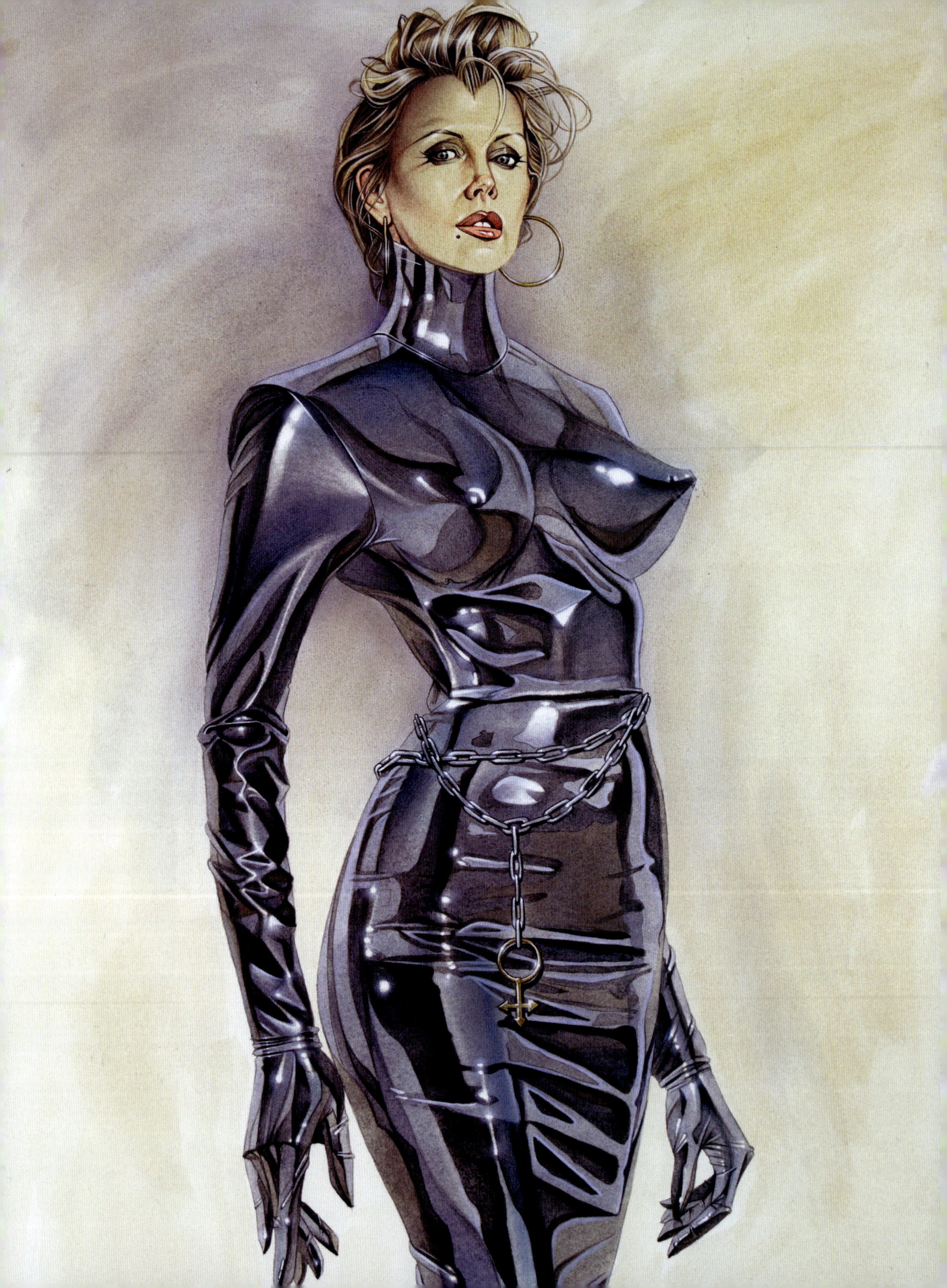

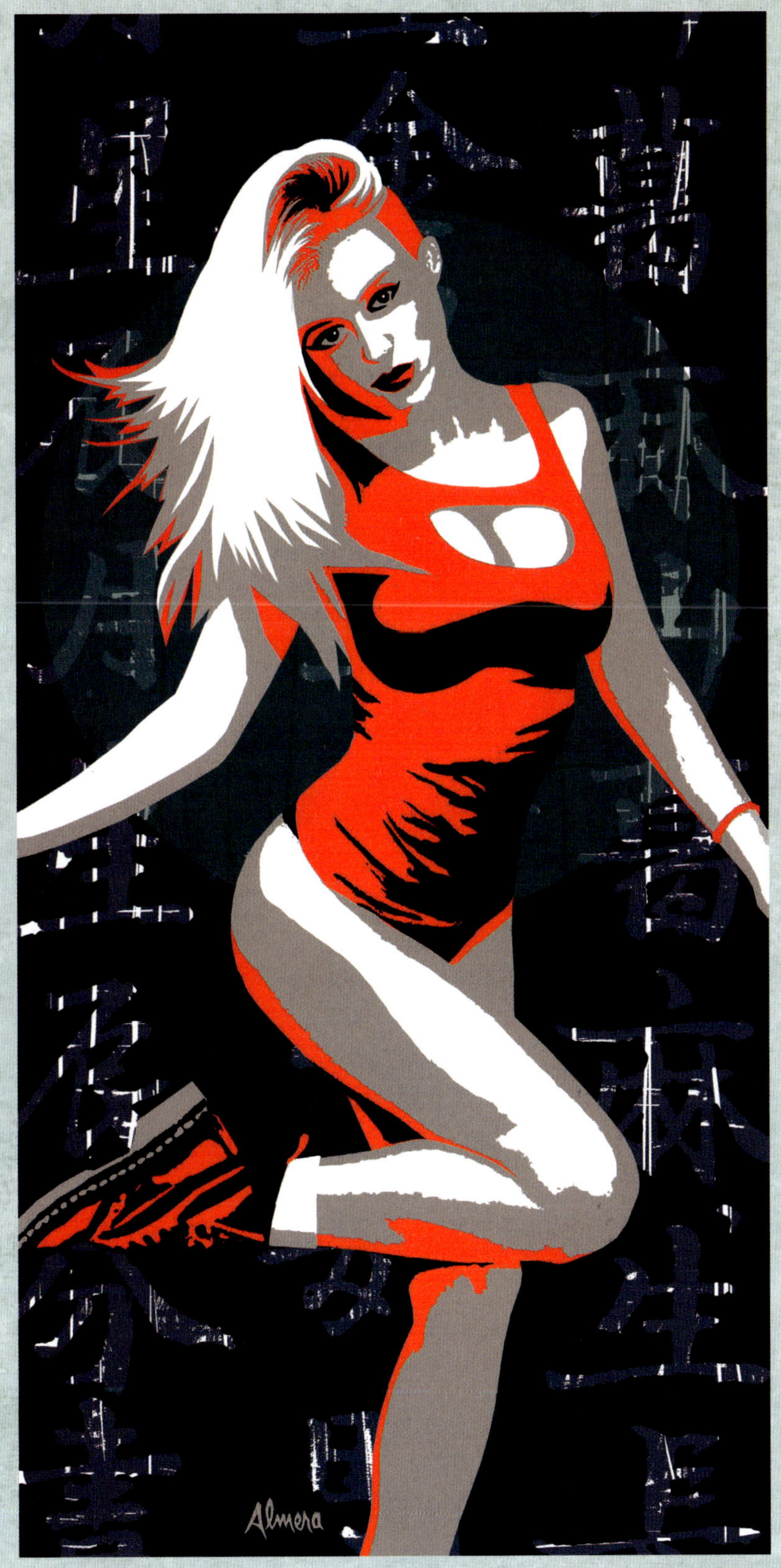

LEFT: ***Long Dress***
Bern Foster

ABOVE: ***Silver***
Marco Almera

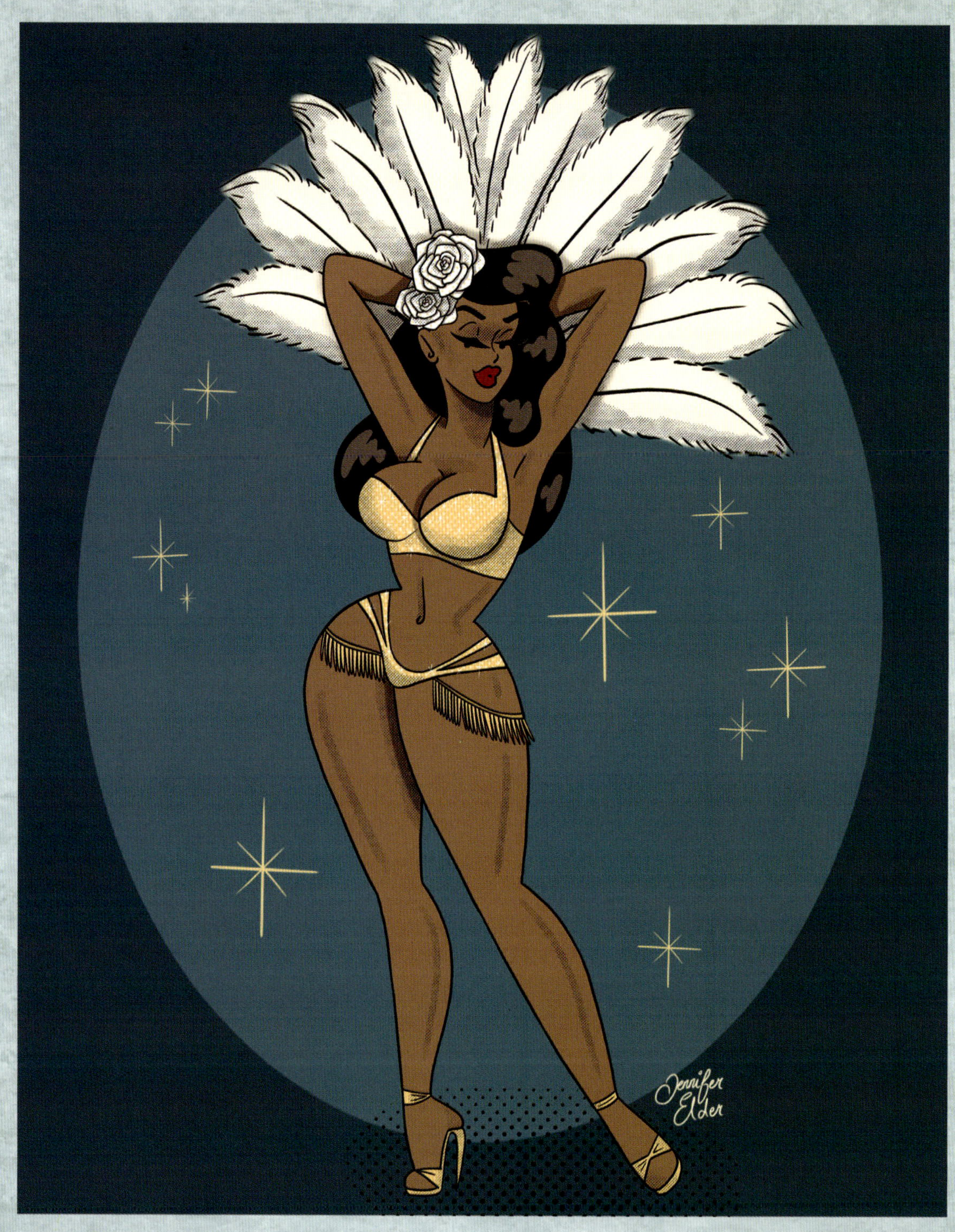

ABOVE: ***Jessebelle Thunder***
Jennifer Elder

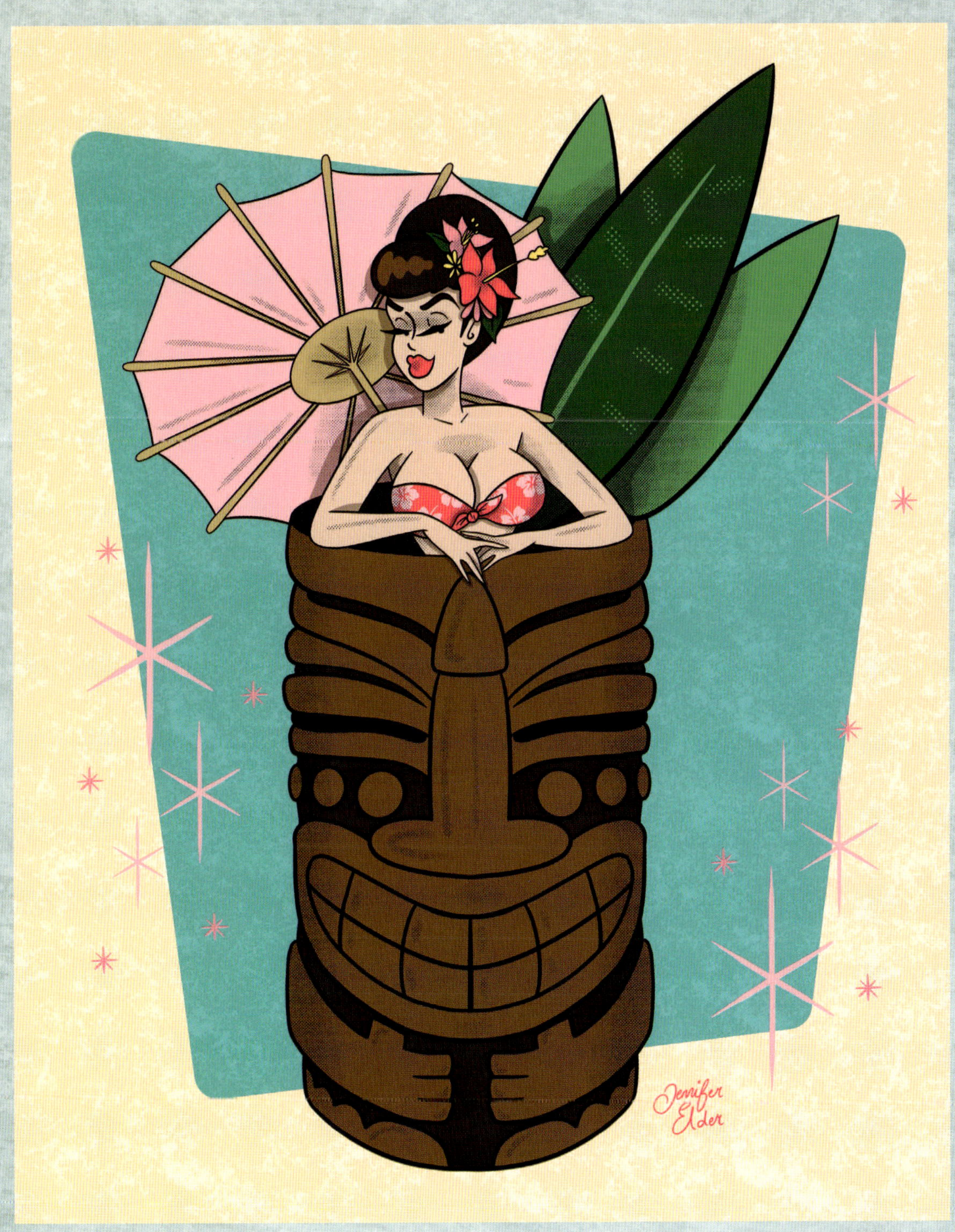

ABOVE: ***Mai Tai Moment***
Jennifer Elder

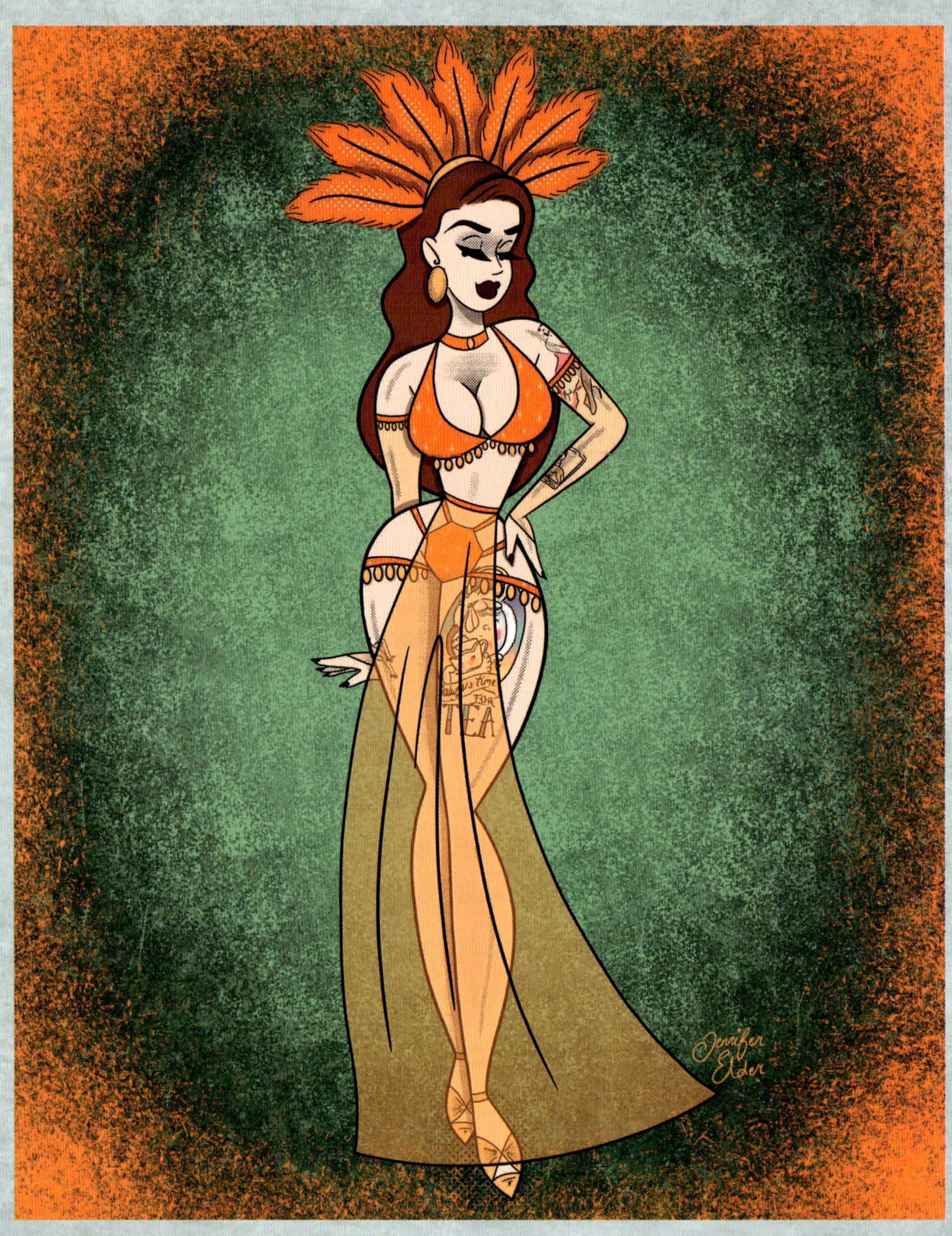

ABOVE: ***Dottie May***
Jennifer Elder

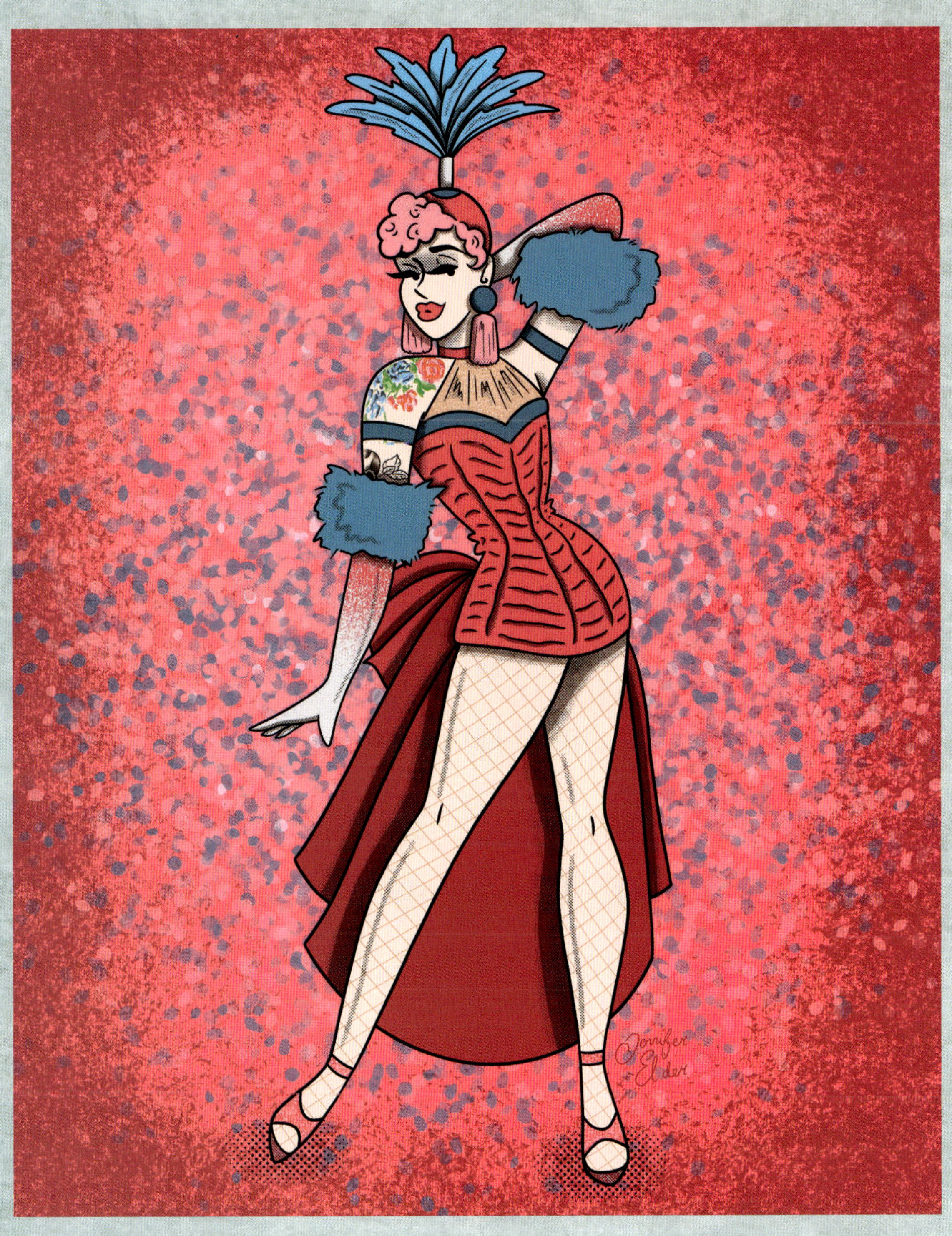

ABOVE: ***Tom Harlow***
Jennifer Elder

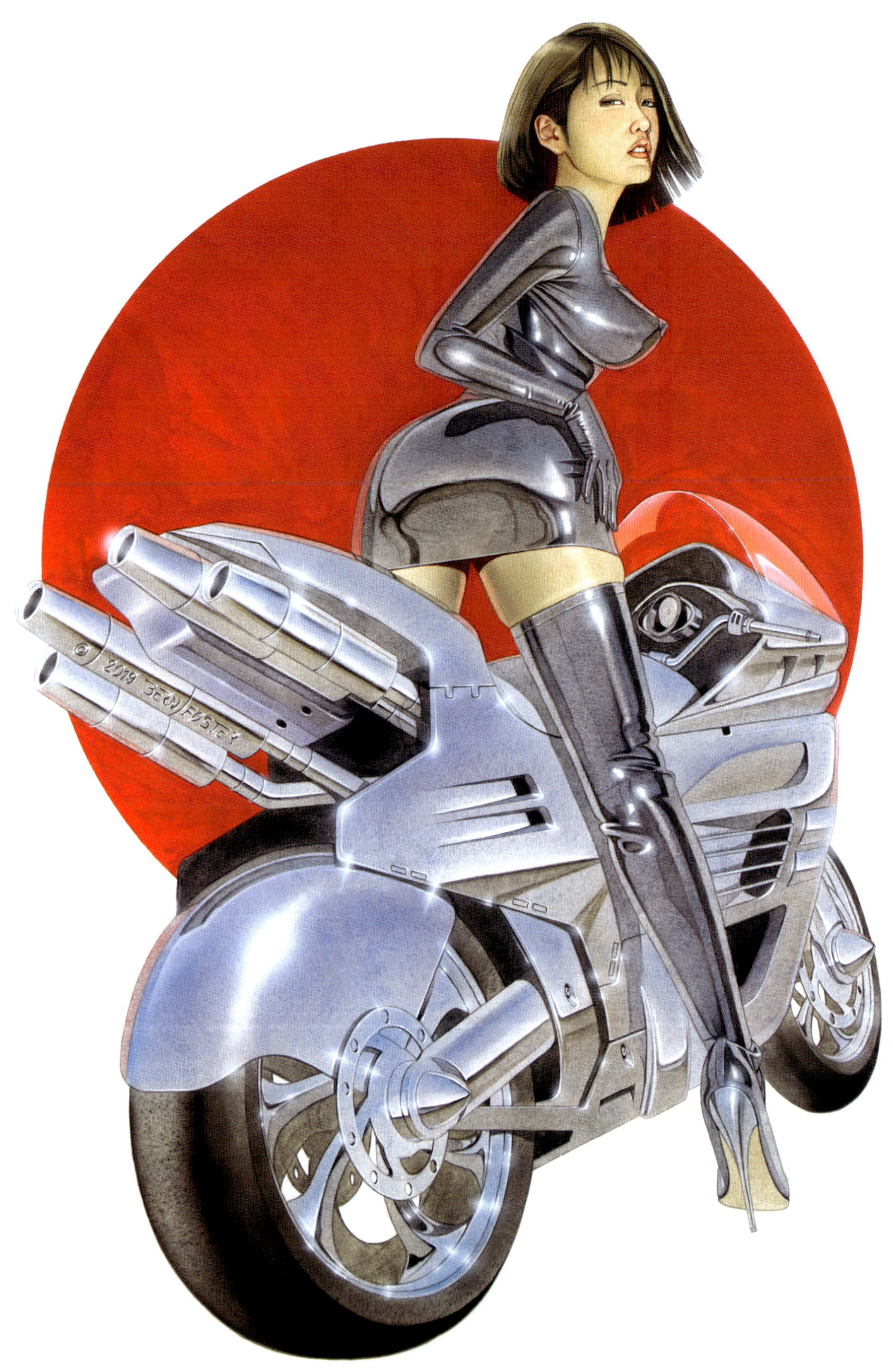
© 2019 BERN FOSTER

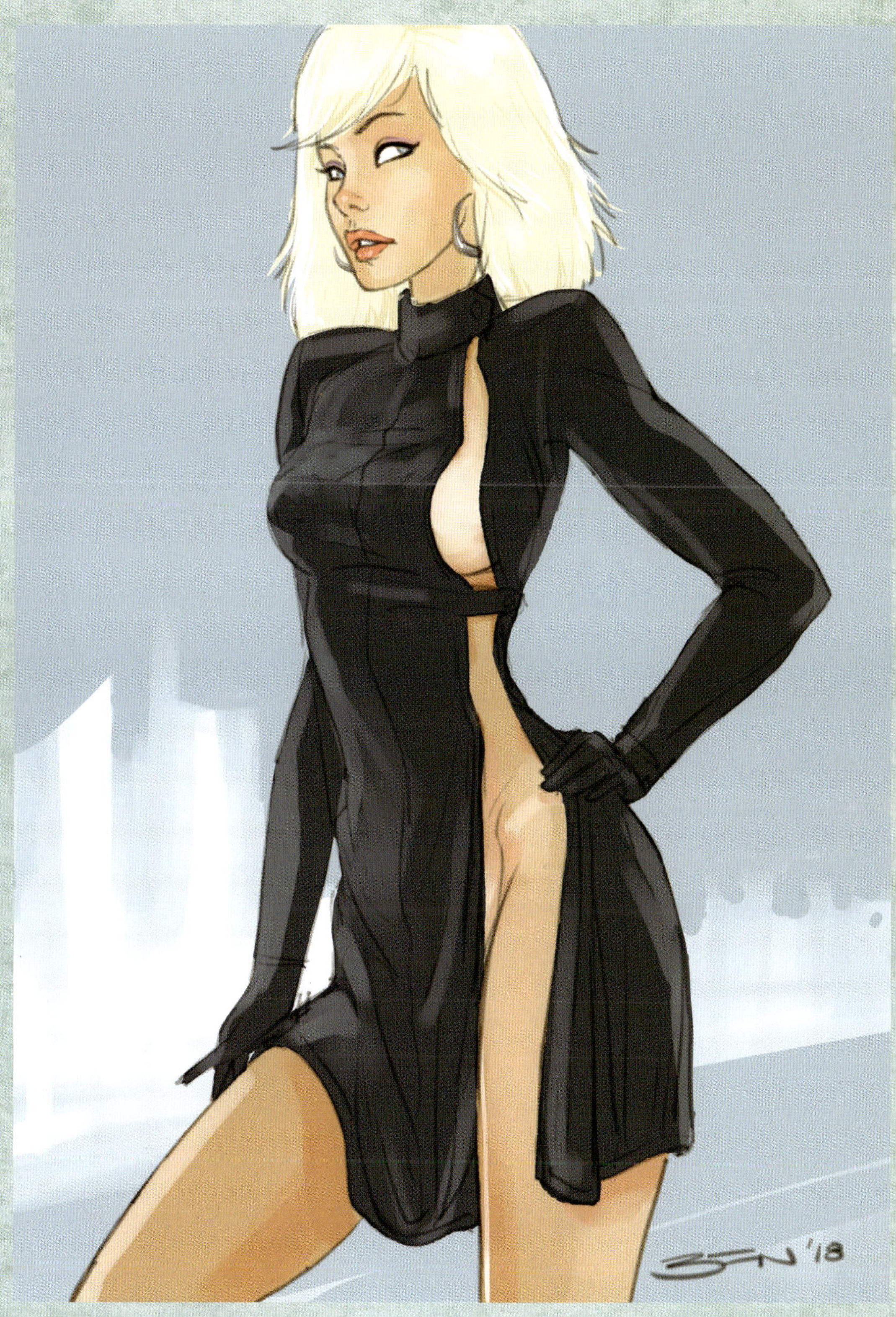

LEFT: ***Tokyo Super Rider***
Bern Foster

ABOVE: ***Slit***
Ben Tan

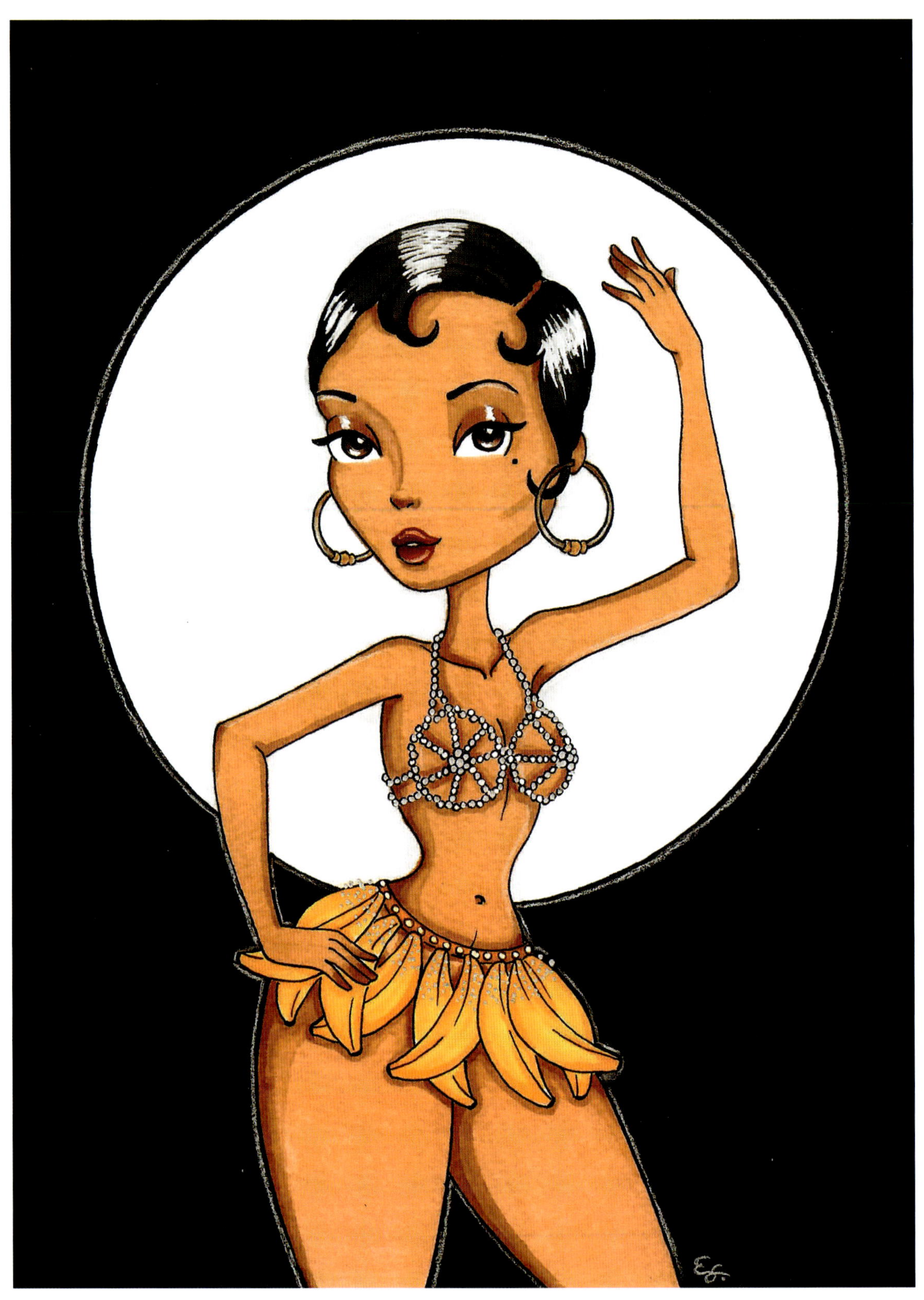

ABOVE: ***Ms Baker***
Erica Lynn Shaw

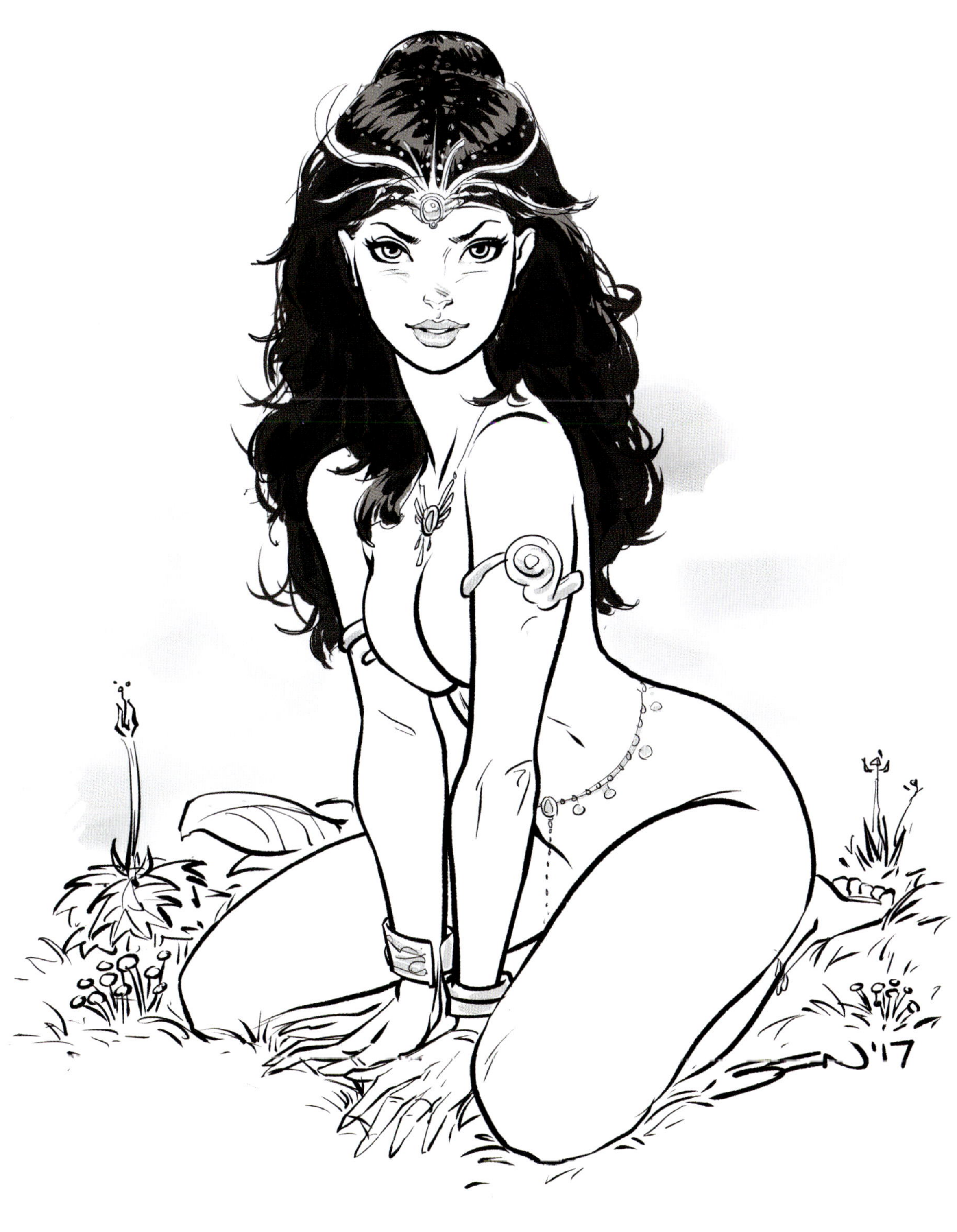

ABOVE: ***Dejah***
Ben Tan

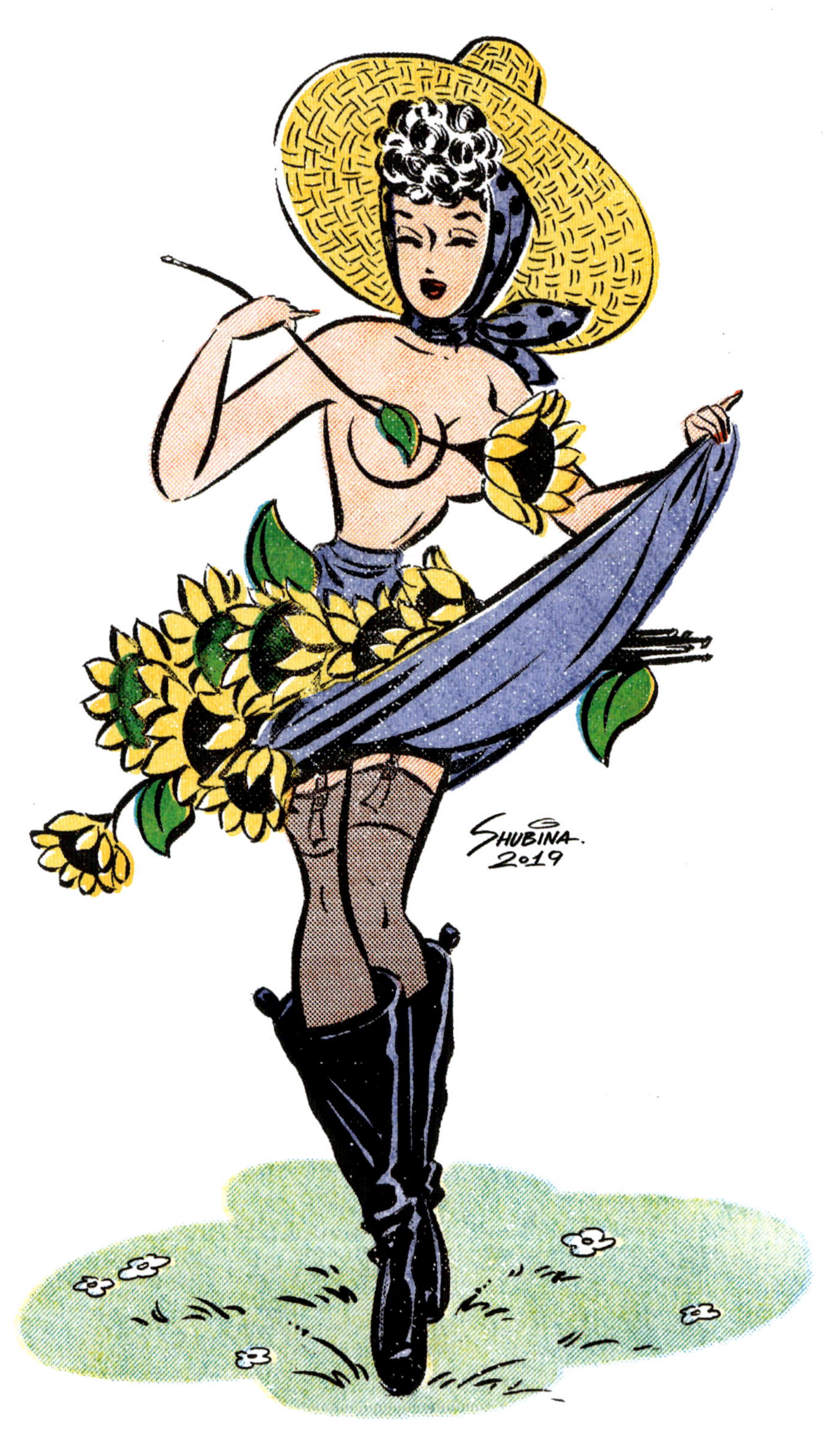

ABOVE: ***Sunflower***
Sveta Shubina

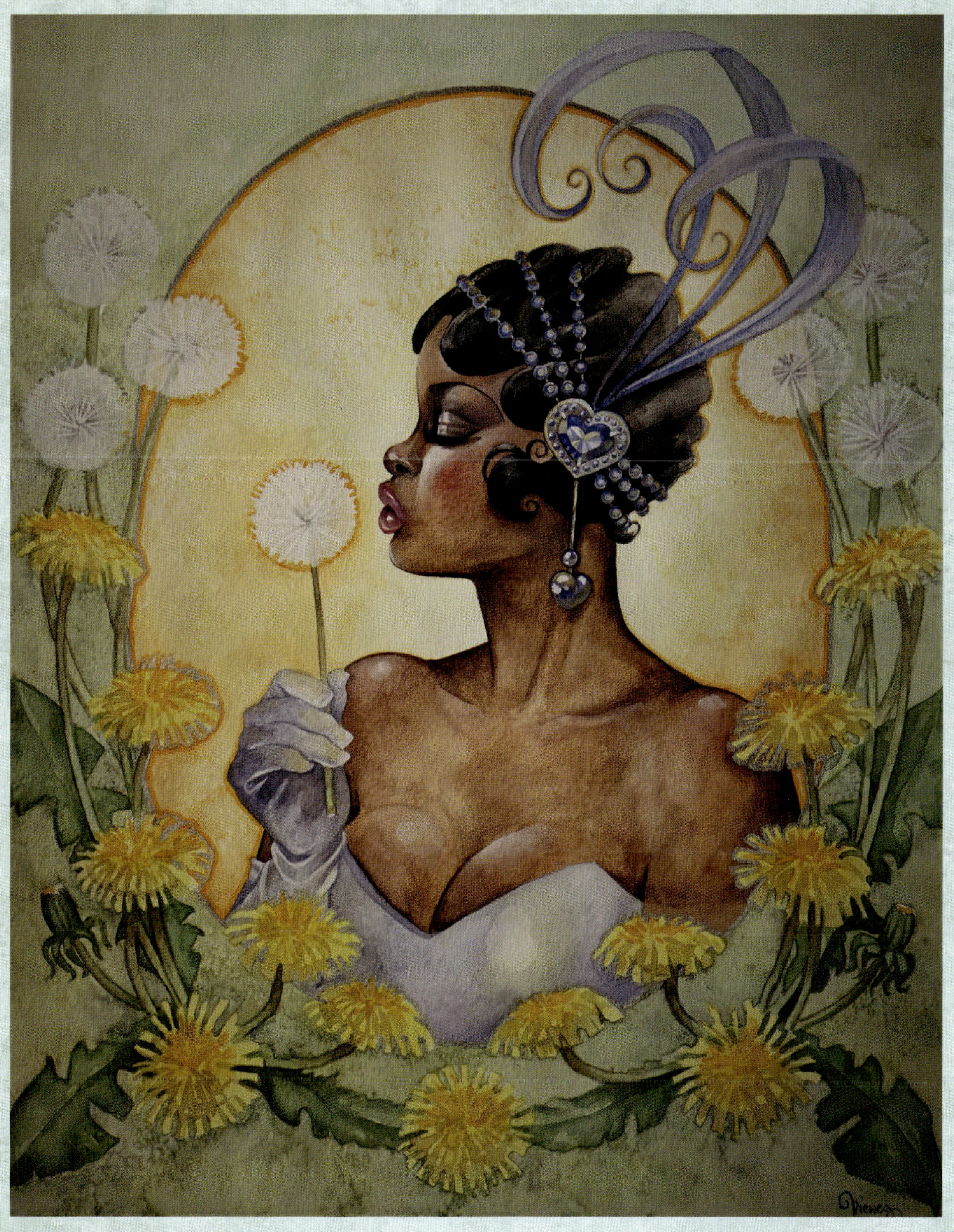

ABOVE: ***Dandelion Queen***
Linda Vieweg Jackson

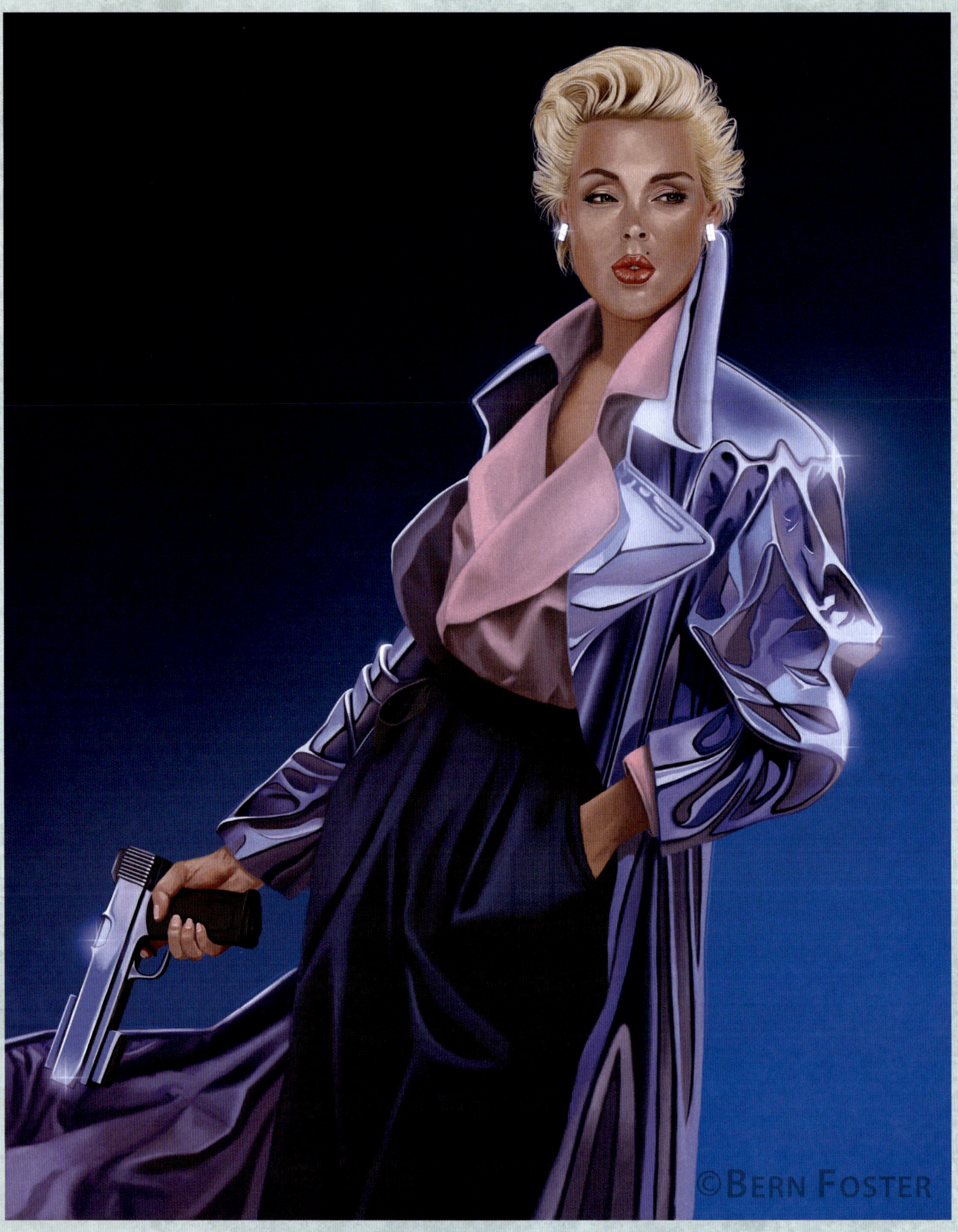
©BERN FOSTER

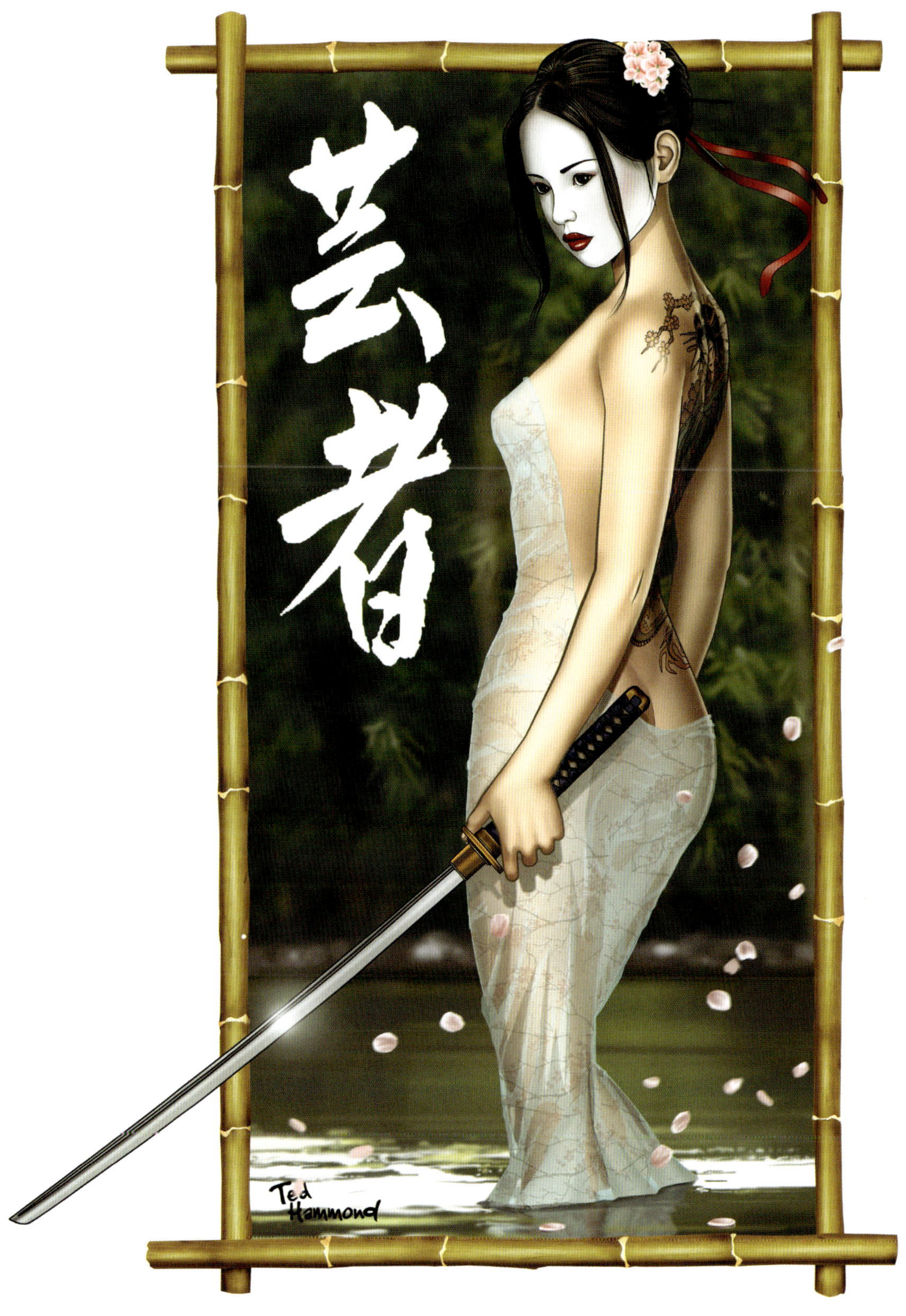

LEFT: ***Lone Justice***
Bern Foster

ABOVE: ***Geisha***
Ted Hammond

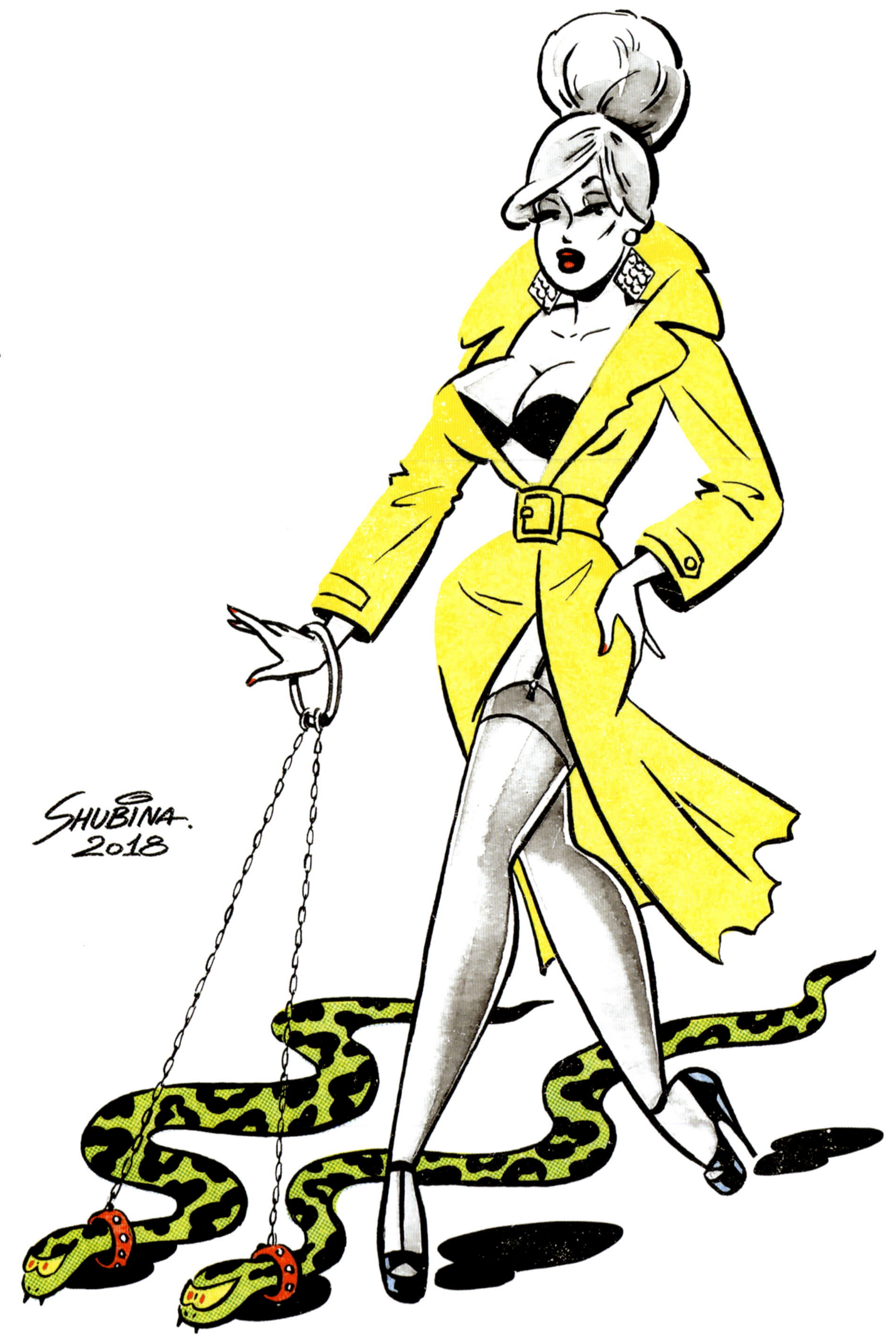
SHUBINA.
2018

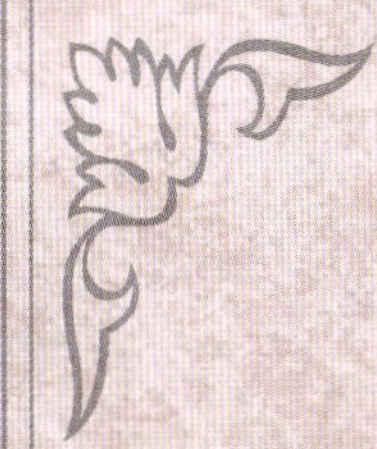

Cartoon & Comic

One need look no further for the original and quintessential cartoon pinup than the incomparable Betty Boop, a sultry caricature of a Jazz flapper. Created by Max Fleischer in the early 1930s, Betty was the first female lead with a provocative edge, from her skimpy dresses, stockings, and heels to her sassy, girlish attitude. Boop presented a heady juxtaposition between the infantine and mondaine–her large baby face with innocent eyes and tiny, pouted lips paired with her small but indubitably womanish body.

Betty's popularity soared and paved the way for this new style of pinup–raunchy yet playful–with newspapers beginning to feature cartoon strips boasting similar characters. Notable examples include British artist Norman Pett's Jane, heroine and 'Queen of the Undie-World' for *The Daily Mirror*, which went on to inspire an American version, *Male Call* by Milton Caniff with memorable characters like Miss Lace and Burma, the gorgeous adventuress from his *Terry and the Pirates* spin-off.

The 1940s saw a turn for the risqué and characters such as the much-loved Torchy from Bill Ward burst onto the scene. Cartoon styles were used for illicit erotica such as *The Tijuana Bibles* which didn't quite conform to the constraints of the Comics Code. In the 1950s, *Playboy* artists such as Harvey Kurtzman, Eldon Dedini, Jules Feiffer, and Shel Silverstein saw the understated power of a simple watercolor with a very cheeky subtext. As the '70s and '80s rolled around, the tight censorship seen in previous decades had all but evaporated. The clean, minimalistic style proved timeless and inspired Patrick Nagel's pop art pinup.

The cartoon coquette remains an admired style that continues to develop to this day, with the innocent yet sensuous Japanese anime girls drawn from that original flirty caricature, Betty Boop. Today, we see 3D animated pinups featured in Disney Pixar films, Elastigirl from The Incredibles being a notable example.

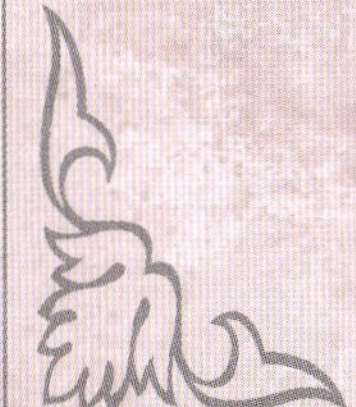

LEFT: ***Serpent***
Sveta Shubina

OVERLEAF: ***Leo***
Sveta Shubina

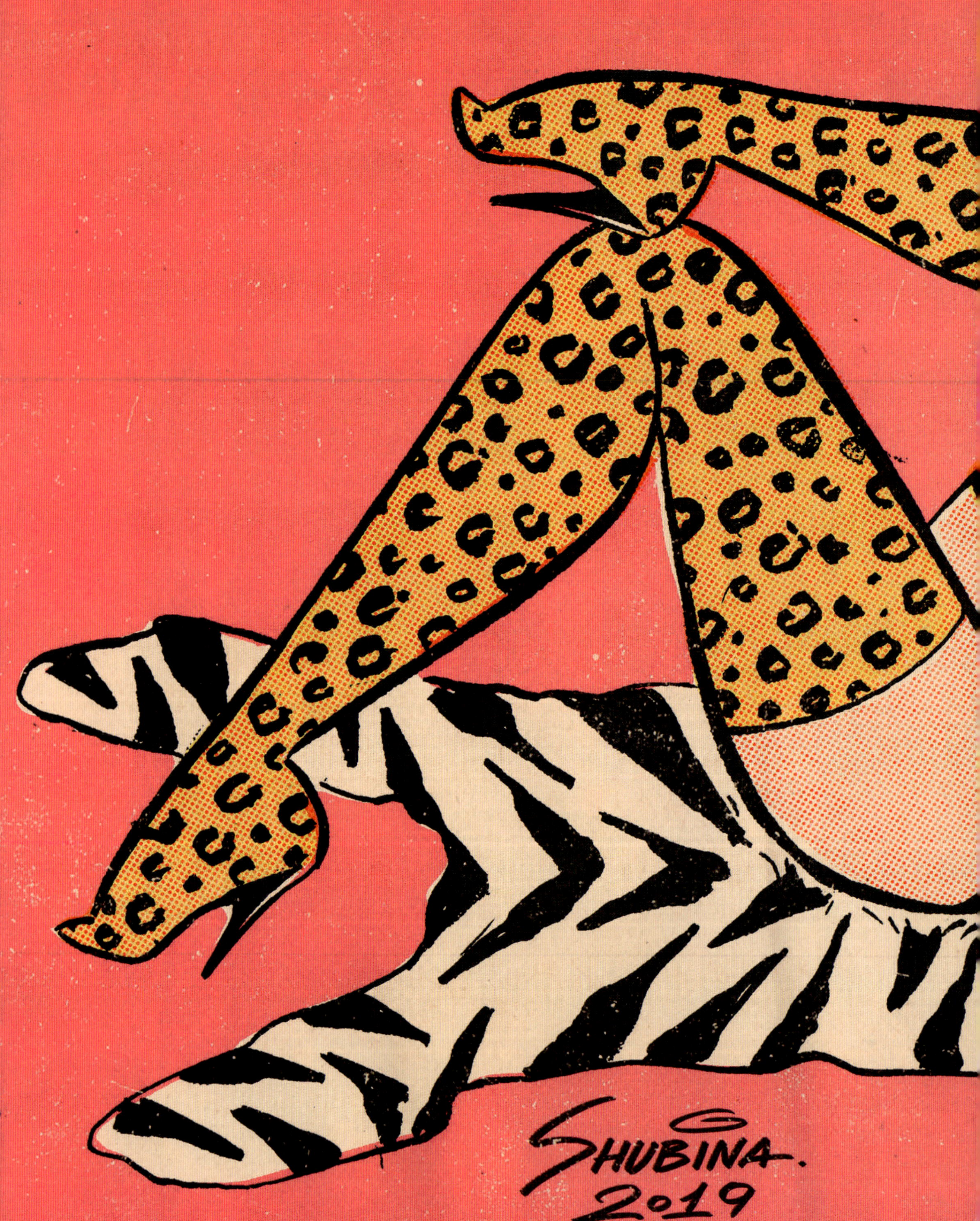
SHUBINA.
2019

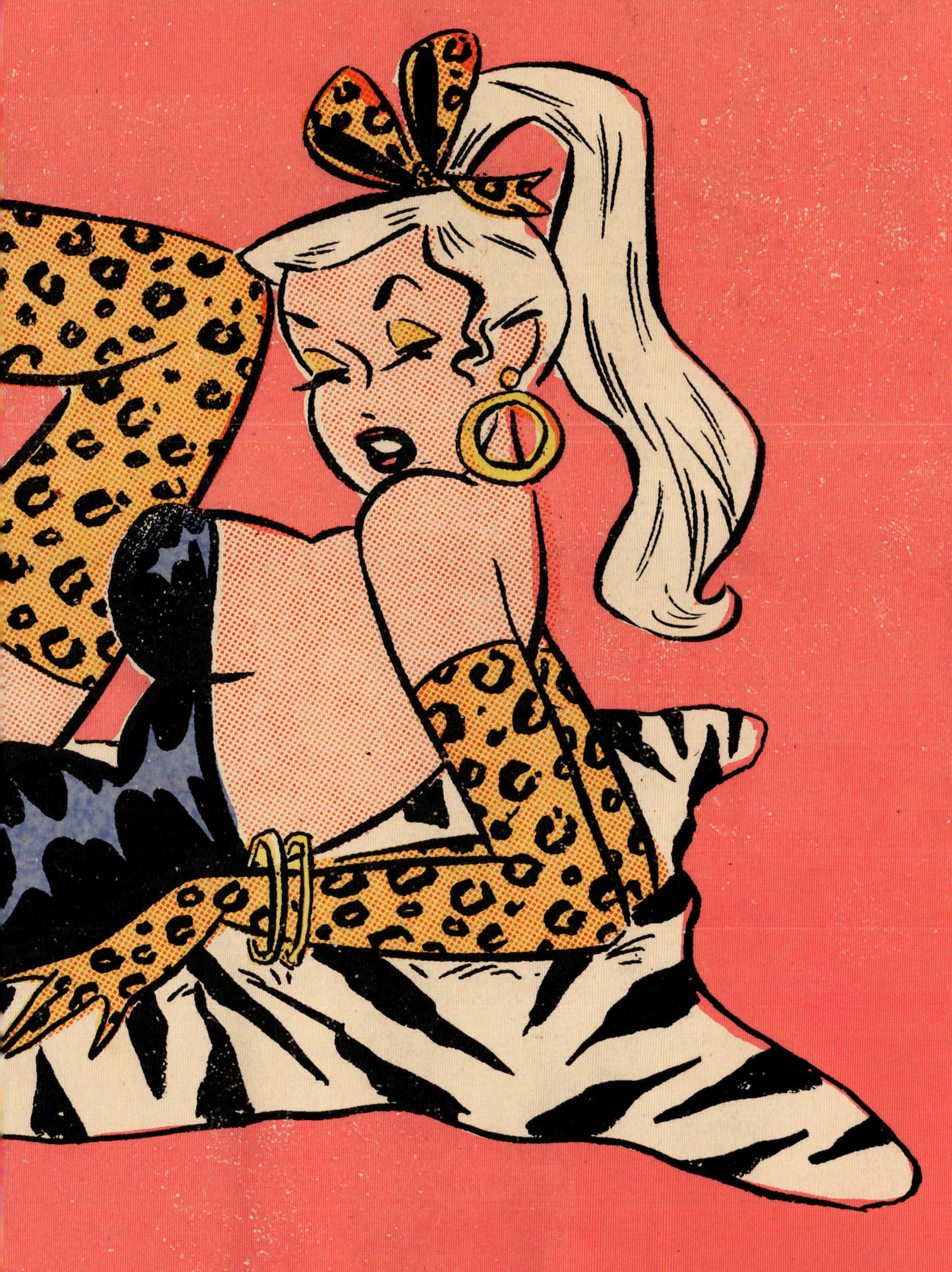

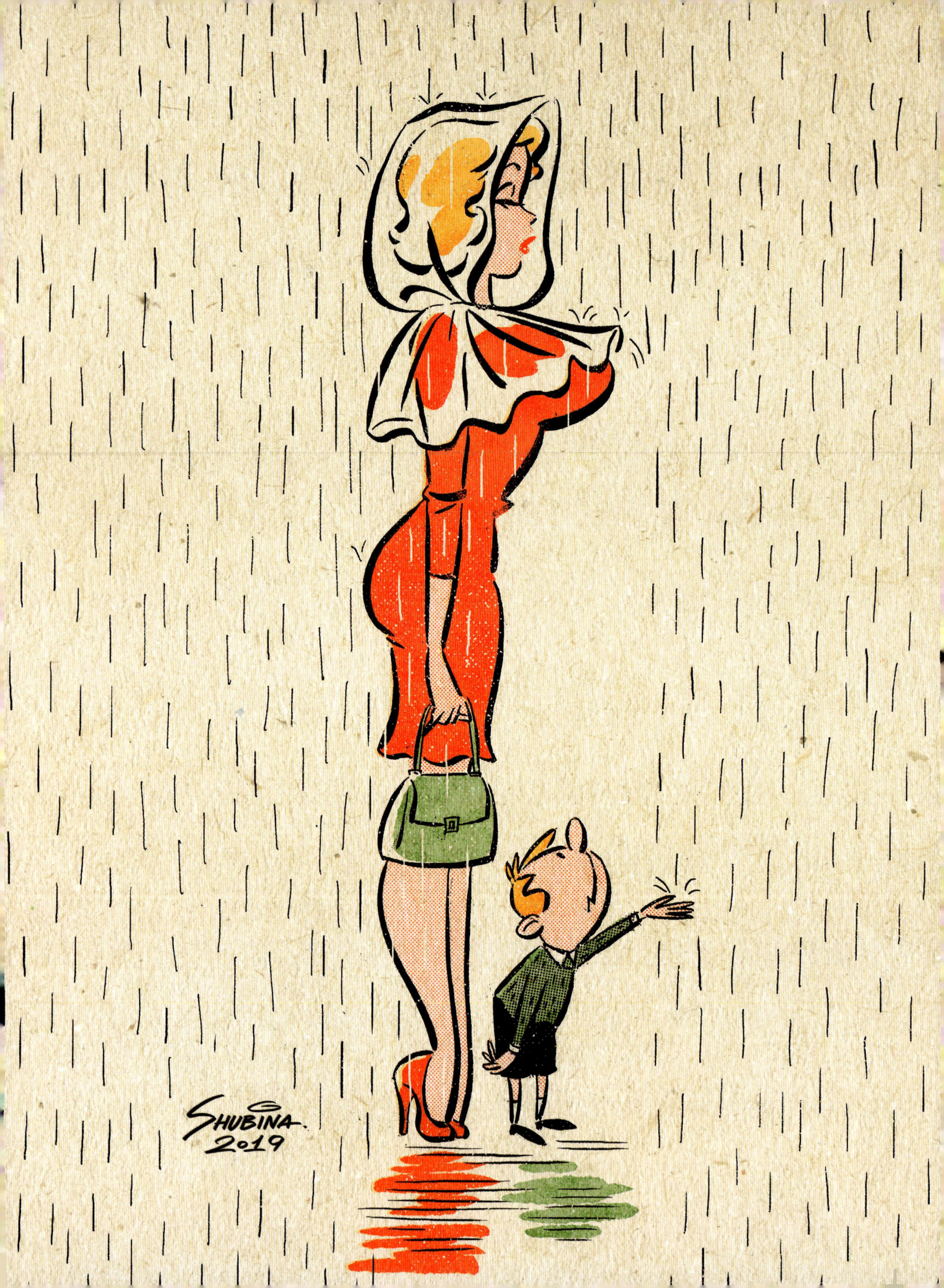
SHUBINA
2019

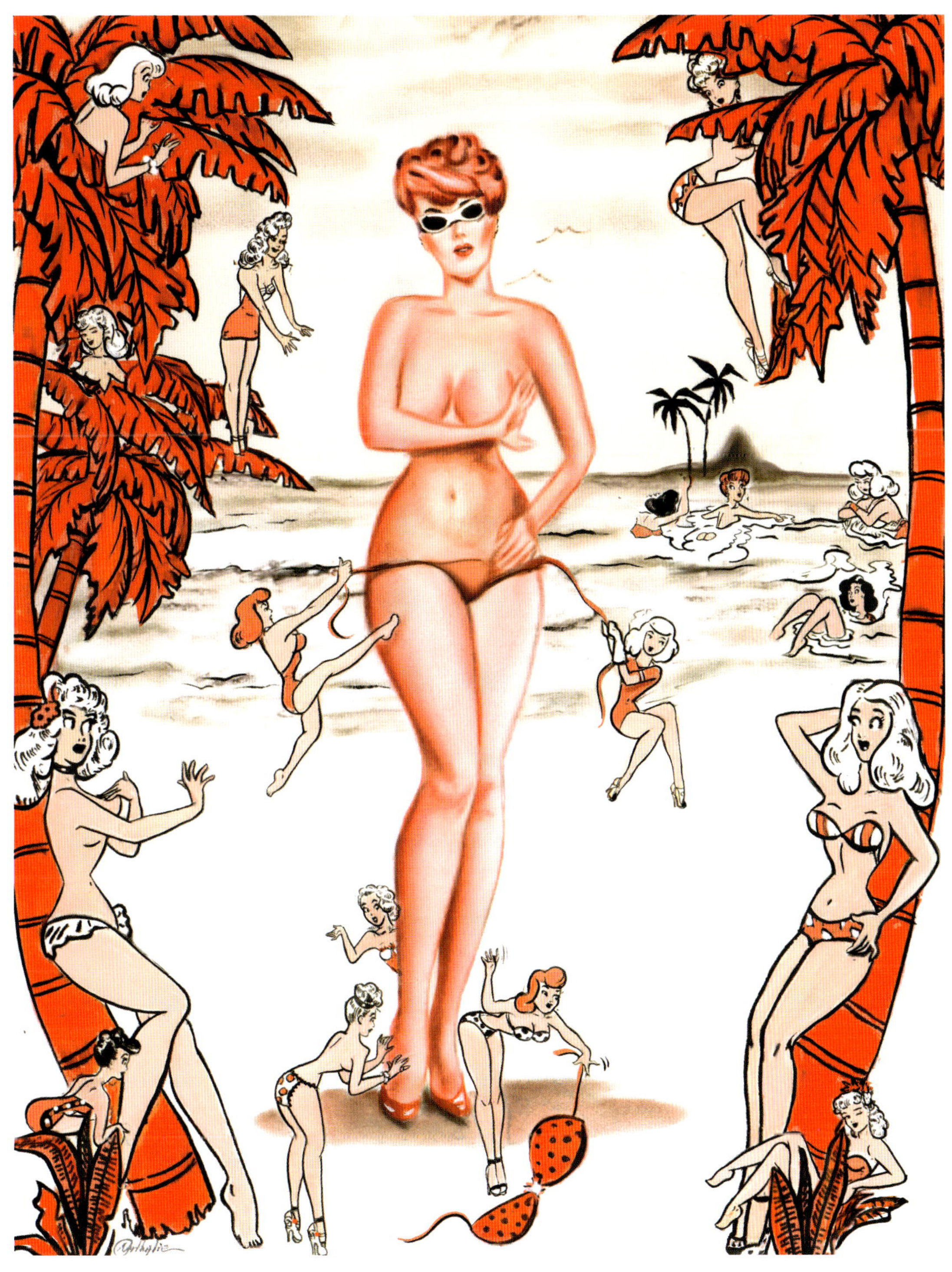

LEFT: ***Rain***
Sveta Shubina

ABOVE: ***The Tiny Lady Gang***
Nathalie Rattner

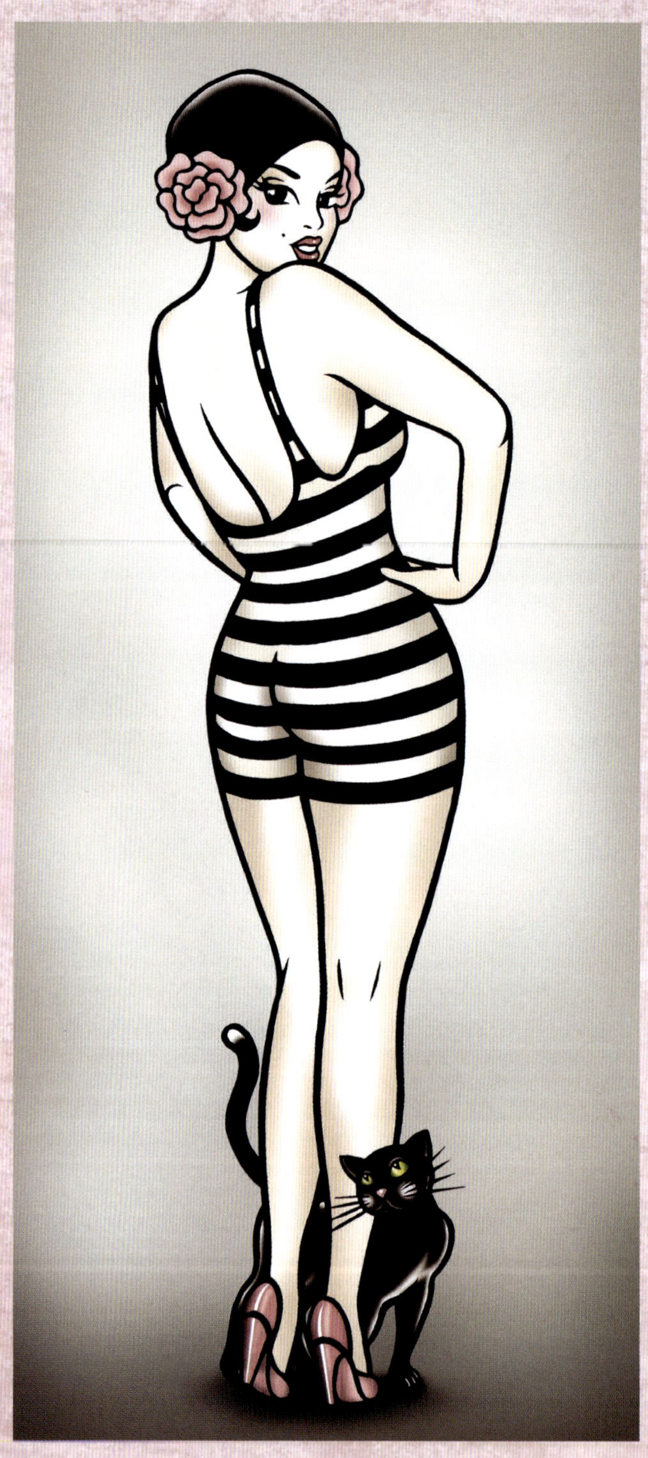

ABOVE: ***Lolita***
Hek

RIGHT: ***Who did it?***
Linda Vieweg Jackson

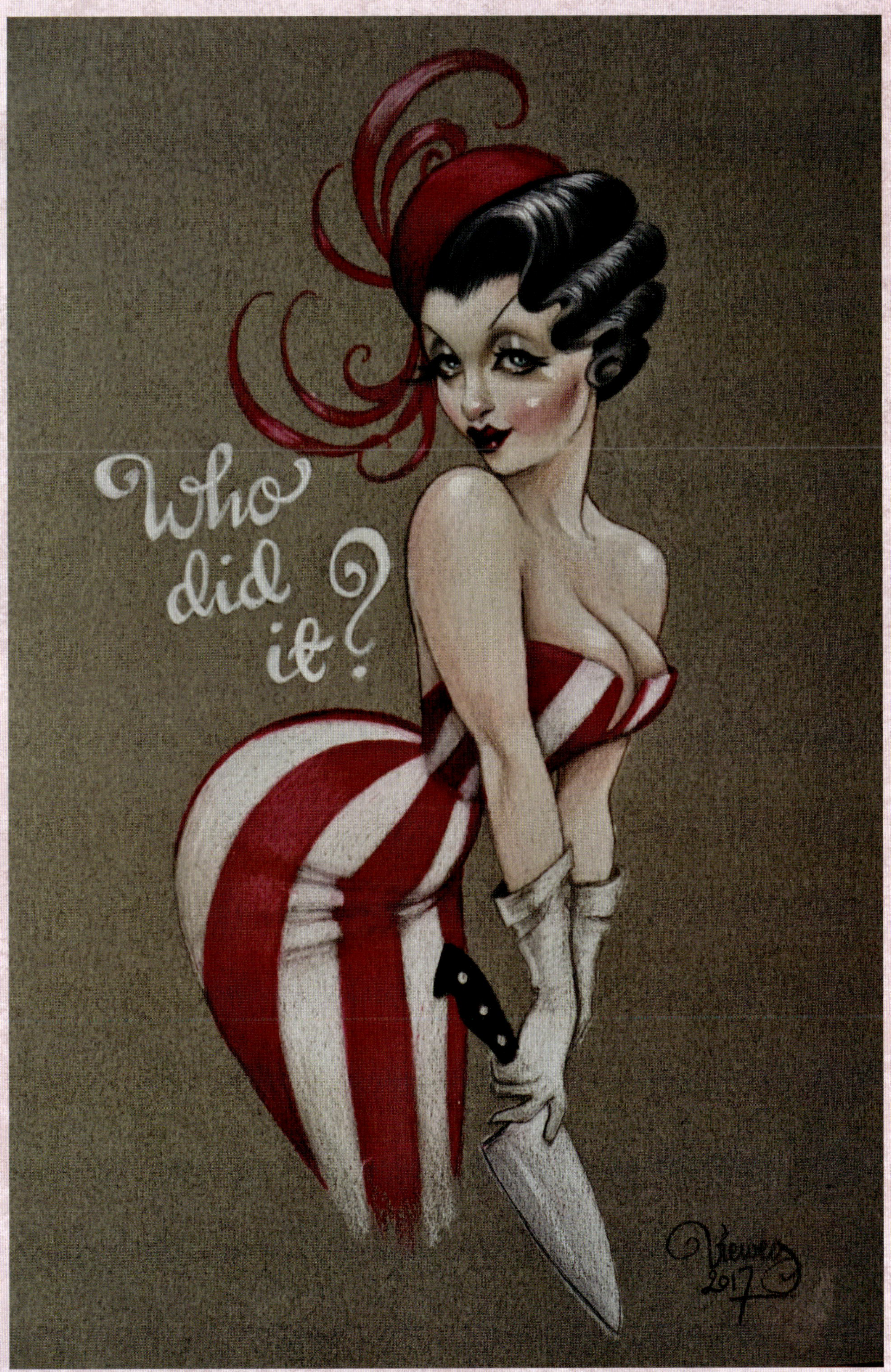
Who did it?
Vieweg 2017

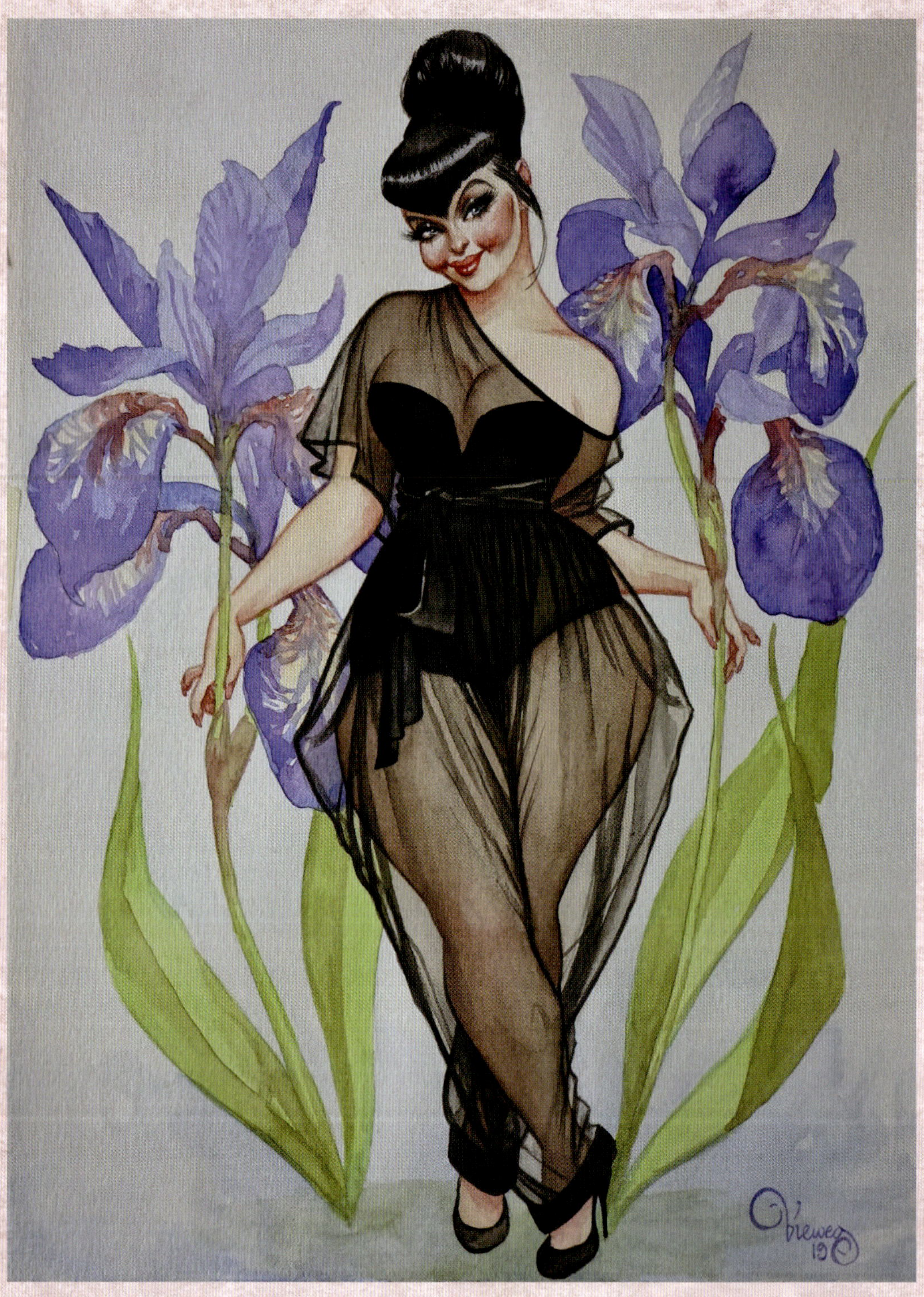

ABOVE: ***Iris***
Linda Vieweg Jackson

RIGHT: ***Perfumed Rose***
Linda Vieweg Jackson

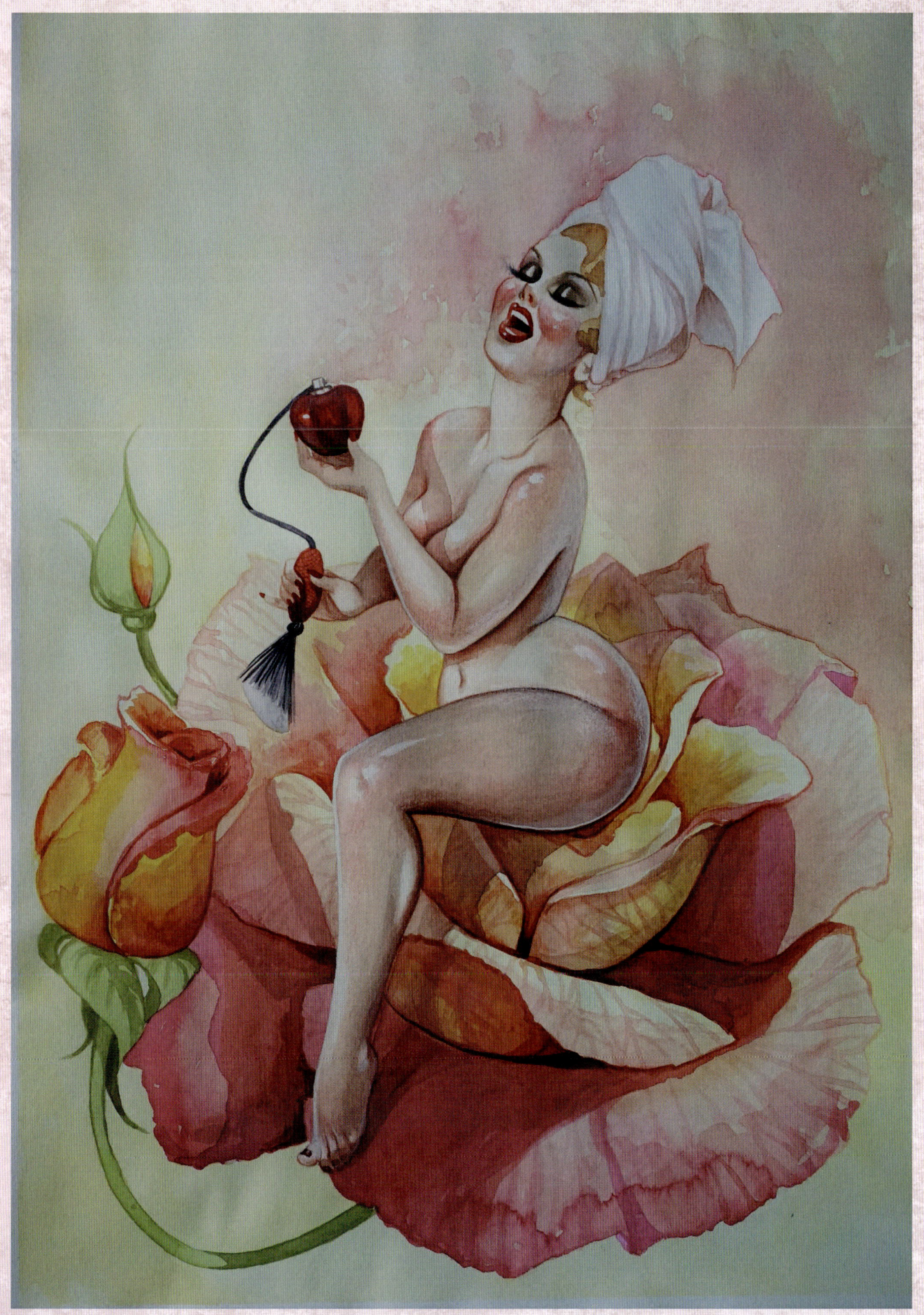

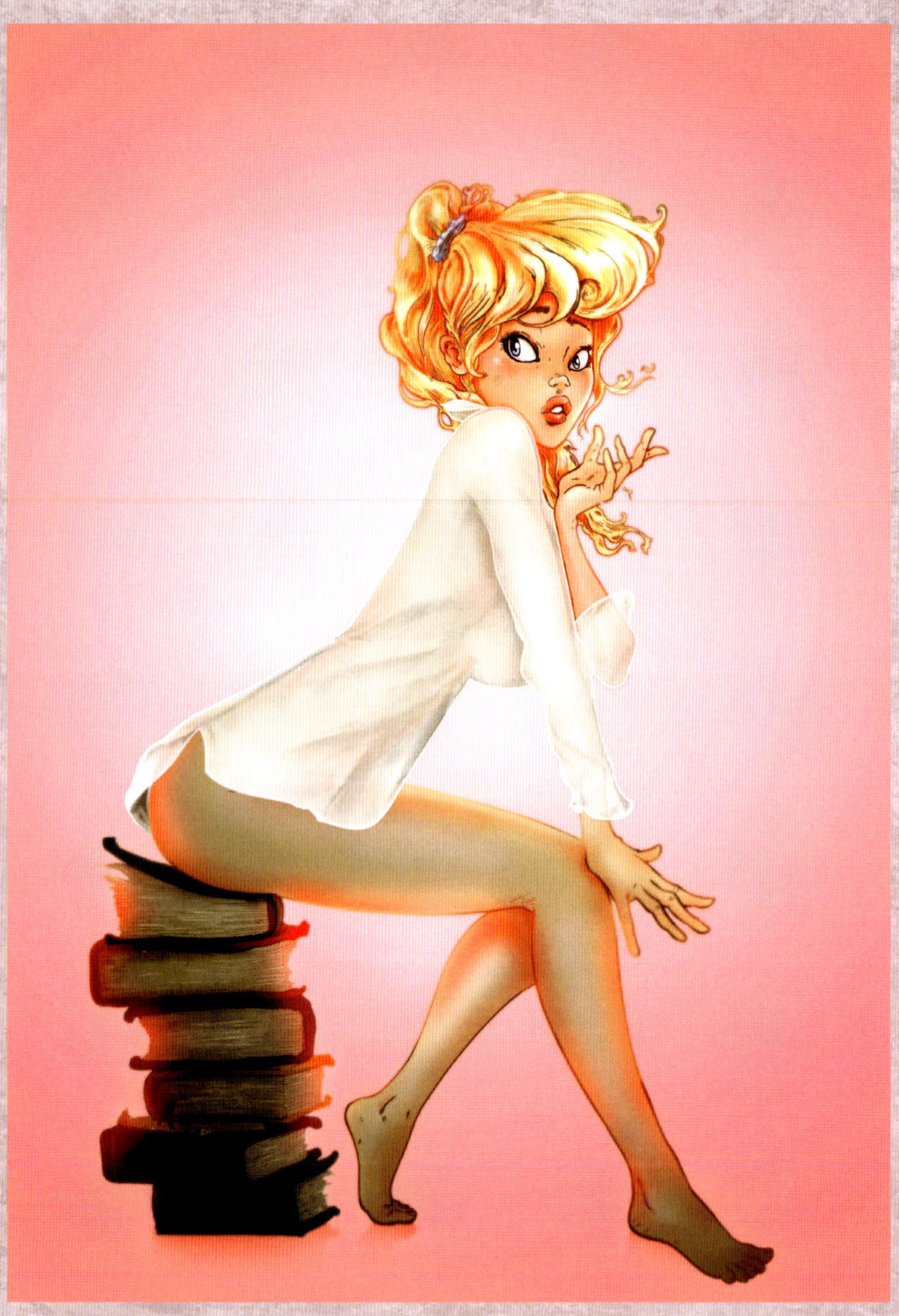

ABOVE: ***Books***
Matthew Britton

RIGHT: ***Milkshake and Fries***
Matthew Britton

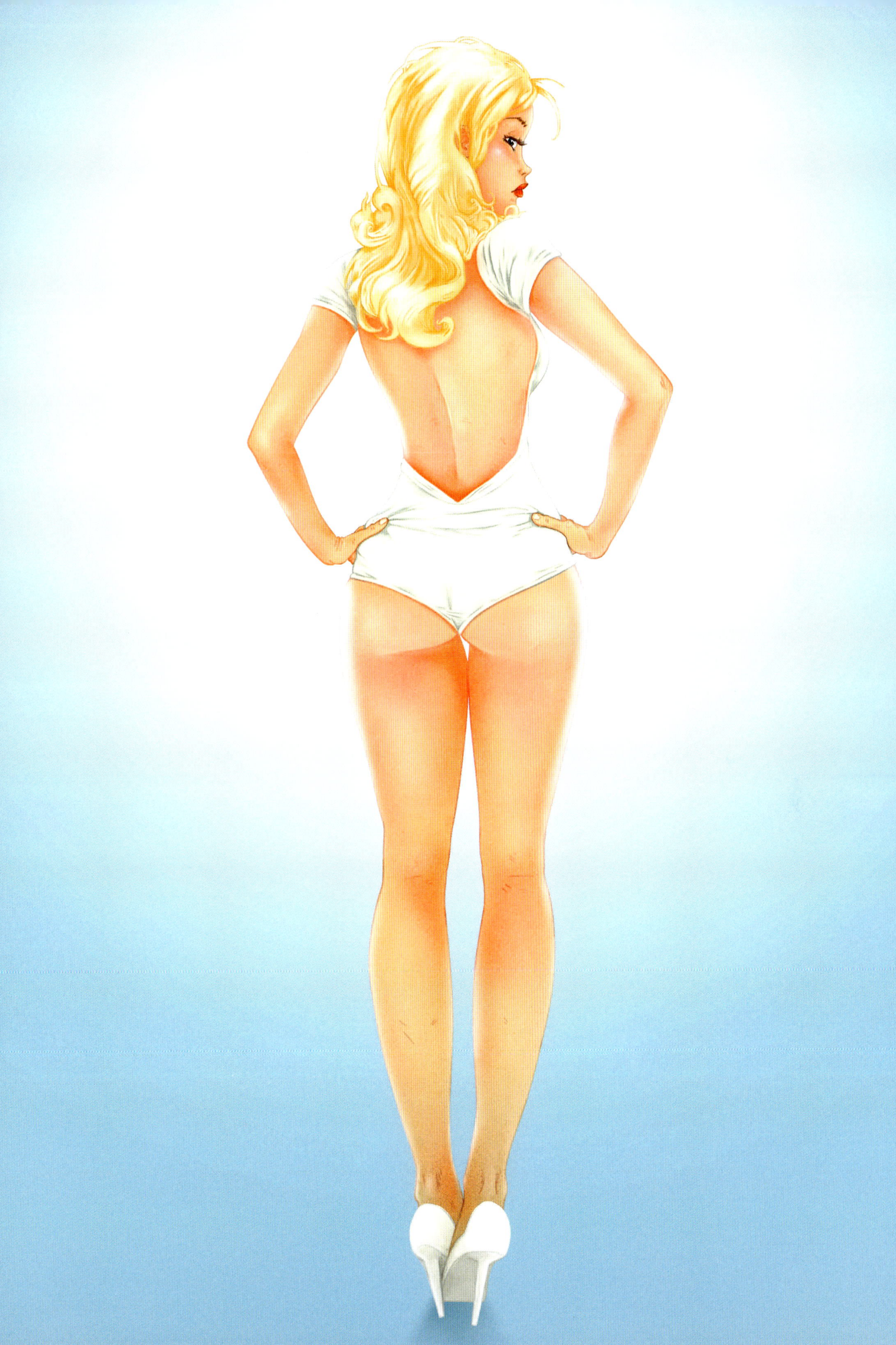

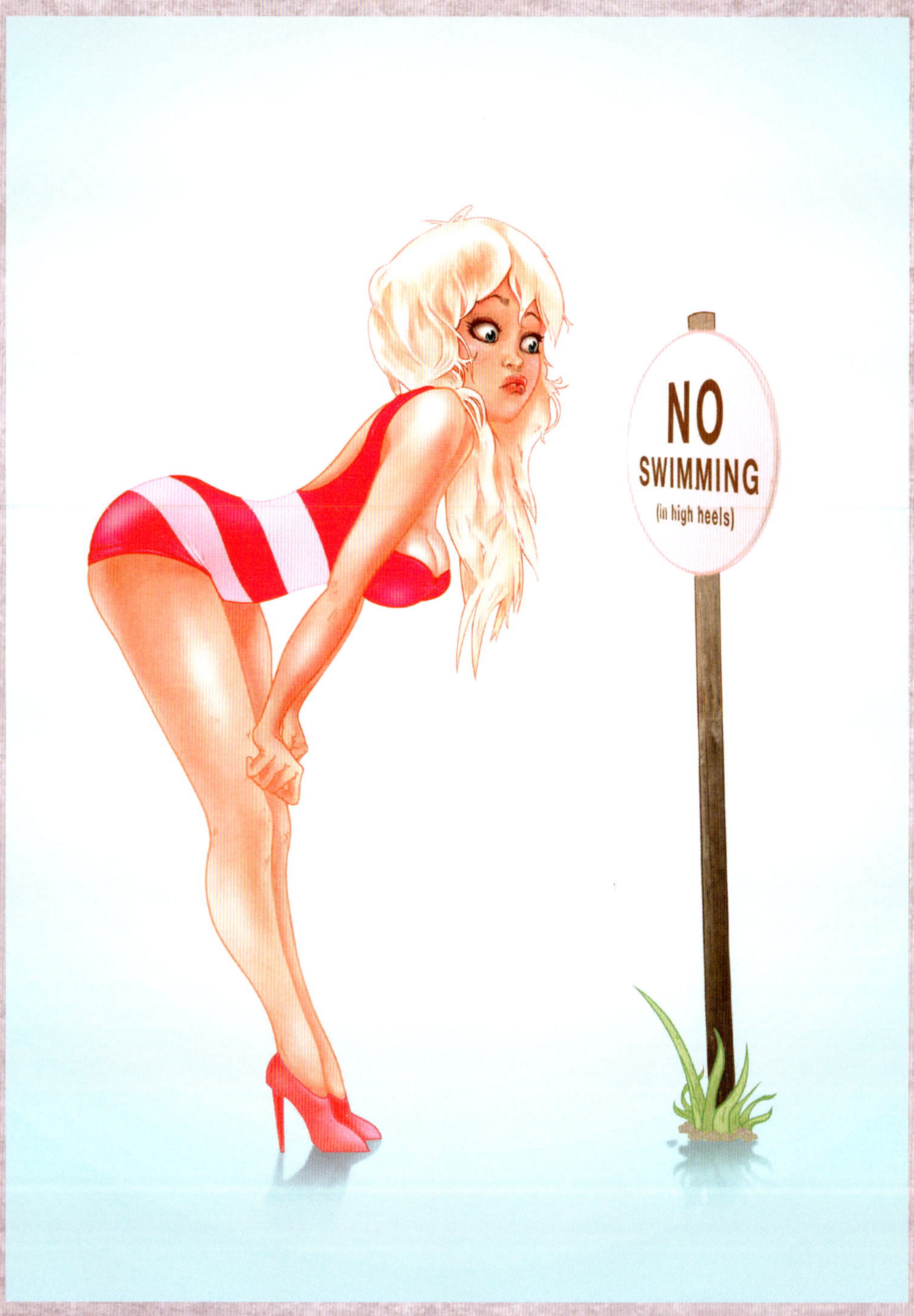

ABOVE: ***No Swimming***
Matthew Britton

RIGHT: ***Roller Derby***
Matthew Britton

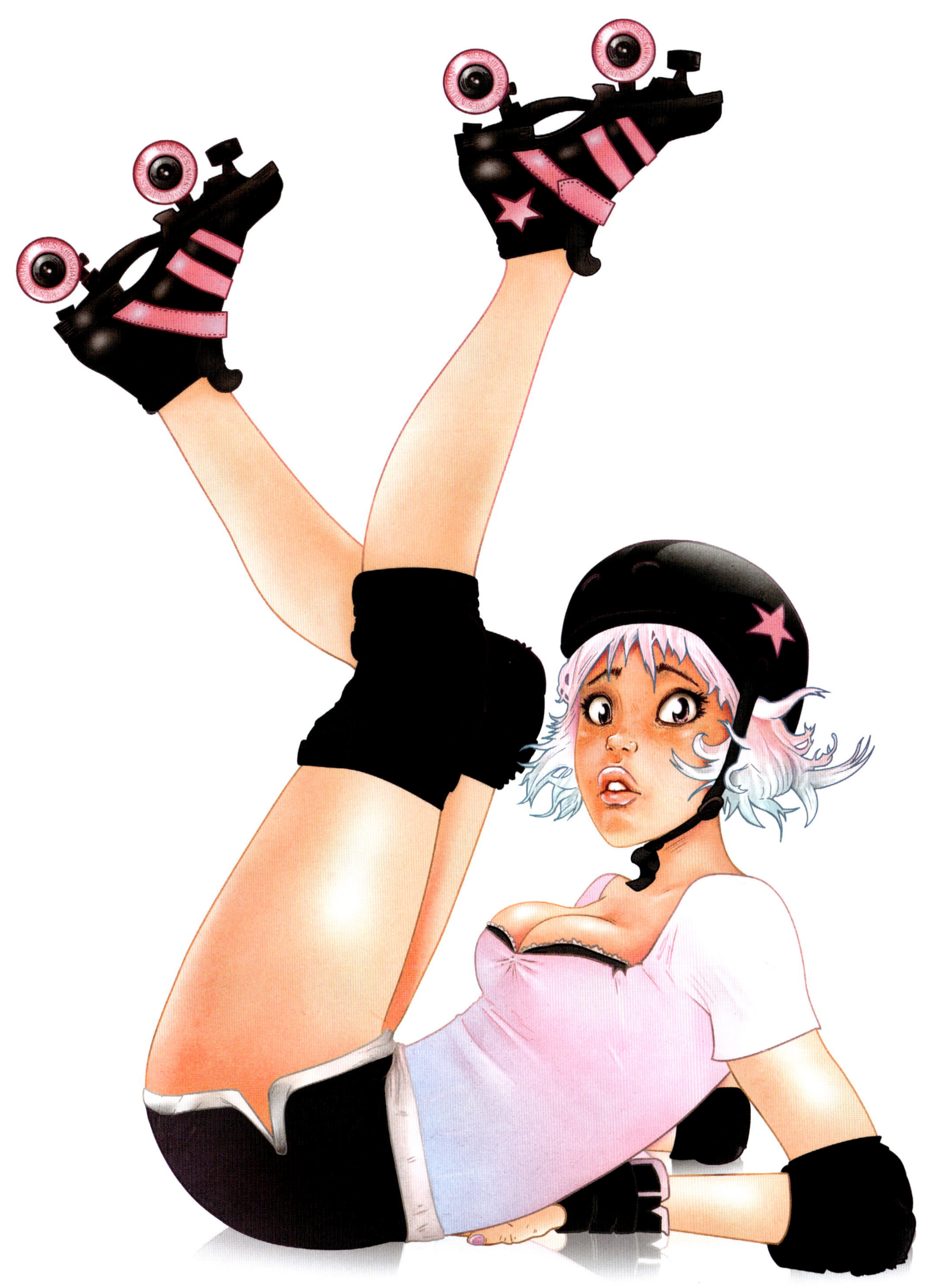

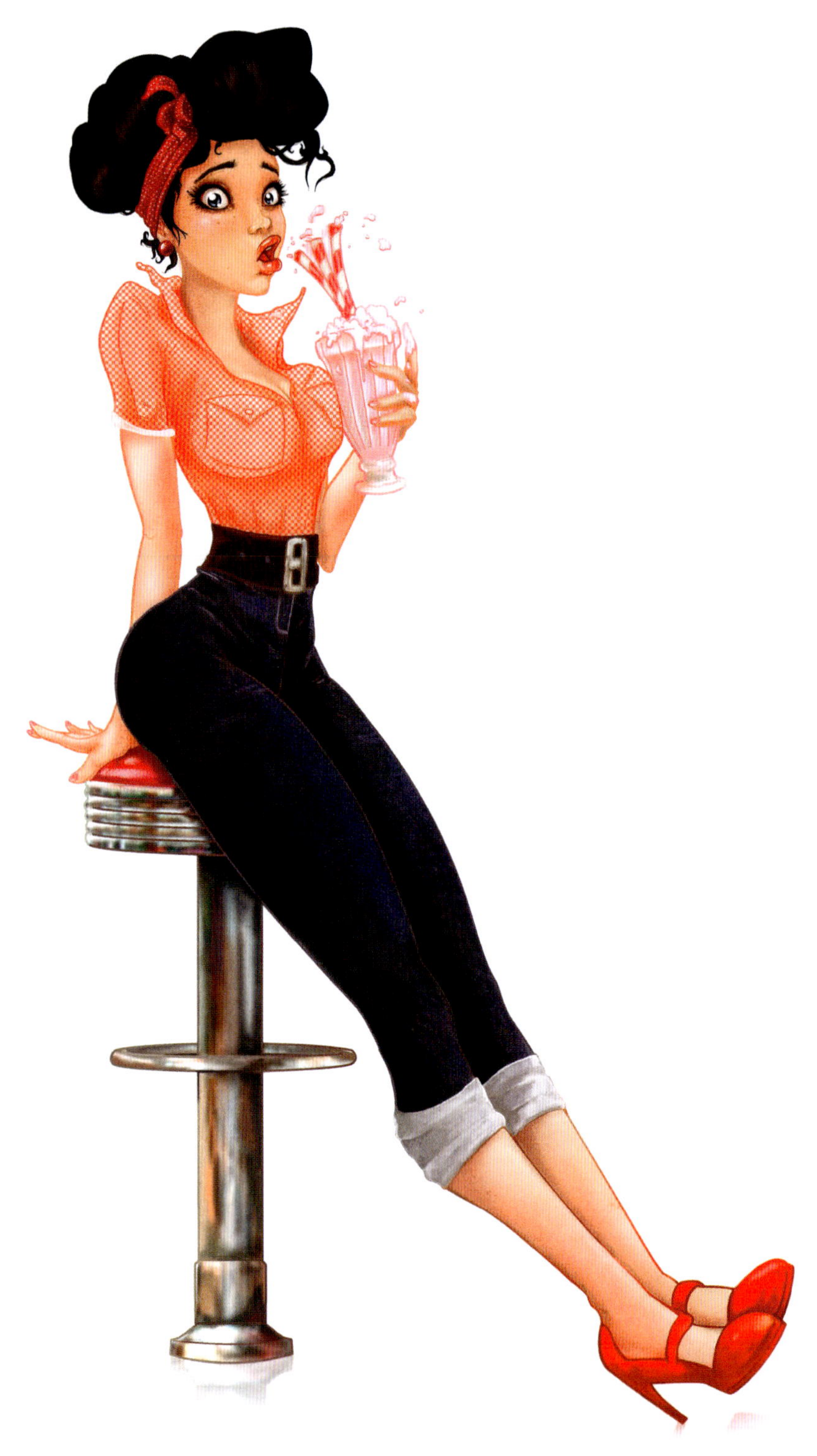

ABOVE: ***Milkshake***
Matthew Britton

RIGHT: ***Waitress***
Matthew Britton

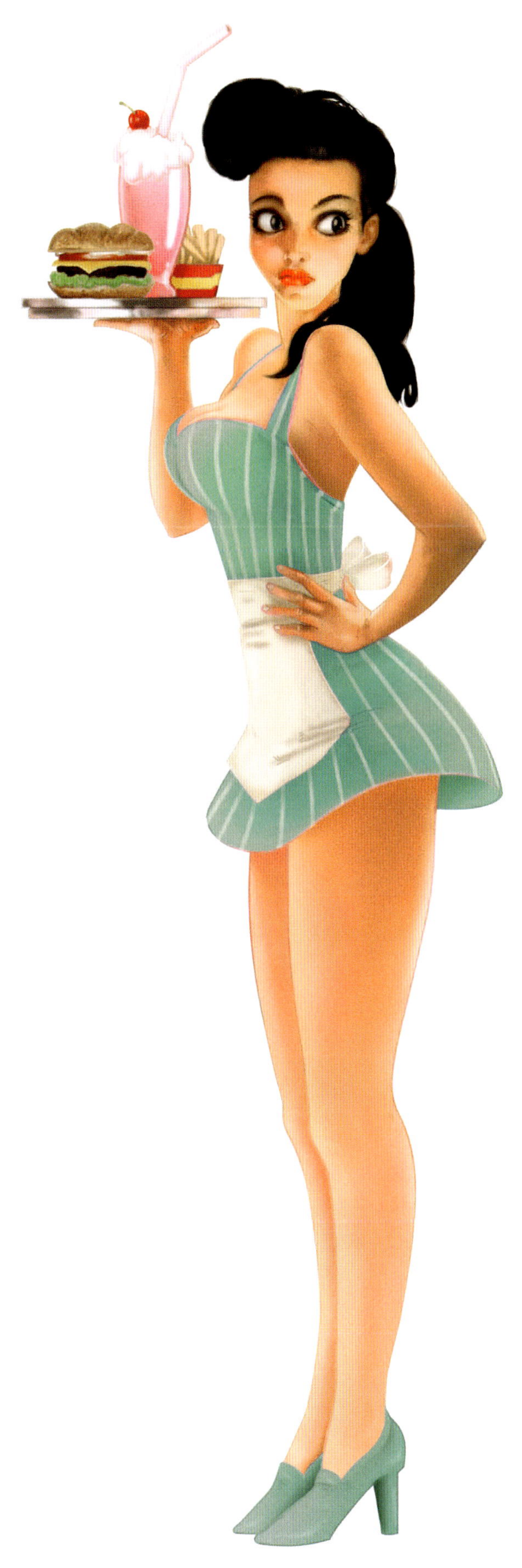

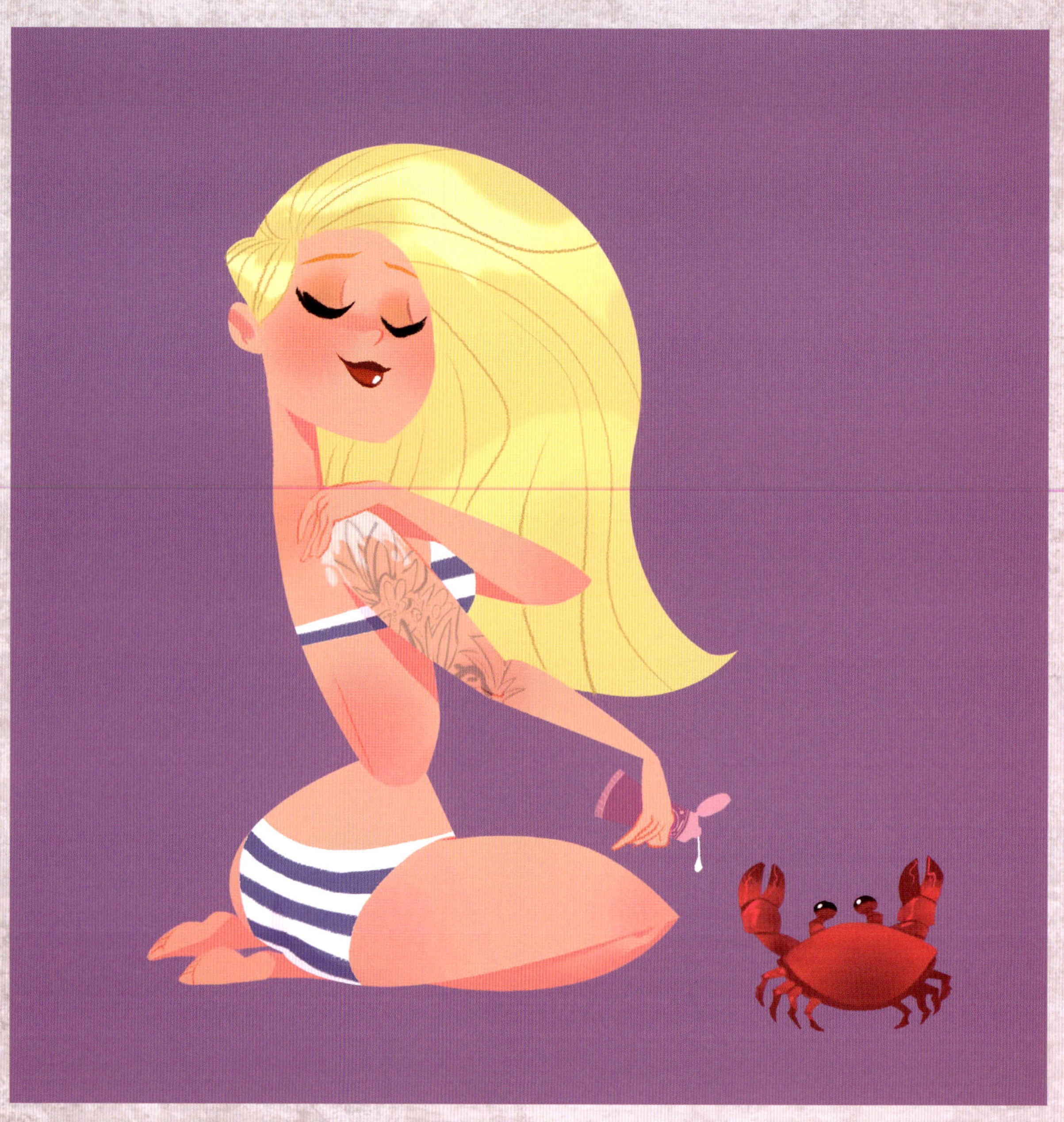

ABOVE: ***Barcelona Girl 6***
Guillaume Poux

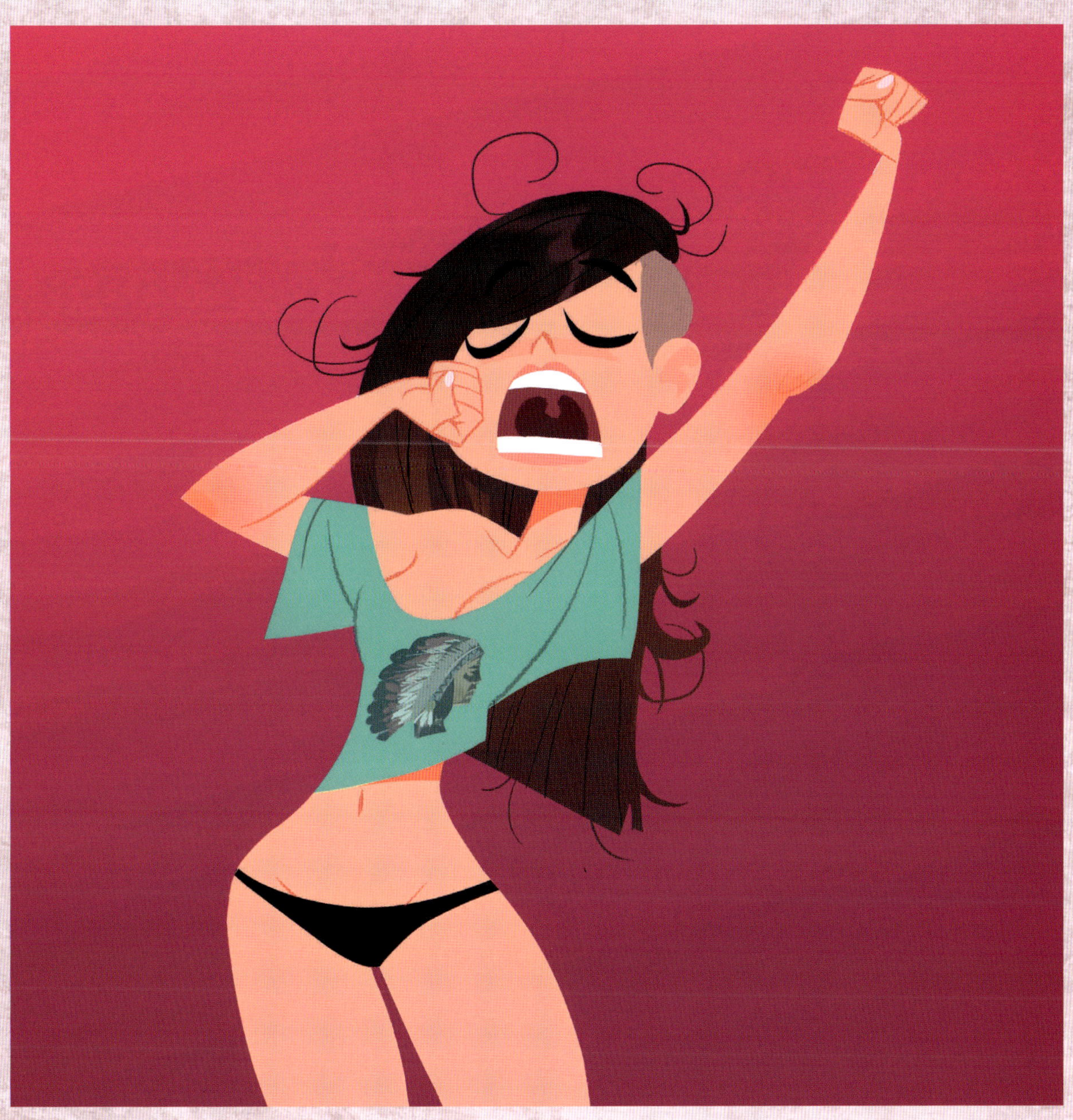

ABOVE: *Barcelona Girl 8*
Guillaume Poux

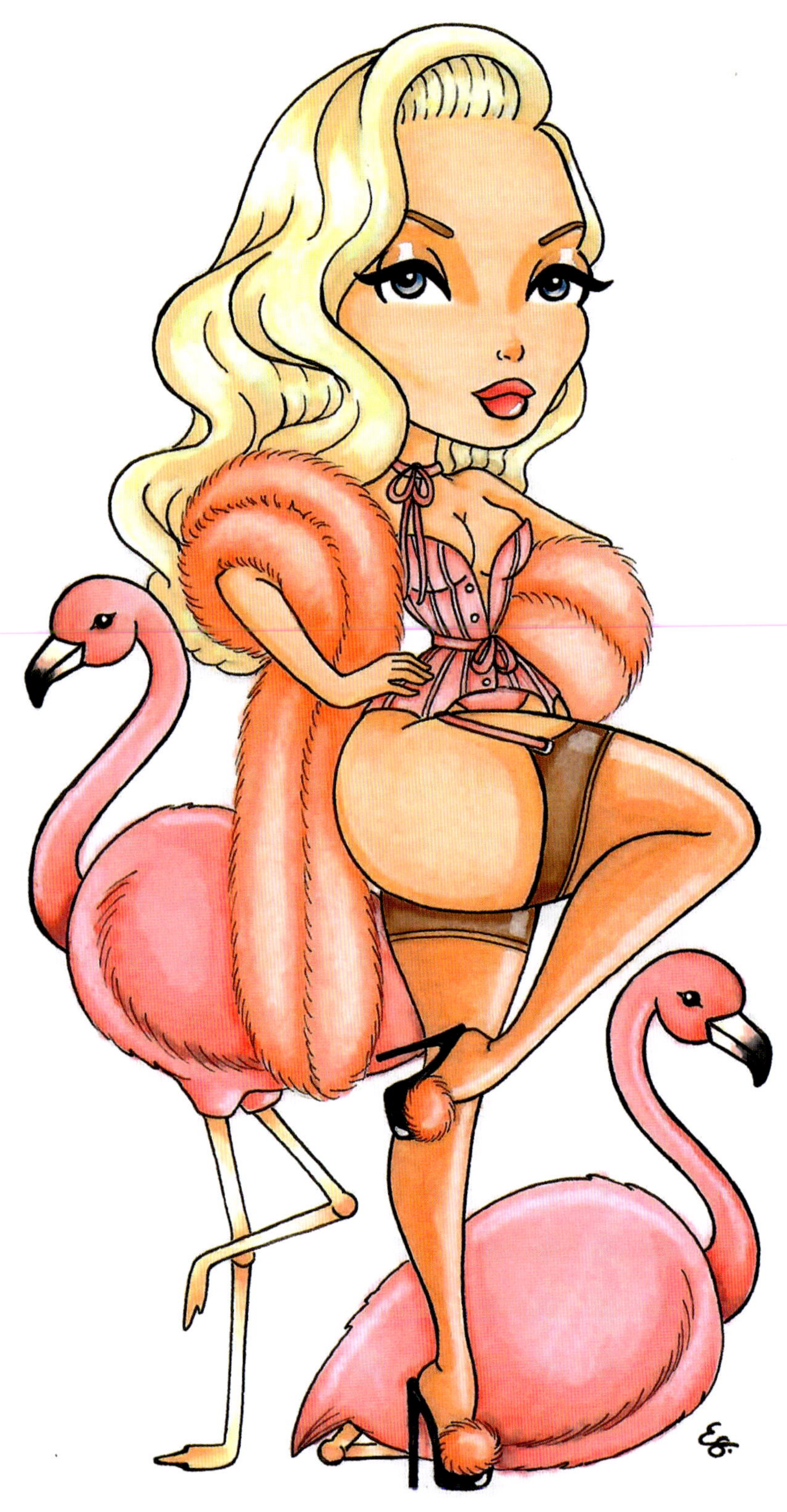

ABOVE: ***Pink Dreams***
Erica Lynn Shaw

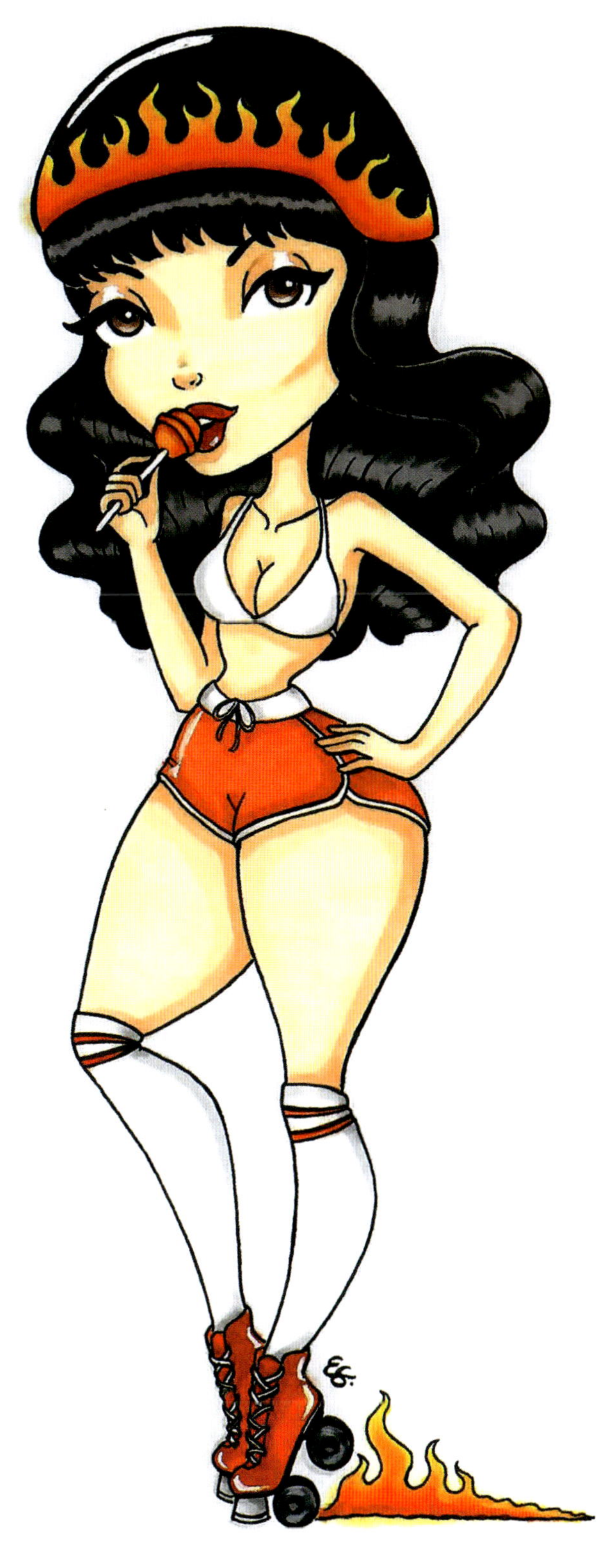

ABOVE: ***Hell on Wheels***
Erica Lynn Shaw

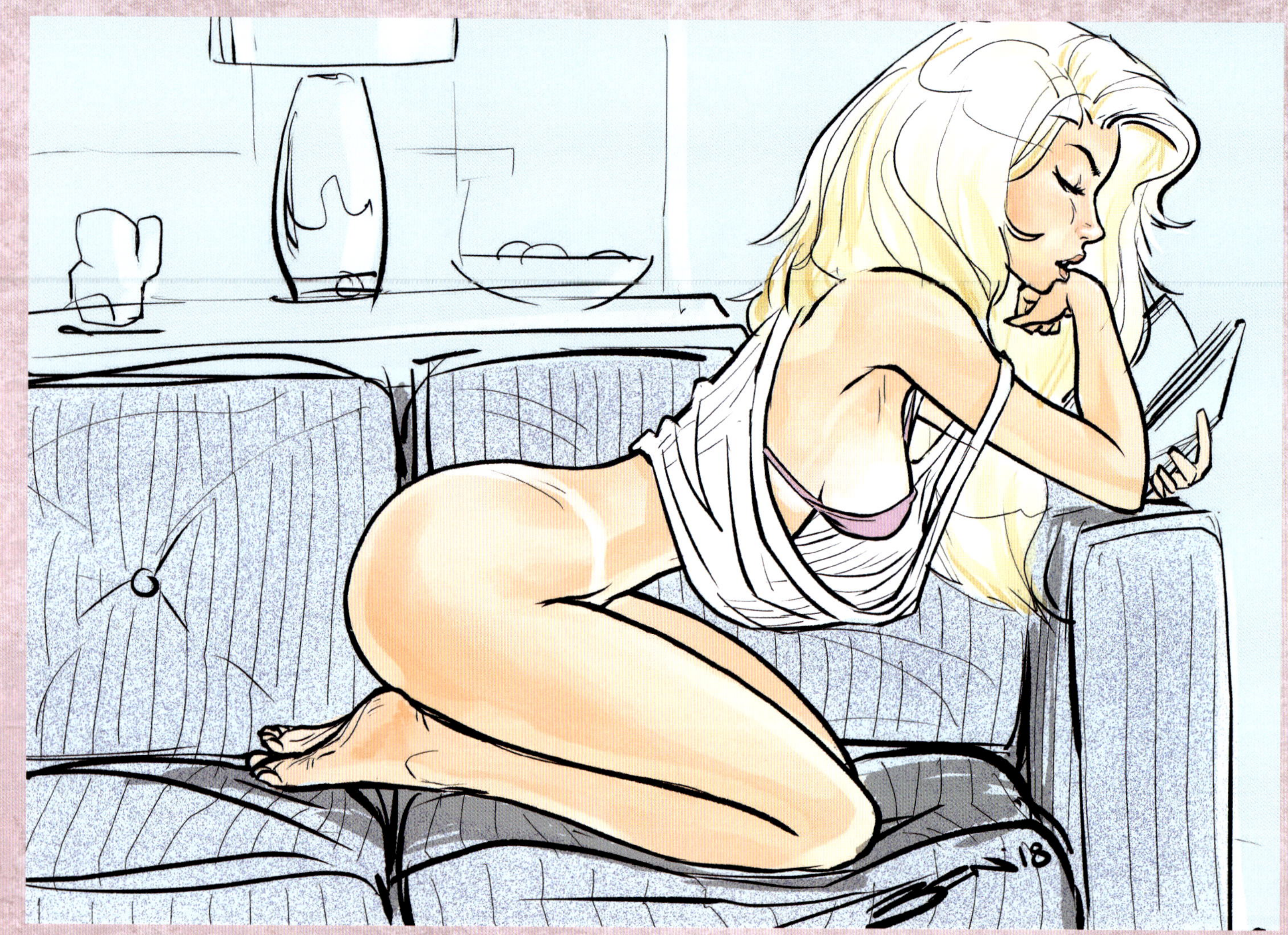

ABOVE: ***Well Read***
Ben Tan

RIGHT: ***Parting the Curtain***
Ben Tan

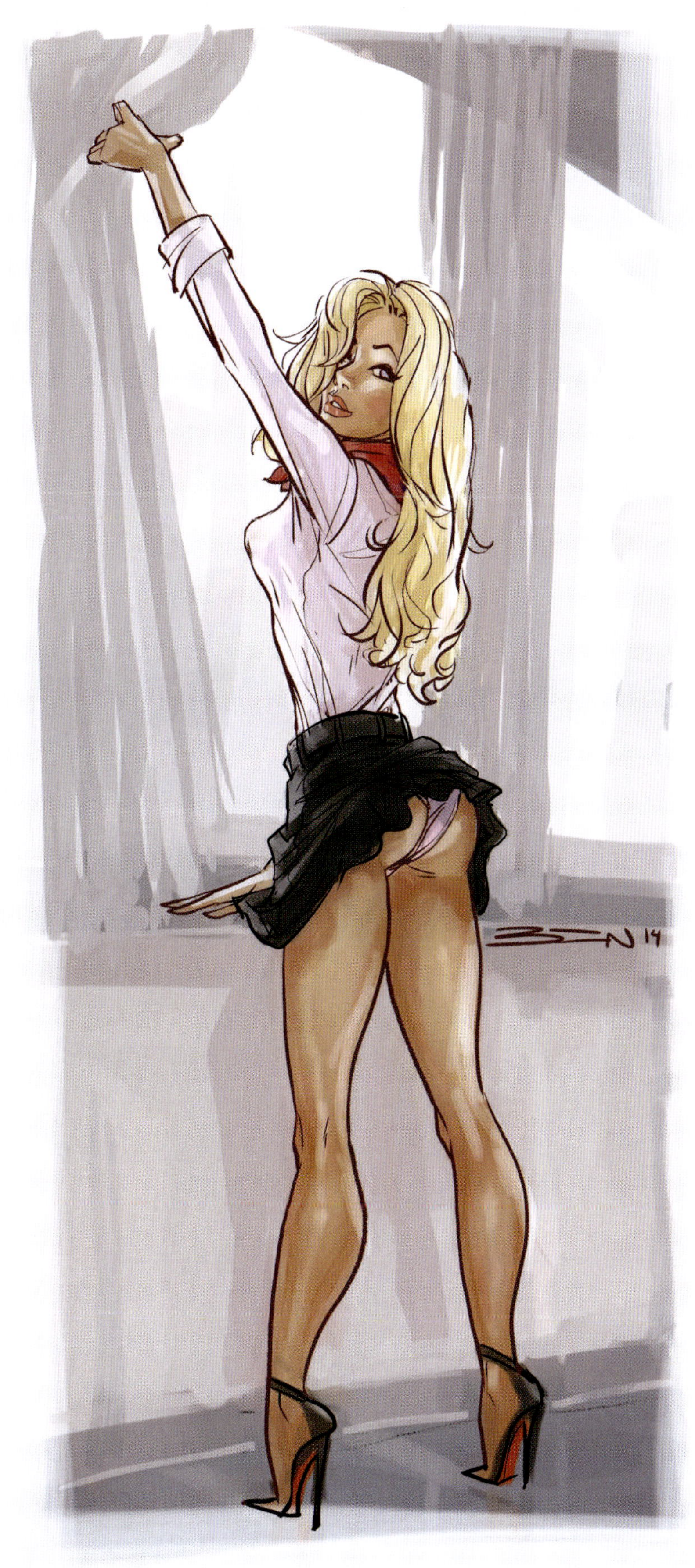

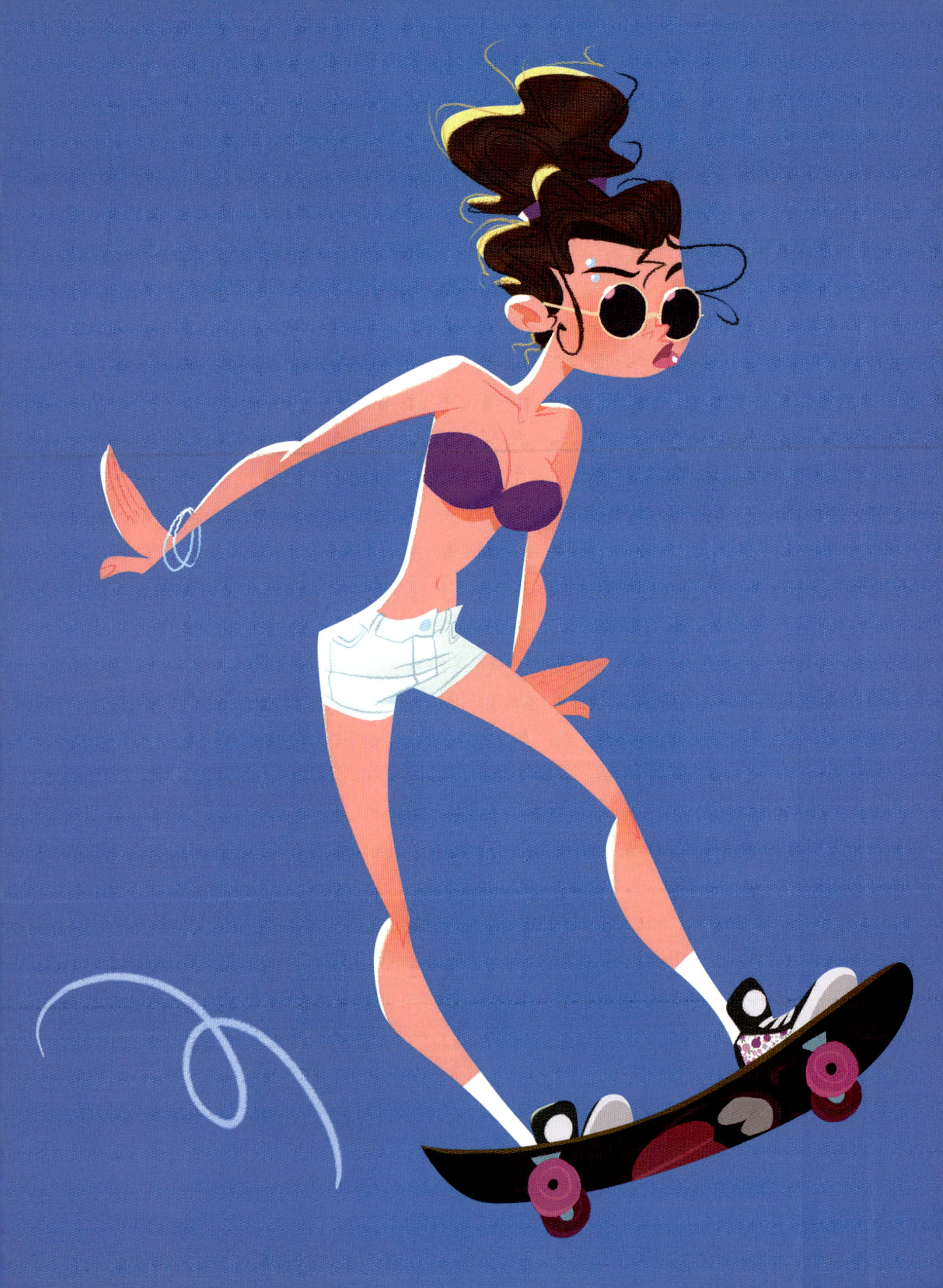

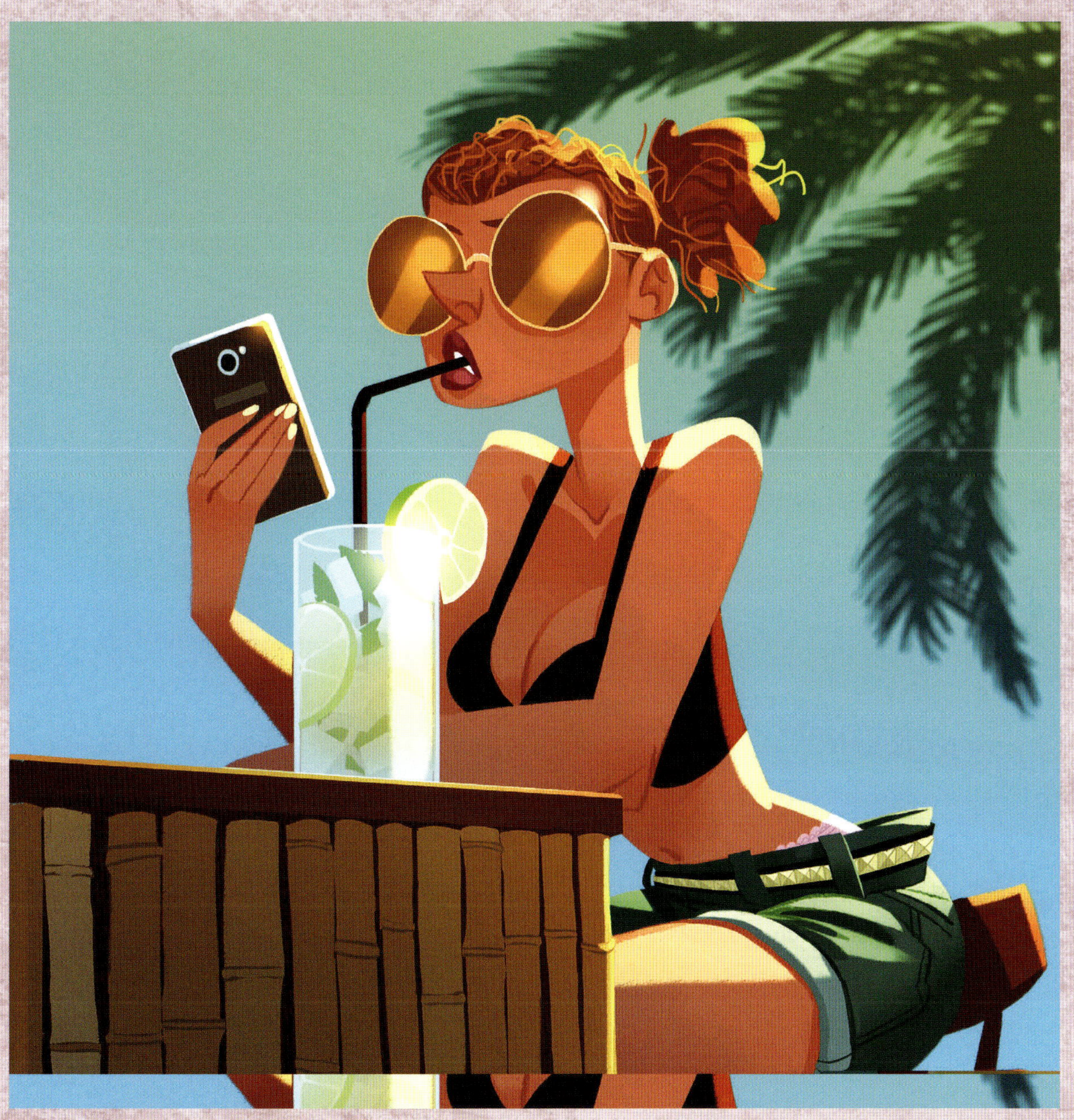

LEFT: ***Barcelona Girl 10***
Guillaume Poux

ABOVE: ***Barcelona Girl 1***
Guillaume Poux

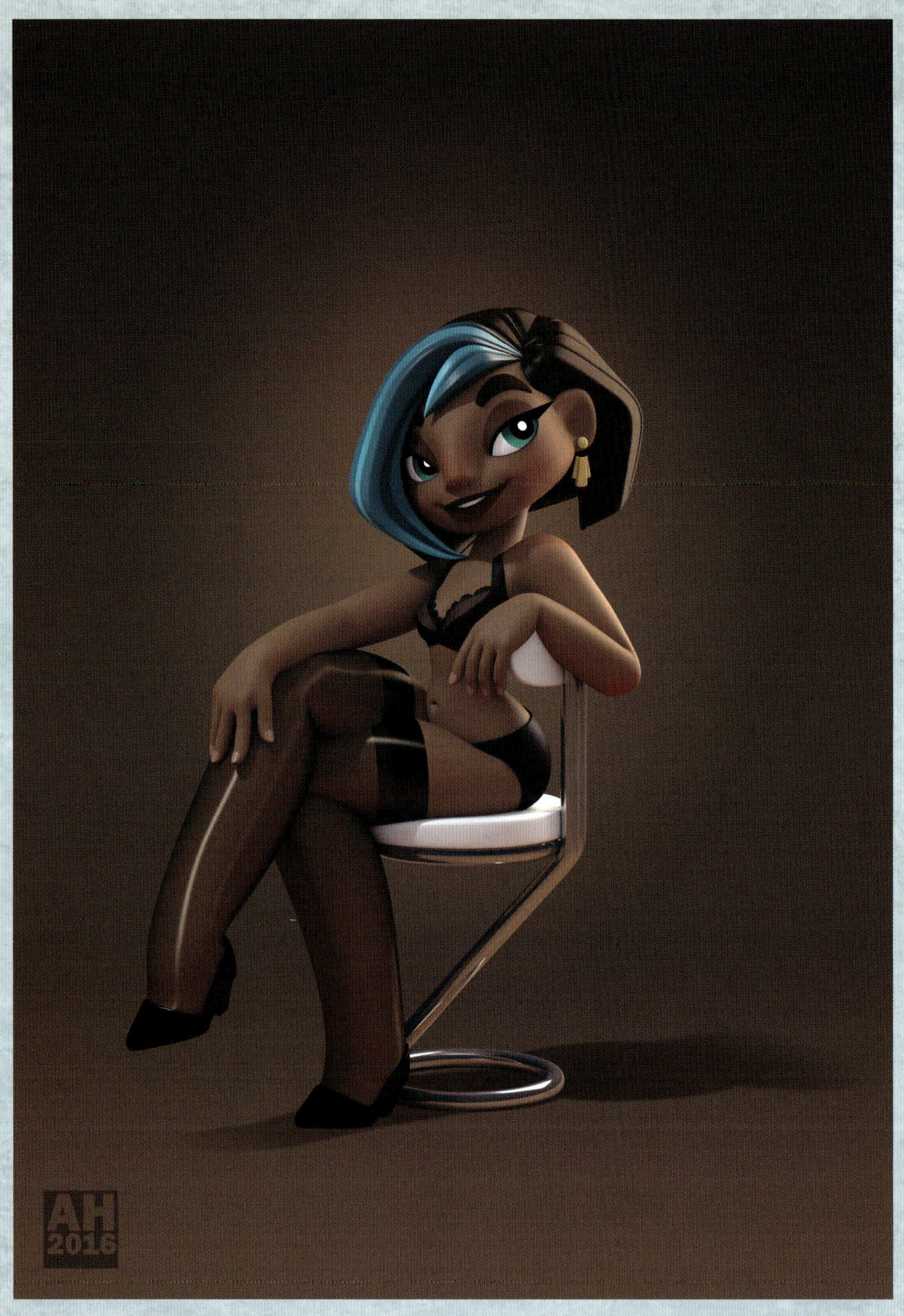

ABOVE: *Rheya*
Andrew Hickinbottom

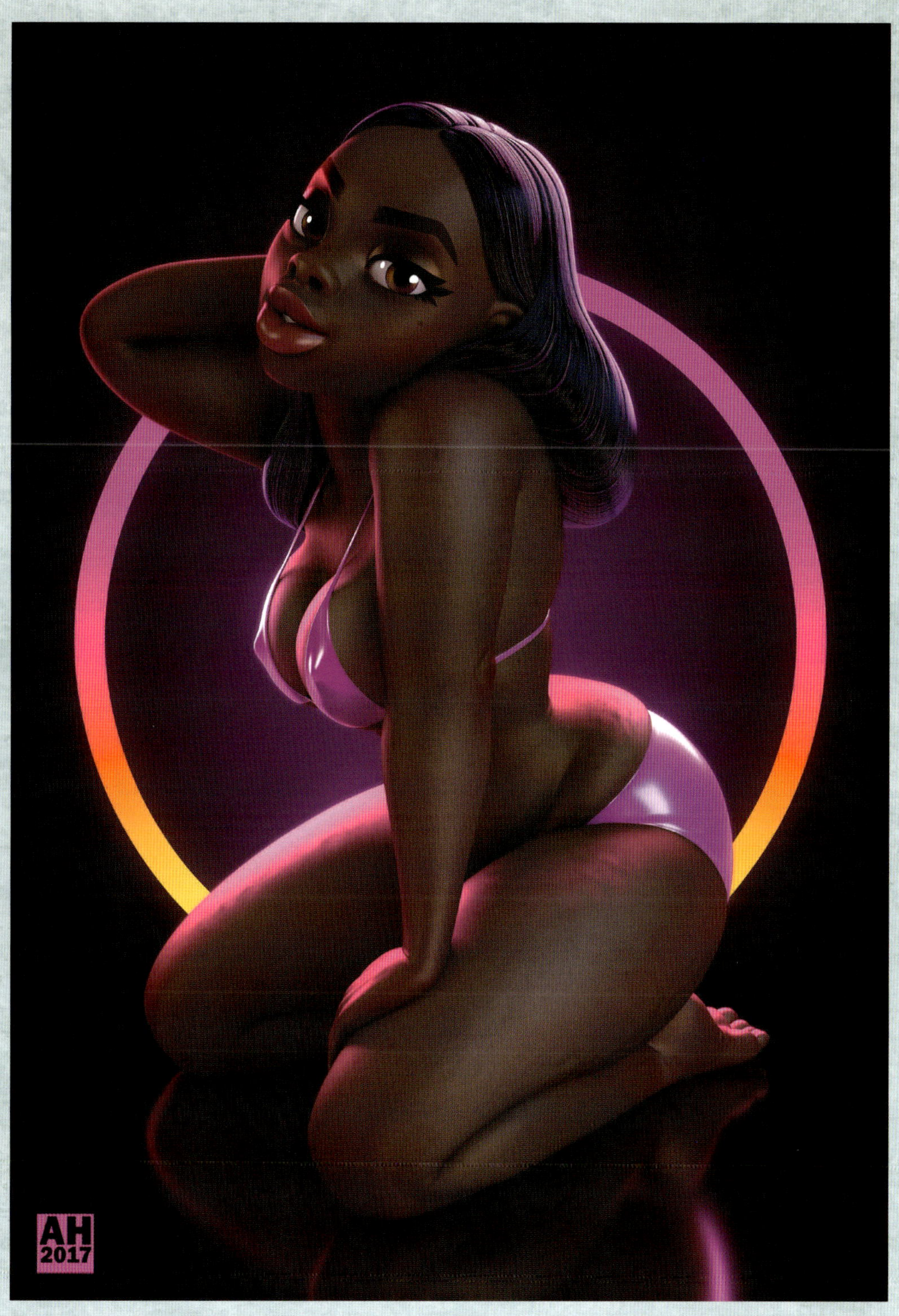

ABOVE: ***Vanessa***
Andrew Hickinbottom

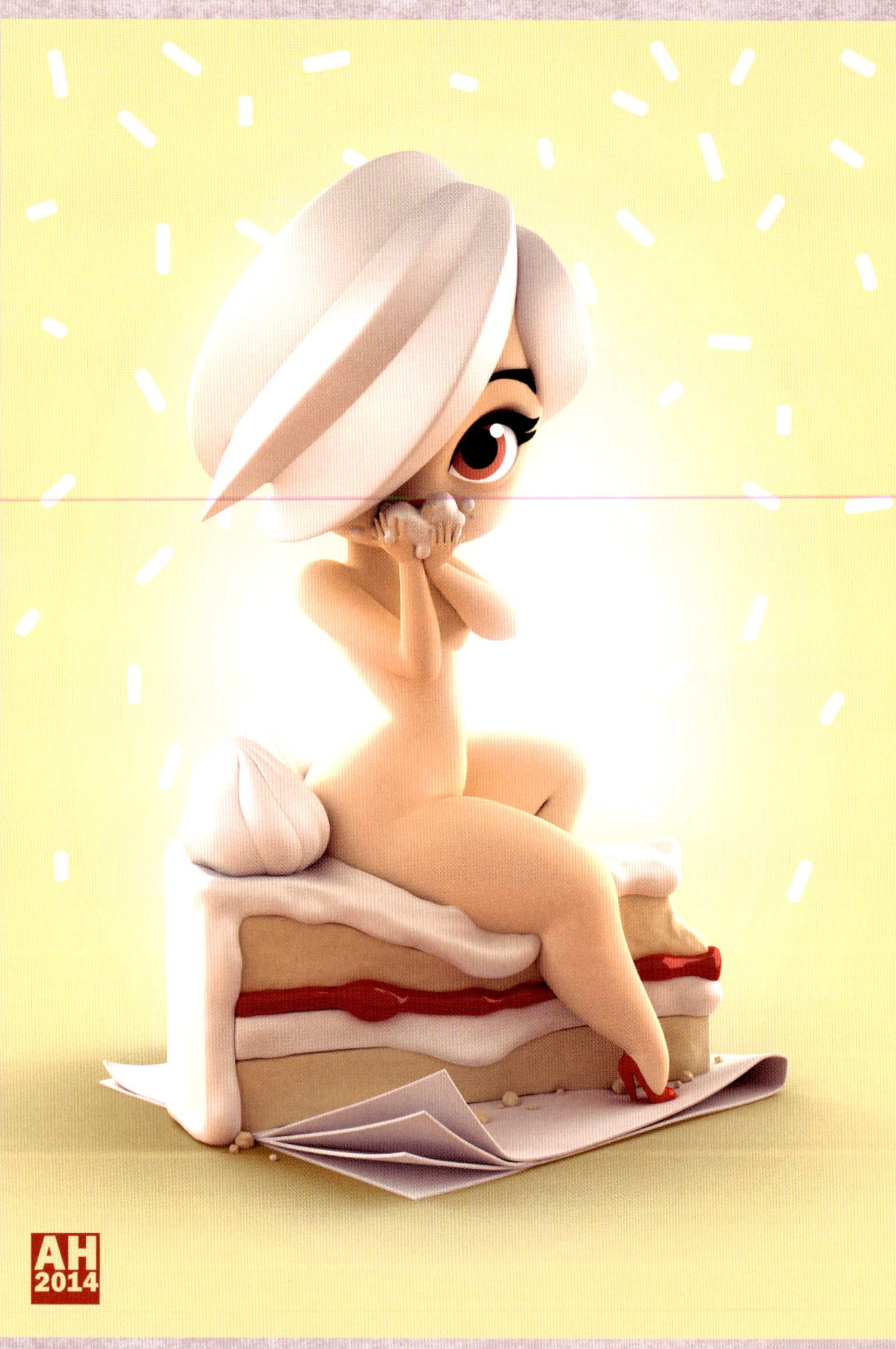

ABOVE: ***Sweet Cheeks***
Andrew Hickinbottom

RIGHT: ***Doris Diner***
Andrew Hickinbottom

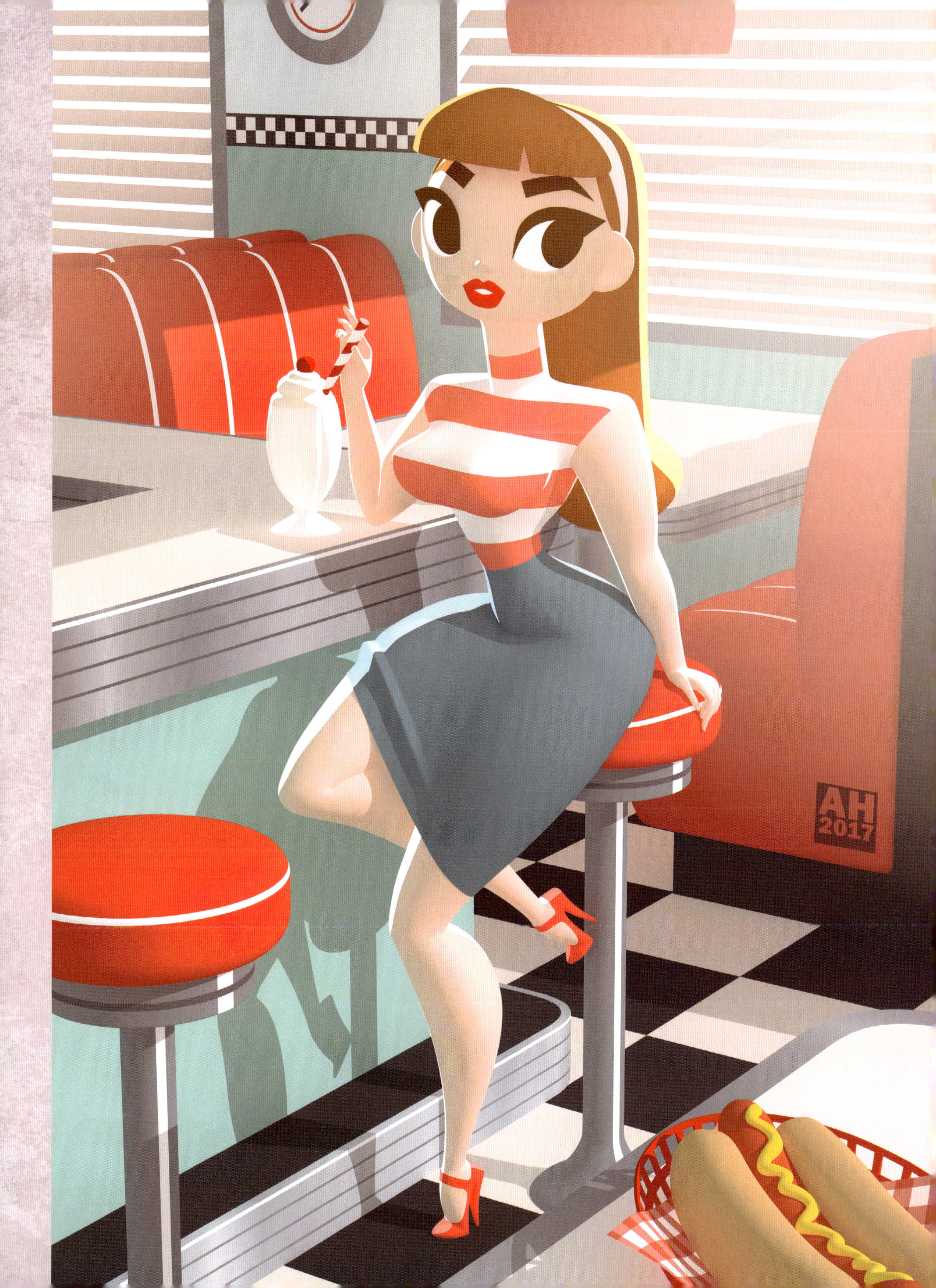
AH
2017

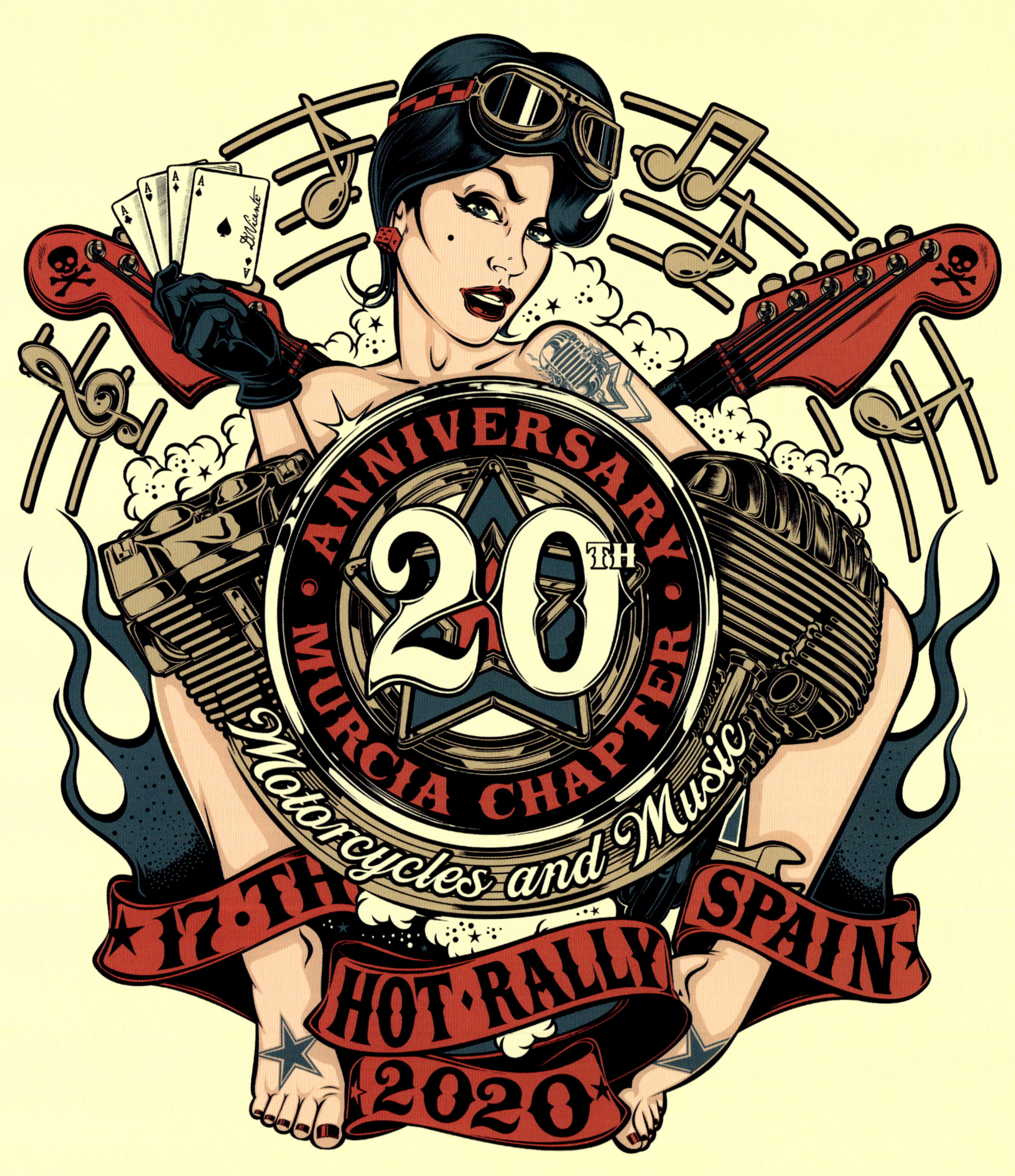

ANNIVERSARY
20TH
MURCIA CHAPTER
Motorcycles and Music
17TH
HOT RALLY
SPAIN
2020

Hot Rod & Badass

Southern California, 1945. The war was won and the celebrated veterans came home with new mechanical know-how thanks to their time in the military, time on their hands and money to burn. Reluctant to buy into the mainstream consumer culture that 40s/50s America was offering and keen to continue the hot rod scene that had begun to take hold just before the war, a new wave of creative expression was born. The classic automobiles so revered by the movement were modified for high performance and improved aerodynamics for the purpose of racing. They were decorated with pin-stripes and flame motifs and despite their risky nature and shaky public opinion, their popularity spread across the nation with dedicated events and magazines being produced in their honour.

It would make sense that the pinup would naturally link up with this rebellious trend - vets had spent the last six years looking at images of gorgeous girls plastered over their living quarters and vehicles, why stop now? The hot-rod pinup is a heady fusion of the classic American pinup girl and the rock 'n' roll, tattooed, anti-establishment persona of the hot rod scene. Their supple, feminine appearance is at delicious odds with the greasy, masculine vibe of the hot rod. These girls were not the coy, kittenish pinups of the former years; they were bold and independent with a devil-may-care attitude and clothes to match.

Tattoo pinups go a little further back. 19th century soldiers in the Spanish-American war had ravishing women tattooed on them to remind them what was waiting for them back home. The trends that were popular then–gypsy, sailor and hula girls in skimpy garb, and those classic cheesecake cuties–remain in favor today, along with a rise of a more modern looking pinup, a sultry mix of big eyes and exaggerated curves to complement the current view of the female ideal.

LEFT: *Murcia Chapter 20th Anniversary*
David Vicente

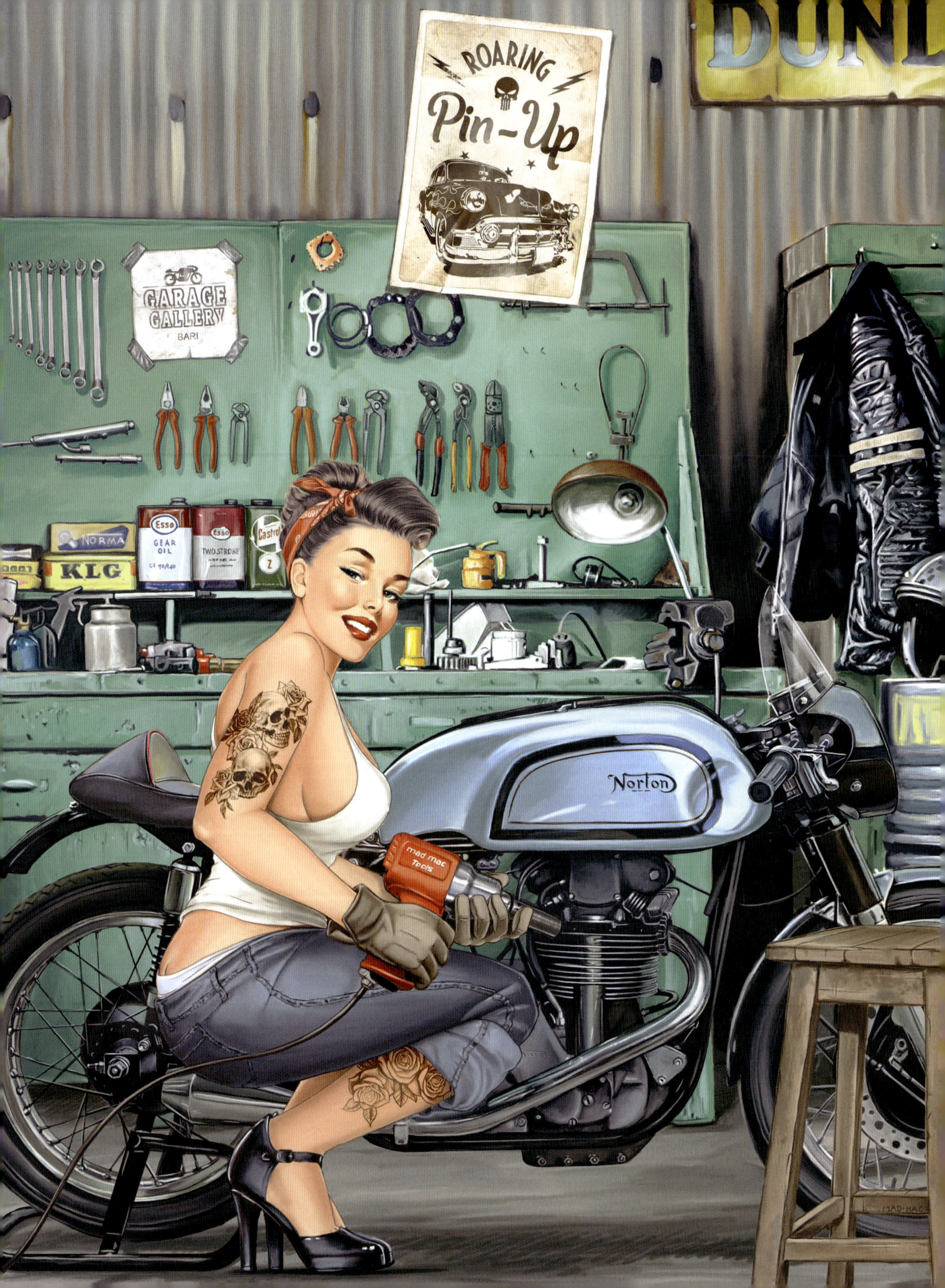
ROARING
Pin-Up
GARAGE GALLERY
BARI
NORMA
KLG
Esso
GEAR OIL
Esso
TWO STROKE
Castrol
Norton
mad mac
Tools

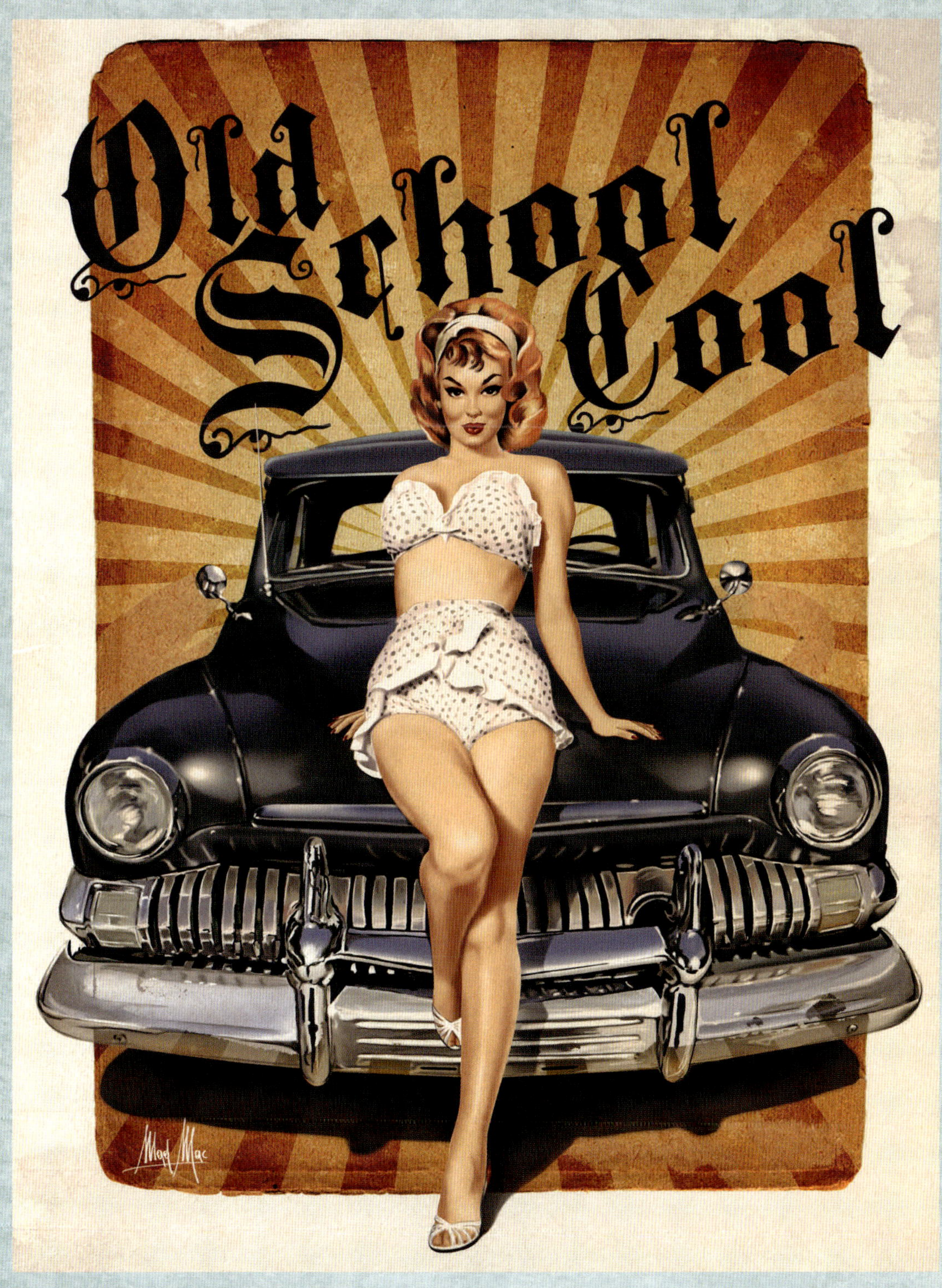

LEFT: ***Sweet Hands***
Mad Mac

ABOVE: ***Old School Cool***
Mad Mac

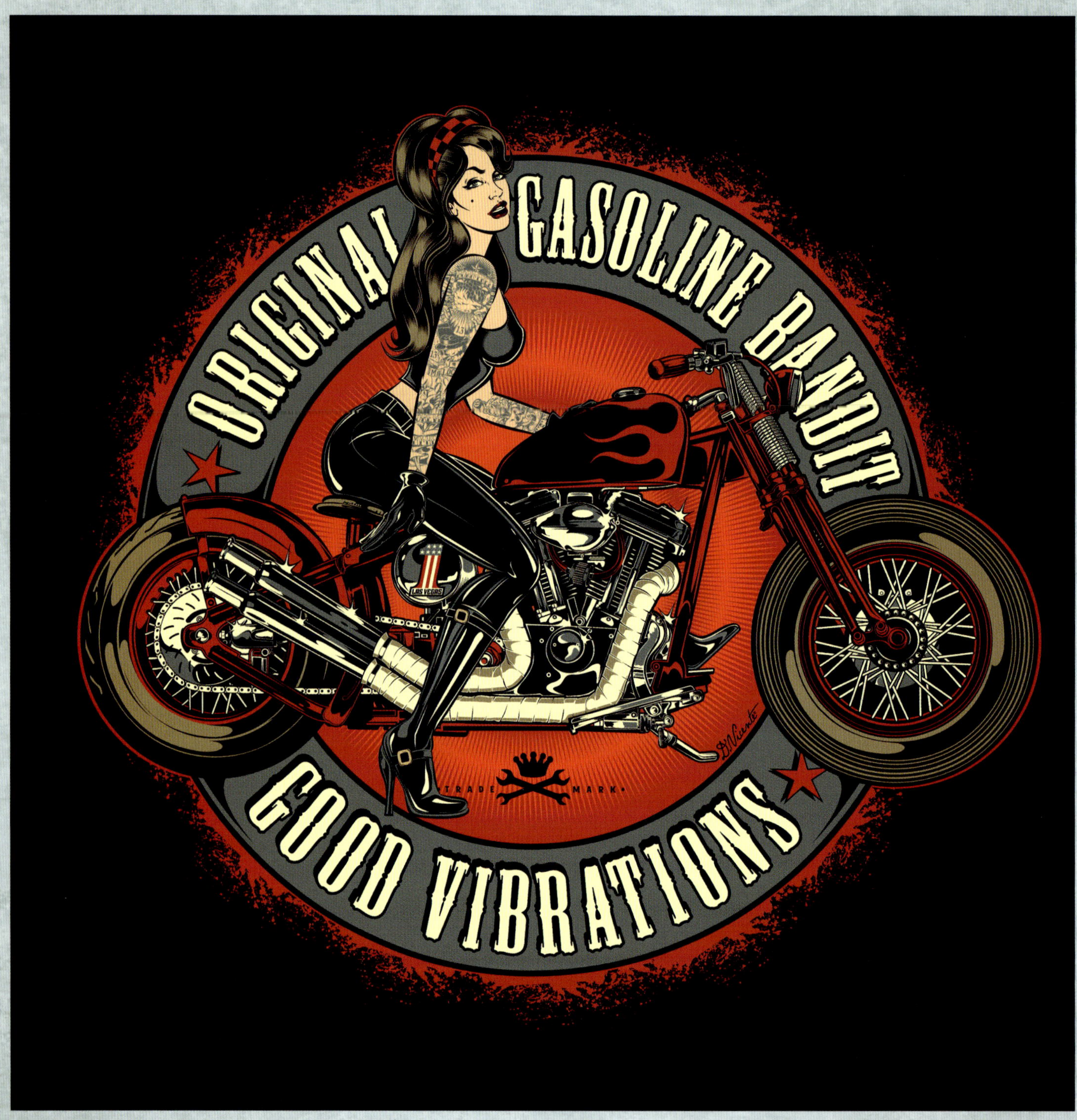

ABOVE: ***Good Vibrations***
David Vicente

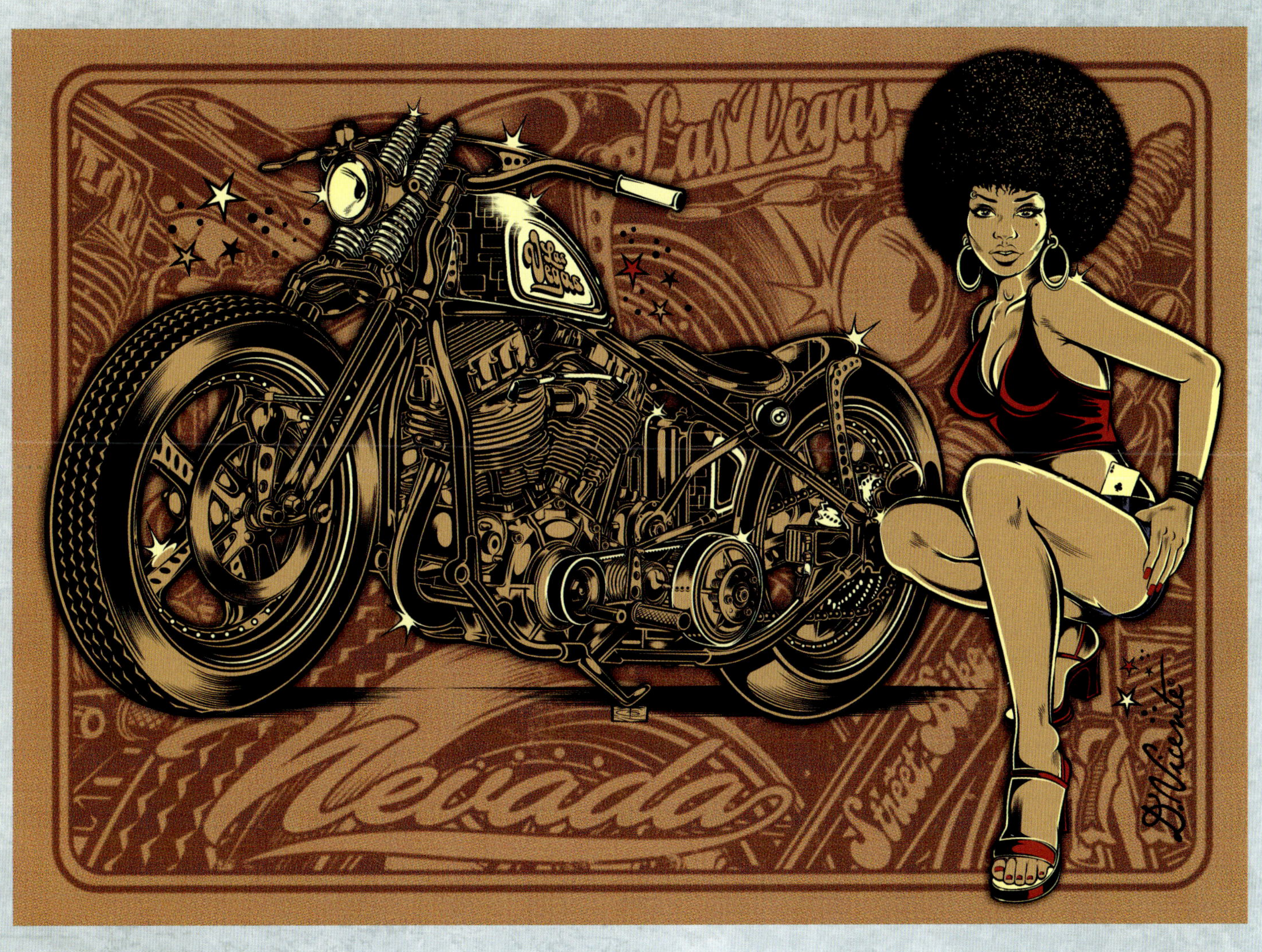

ABOVE: ***Street Bike 77***
David Vicente

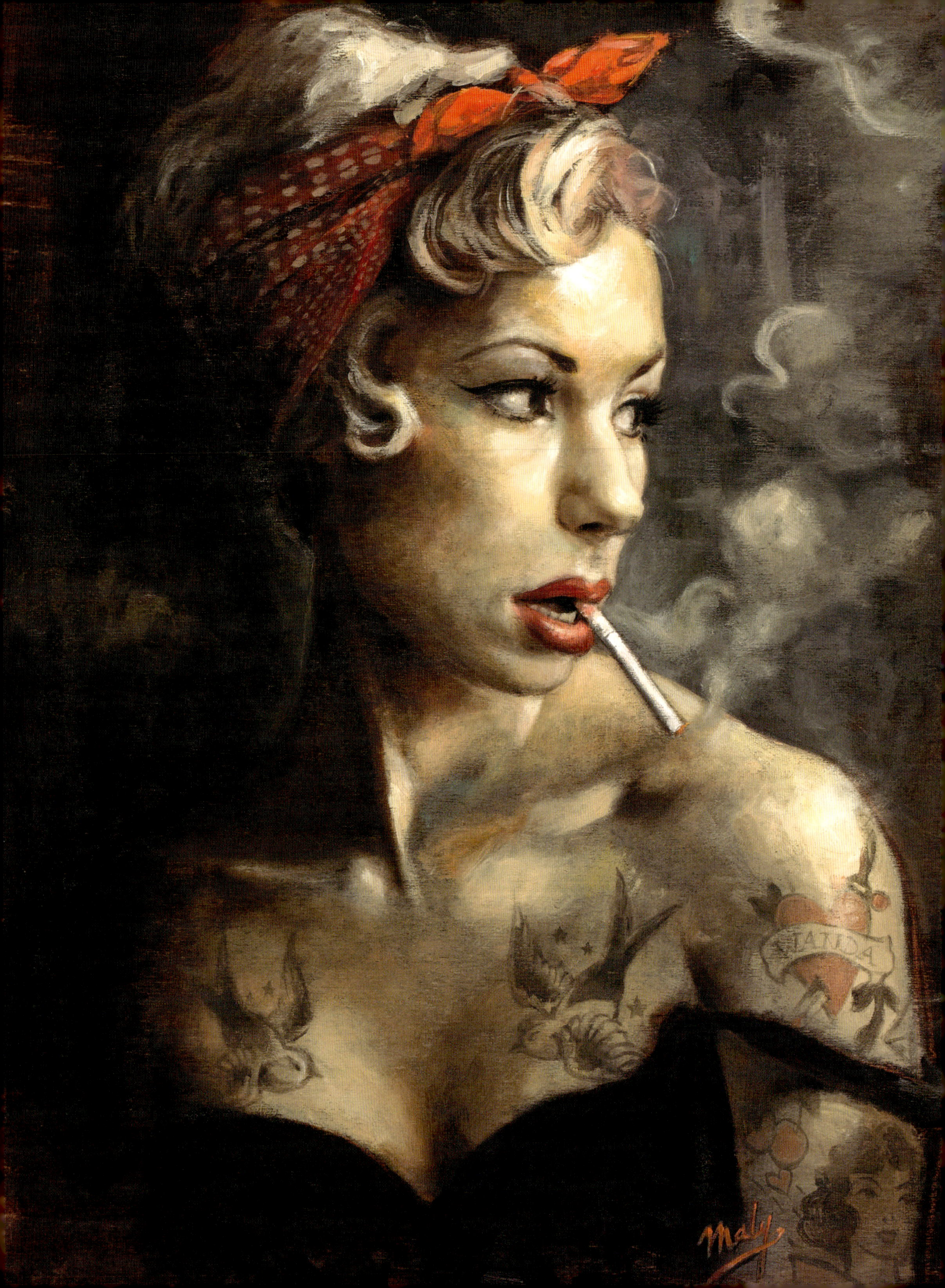
Maly

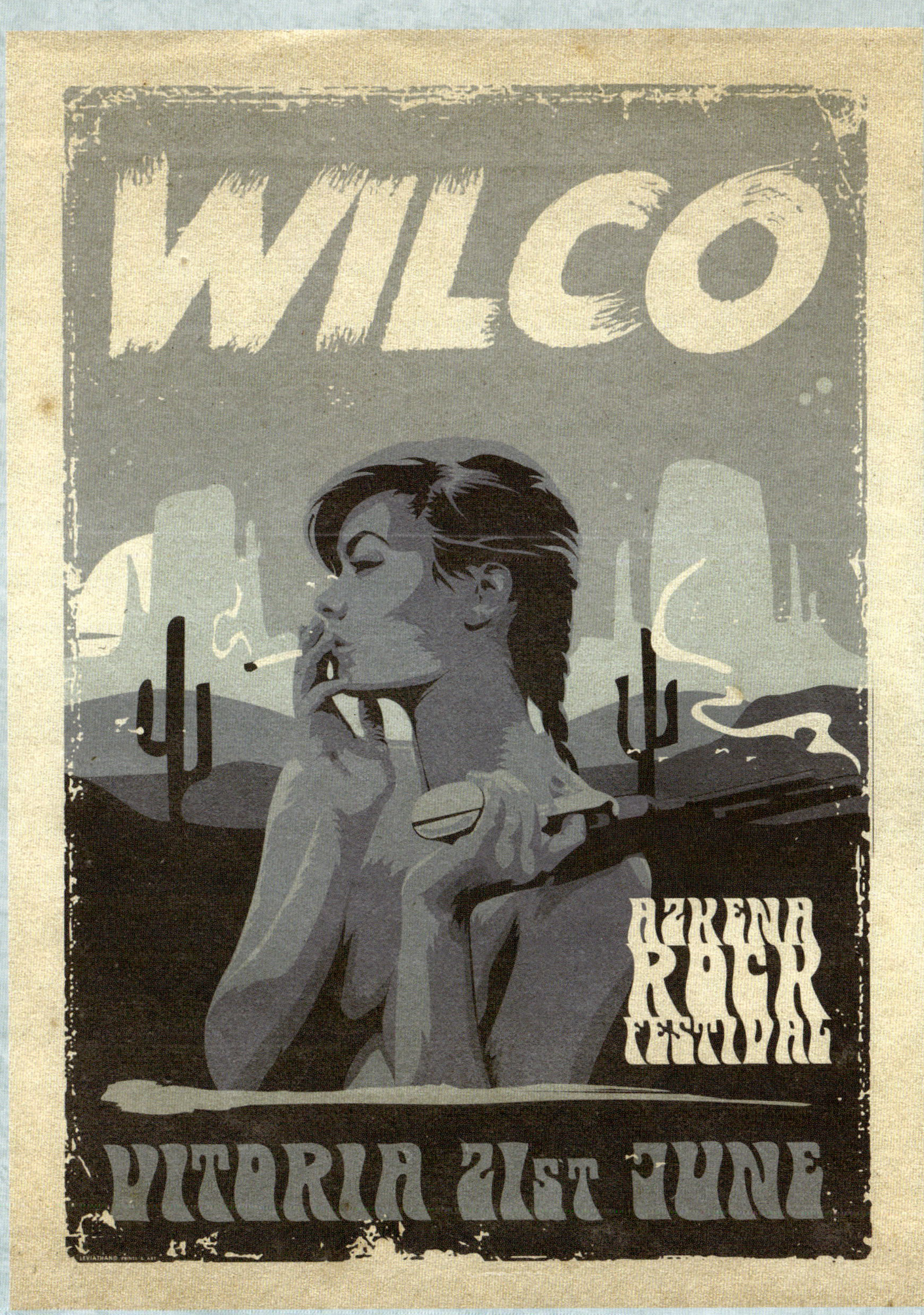

LEFT: ***I Love Wanda***
Maly Siri

ABOVE: ***Wilco***
Leviathan

OVERLEAF: ***It Ain't Me***
Leviathan

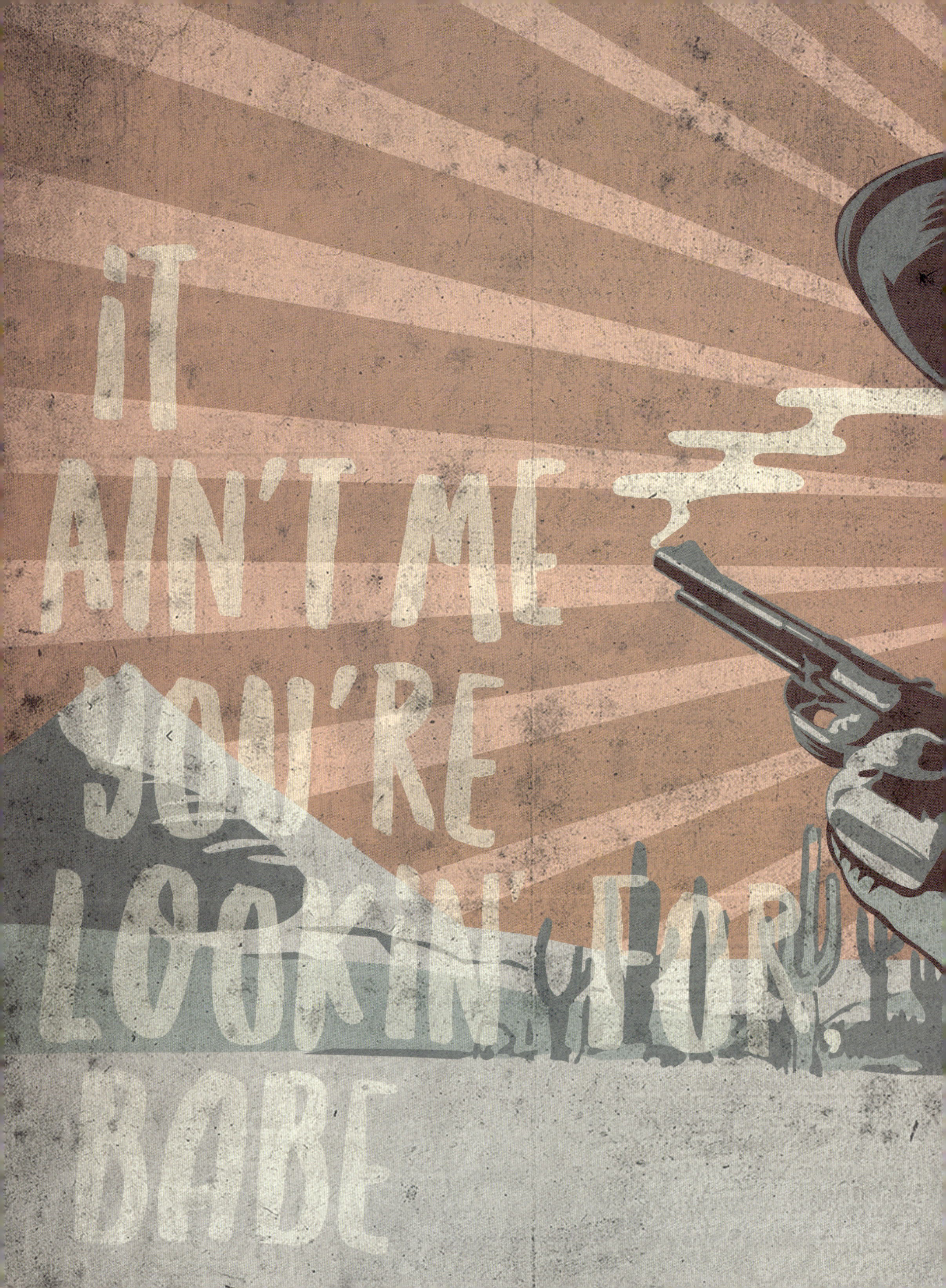
iT
AIN'T ME
YOU'RE
LOOKIN' FOR
BABE

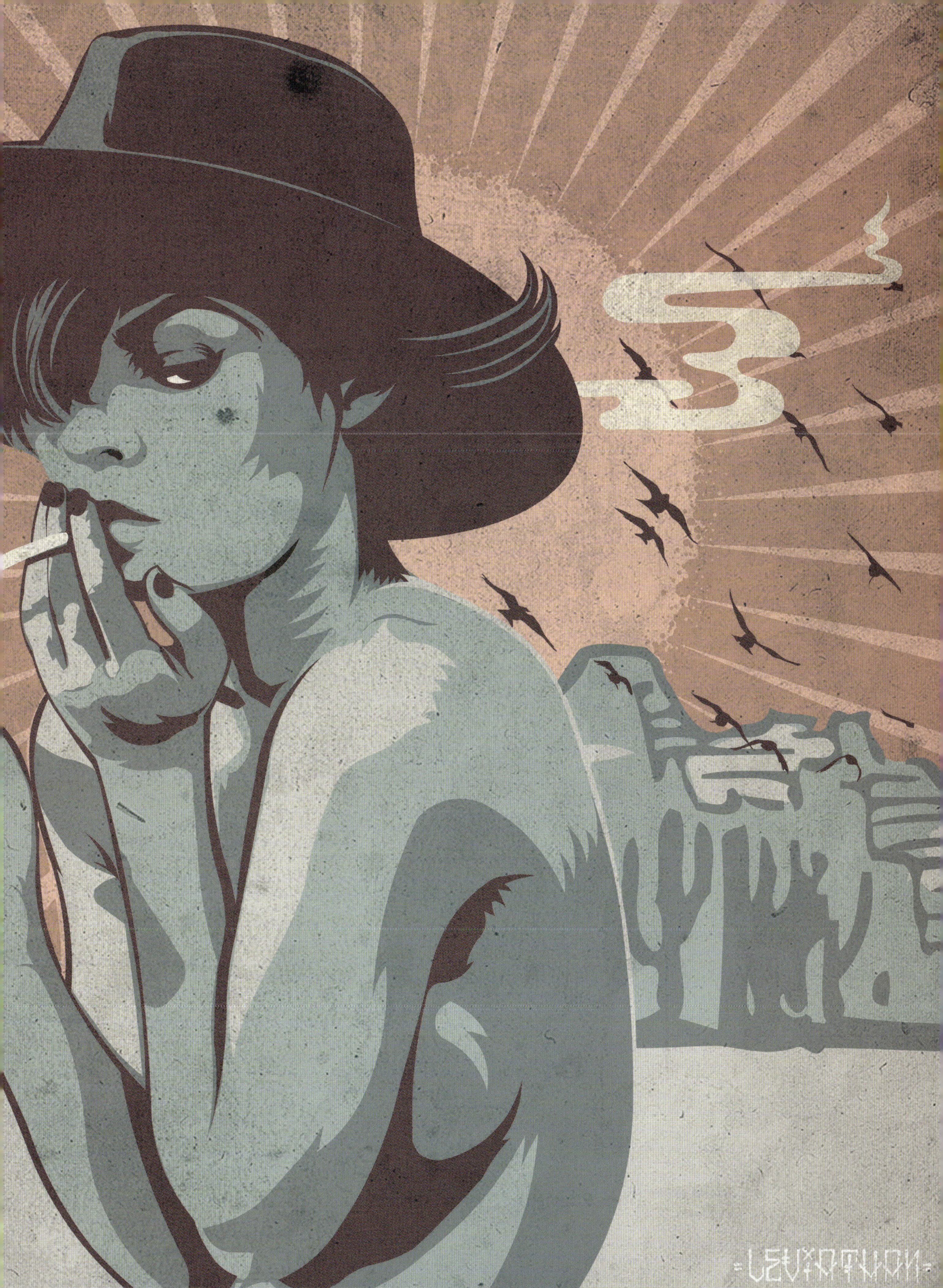

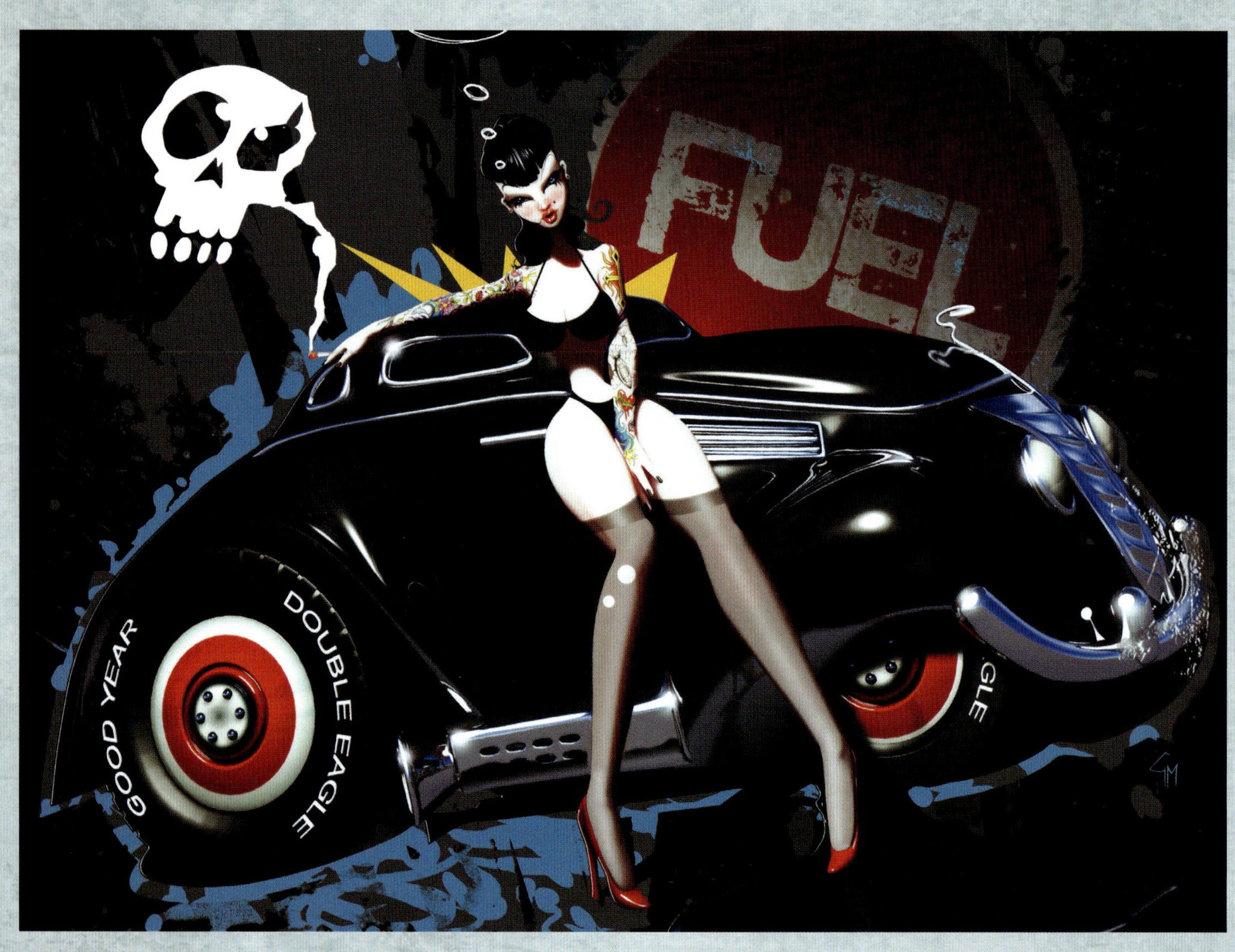

ABOVE: *Fuel*
Gianluca Mattia

RIGHT: *Degree XIII*
Lorenzo Sperlonga

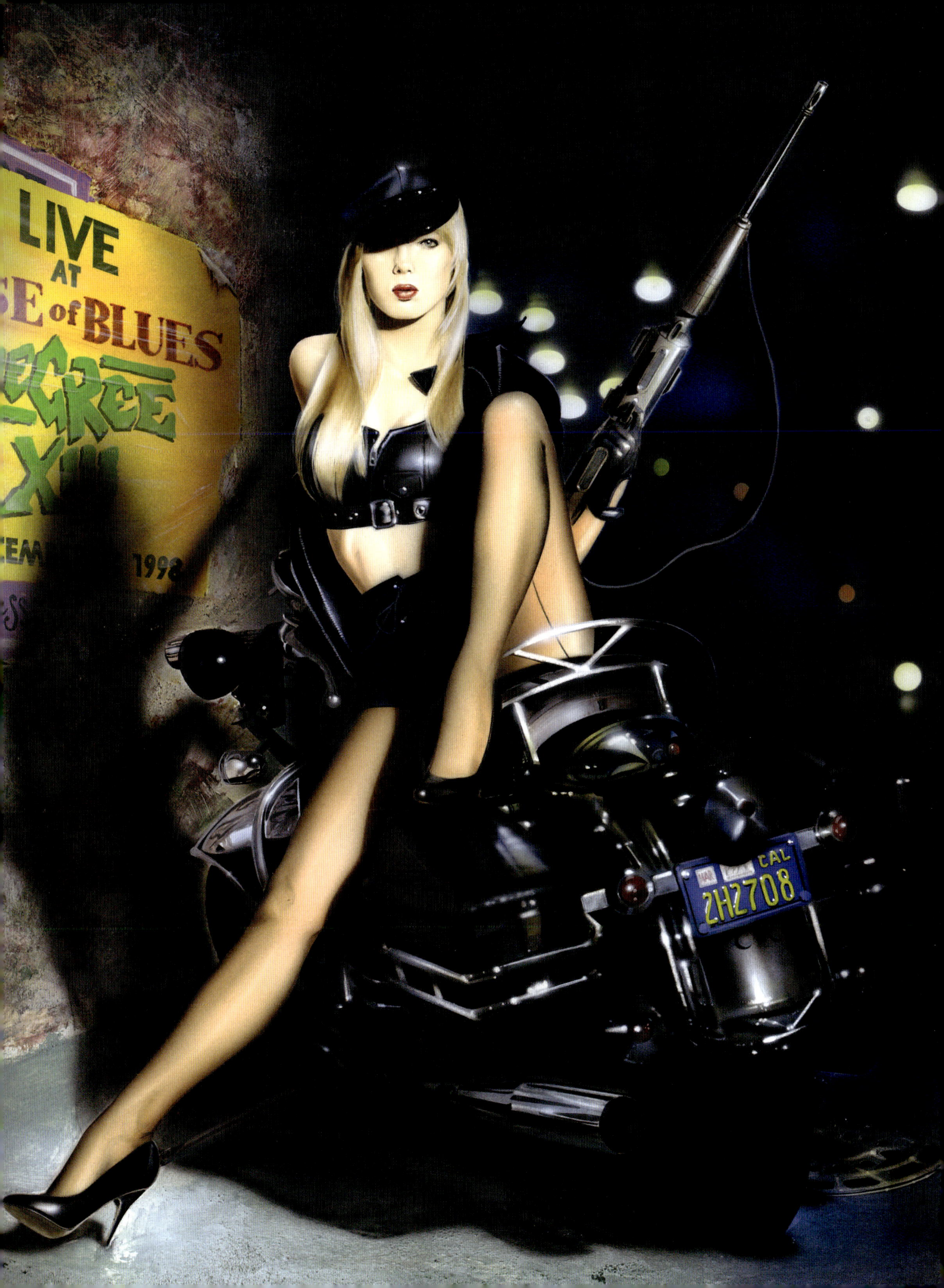
LIVE
AT
SE of BLUES
1998
CAL
2HZ708

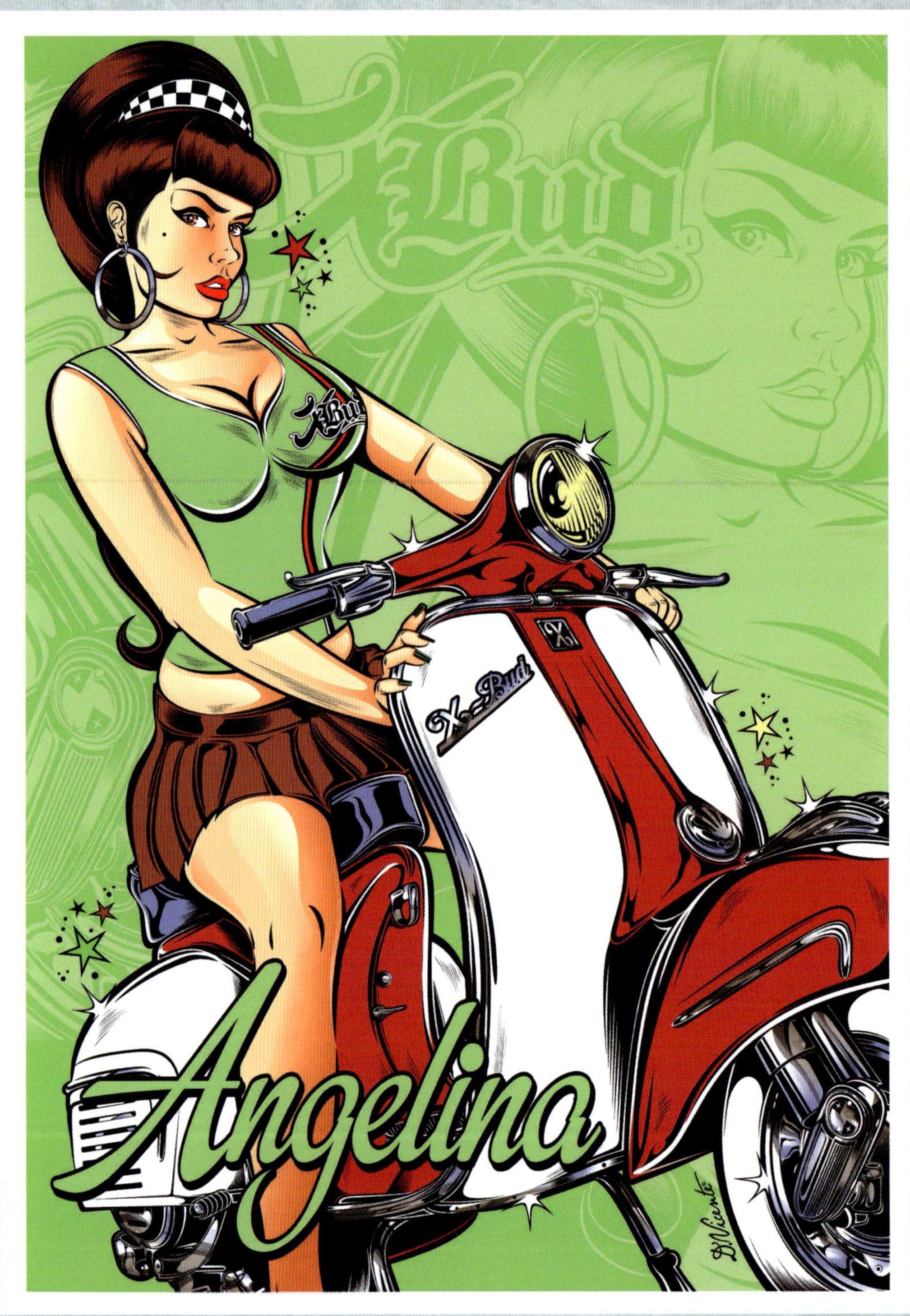

ABOVE: ***Angelina***
David Vicente

RIGHT: ***Spritz Run***
David Vicente

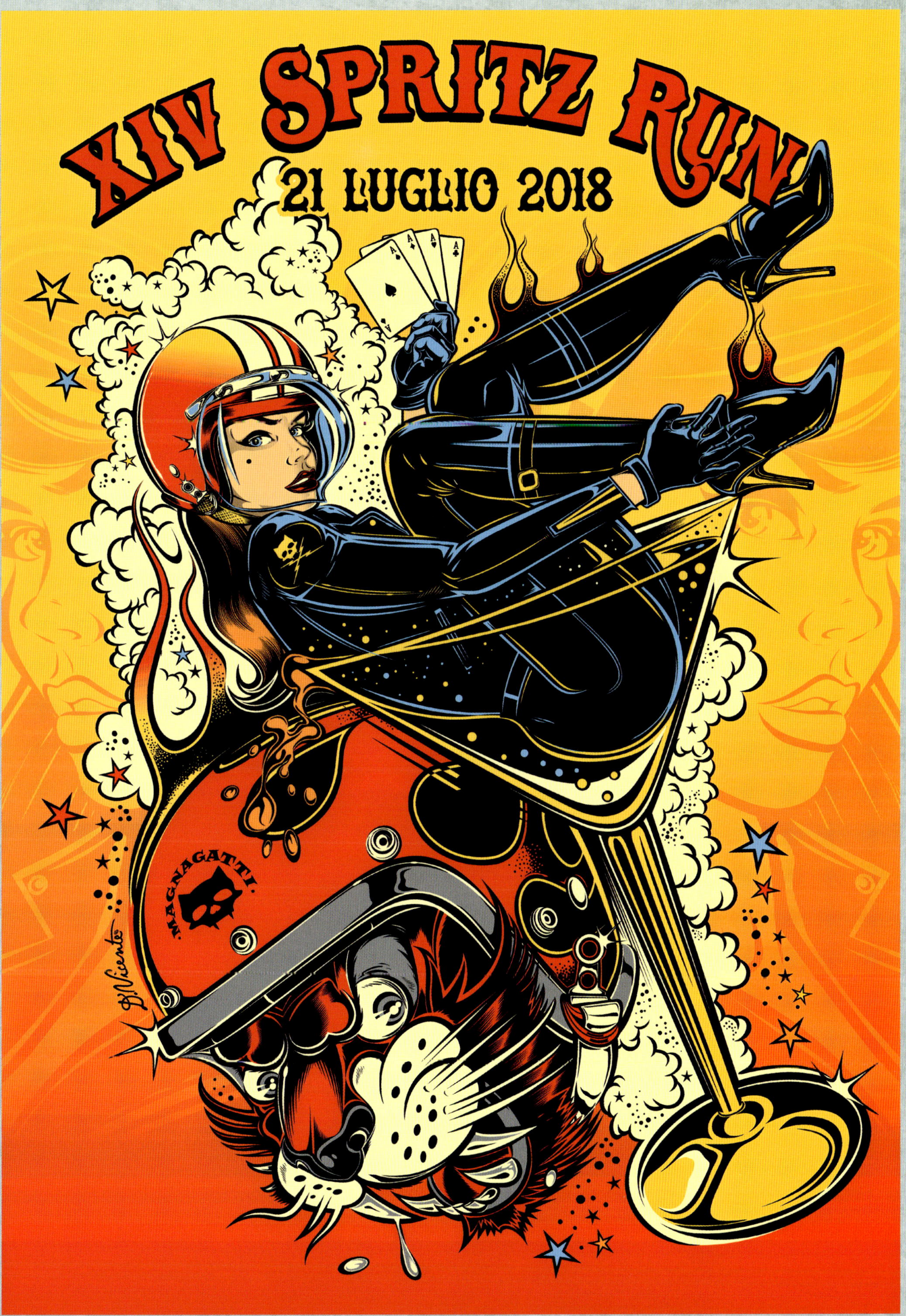
XIV SPRITZ RUN
21 LUGLIO 2018
MAGNAGATTI

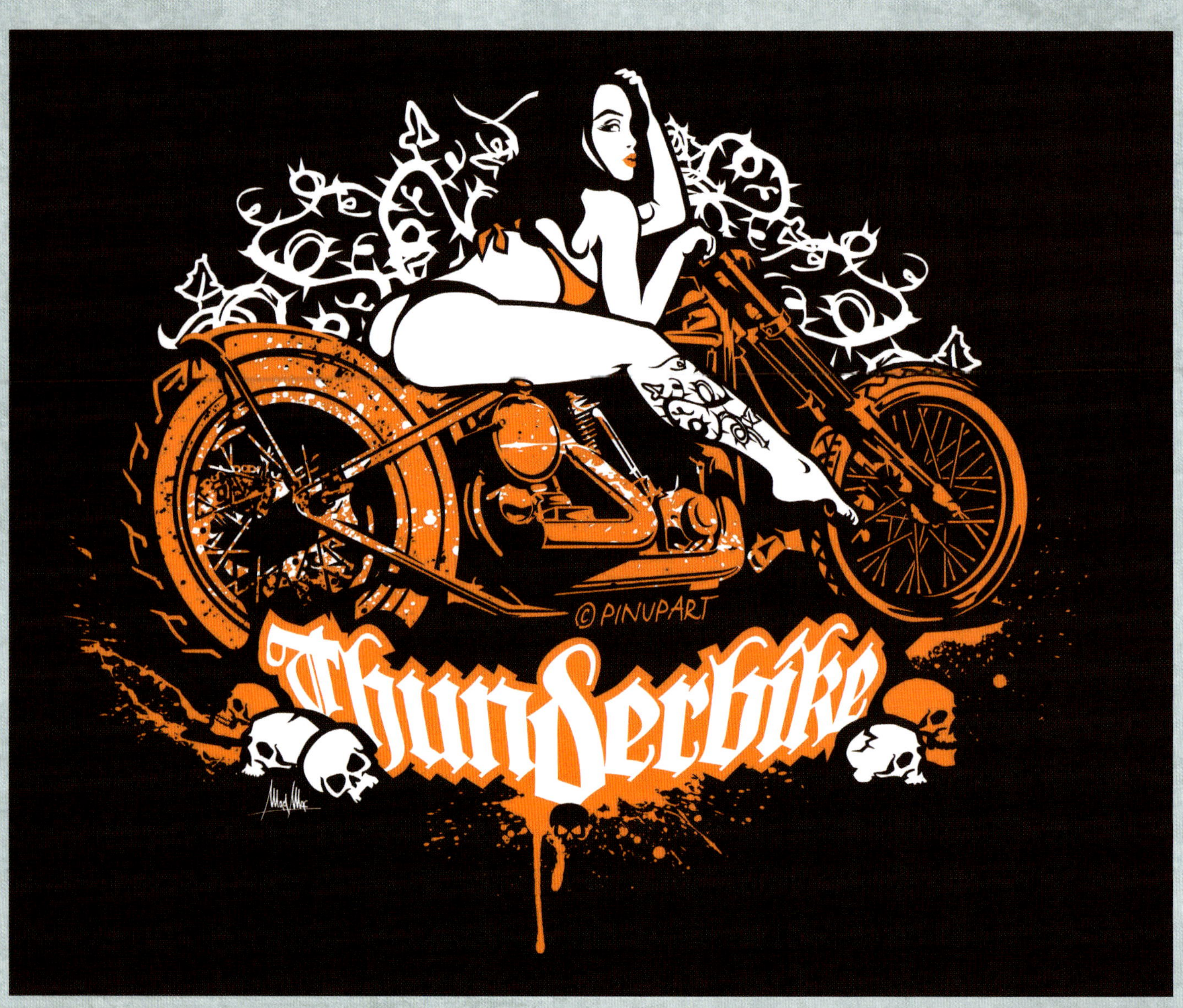

ABOVE: **Thunderbike**
Mad Mac

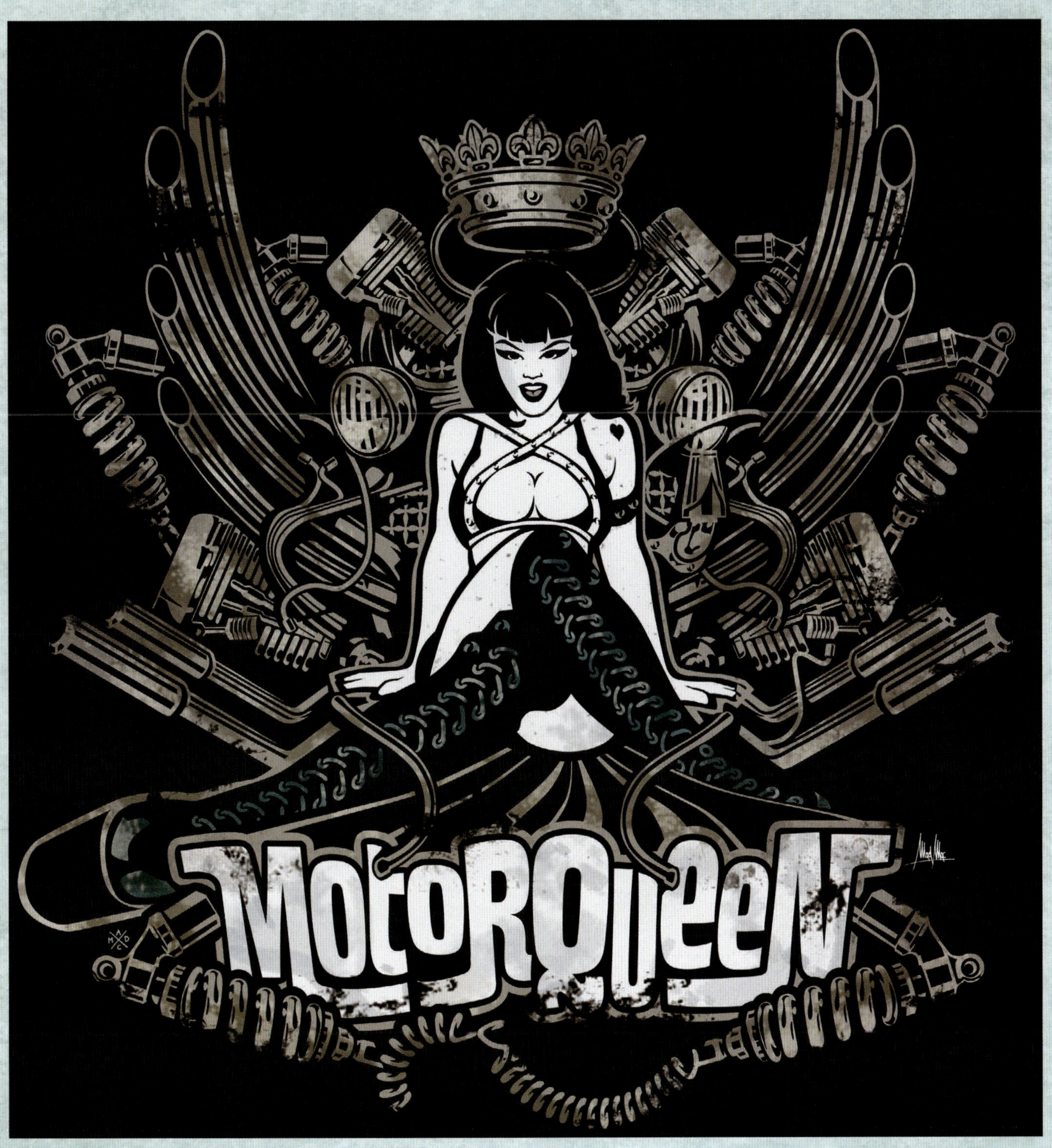

ABOVE: ***Motor Queen***
Mad Mac

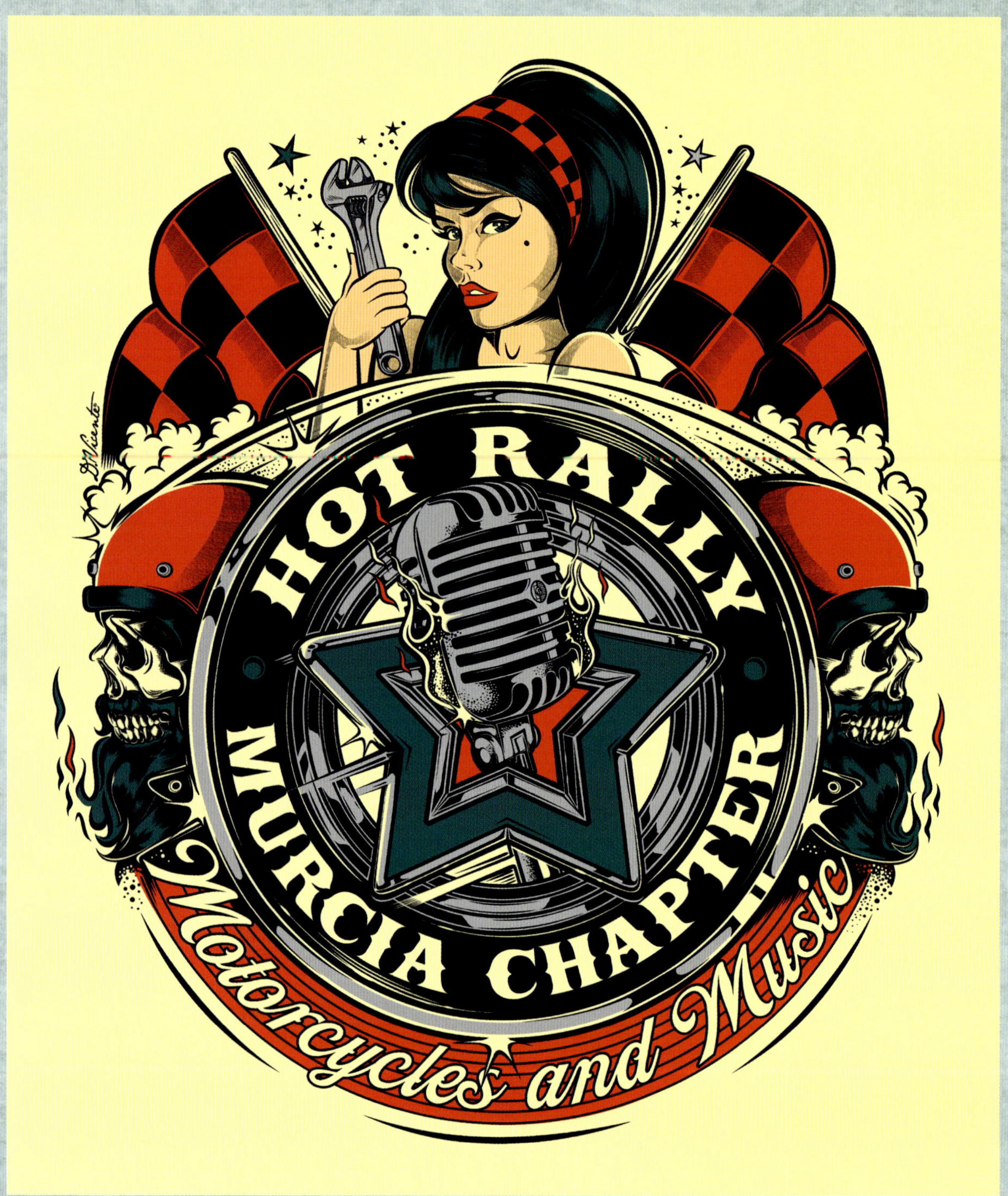

ABOVE: ***Hot Rally***
David Vicente

RIGHT: ***Lucky Games***
David Vicente

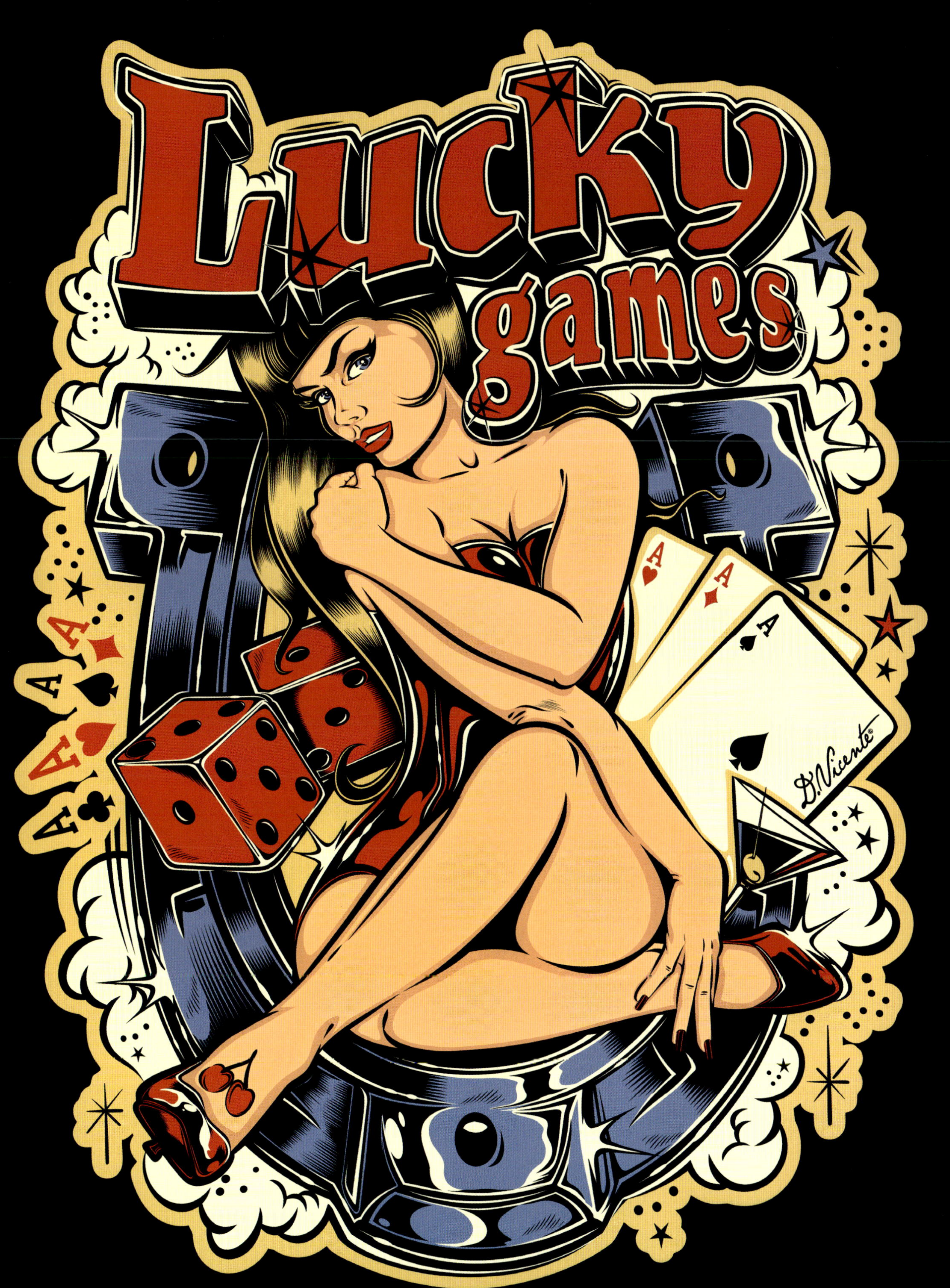
Lucky
games
D. Vicente

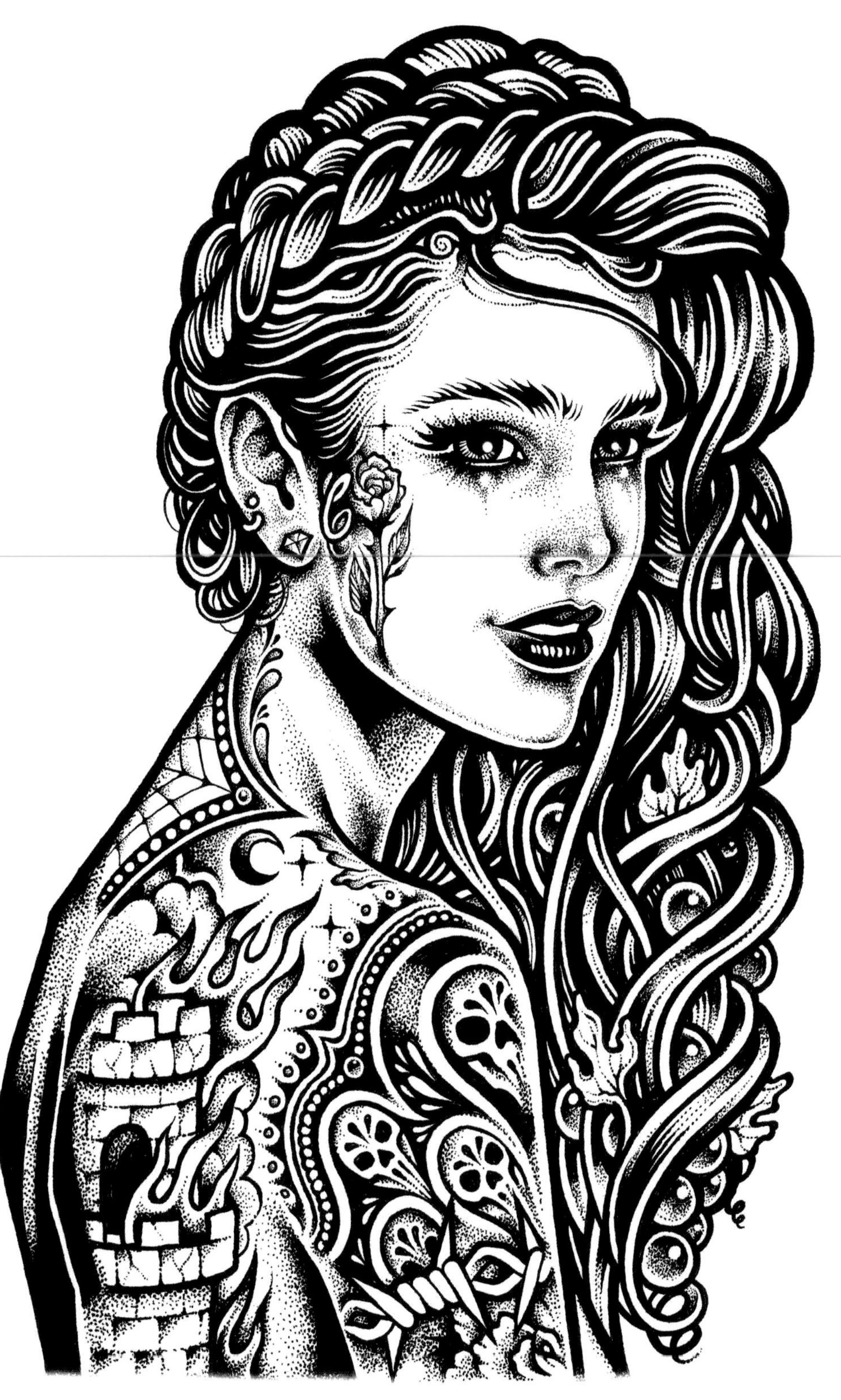

ABOVE: ***Red Wine***
Adam Isaac Jackson

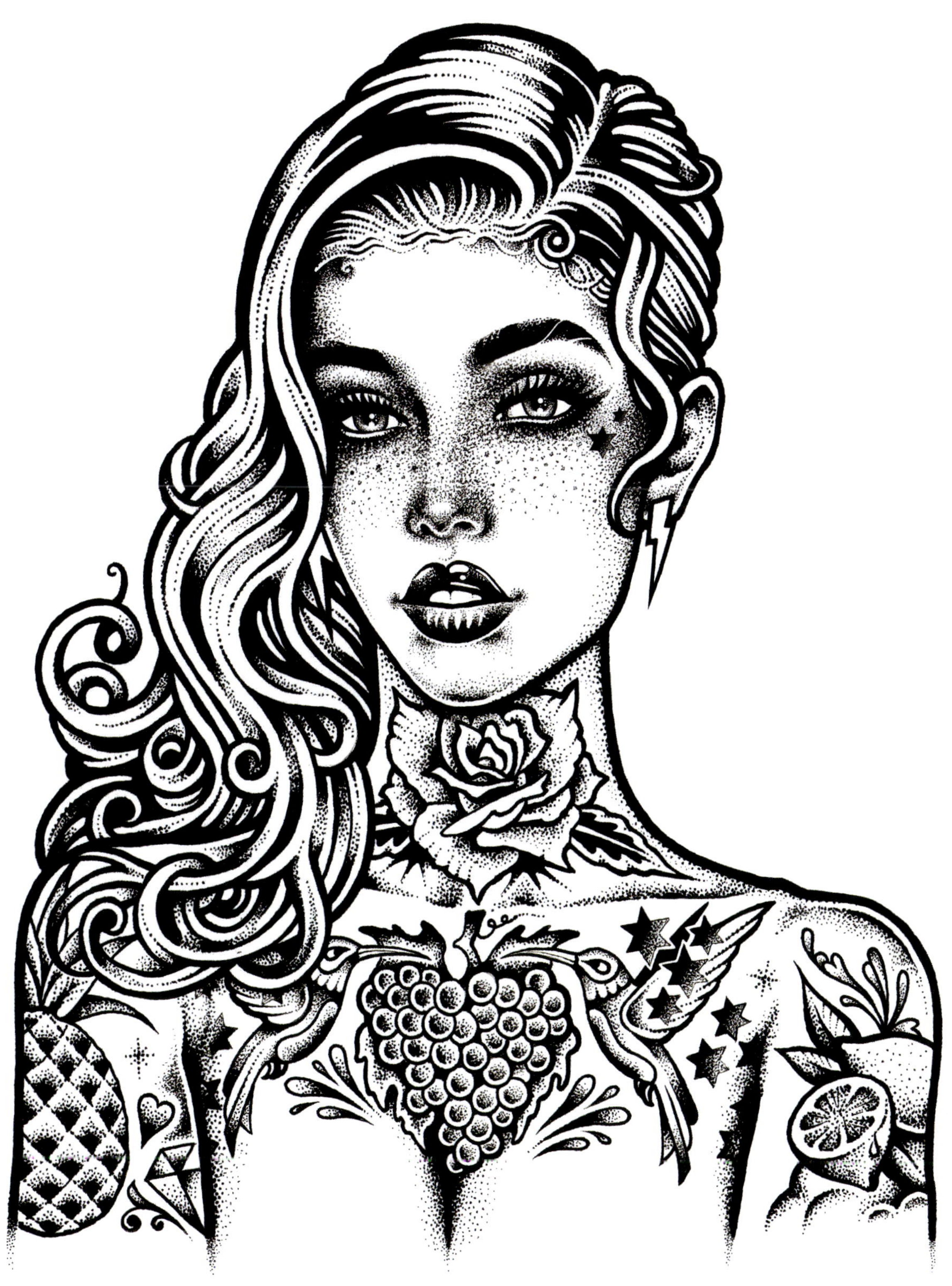

ABOVE: ***Chardonnay***
Adam Isaac Jackson

OVERLEAF: ***Hot Rod Pinup***
Mad Mac

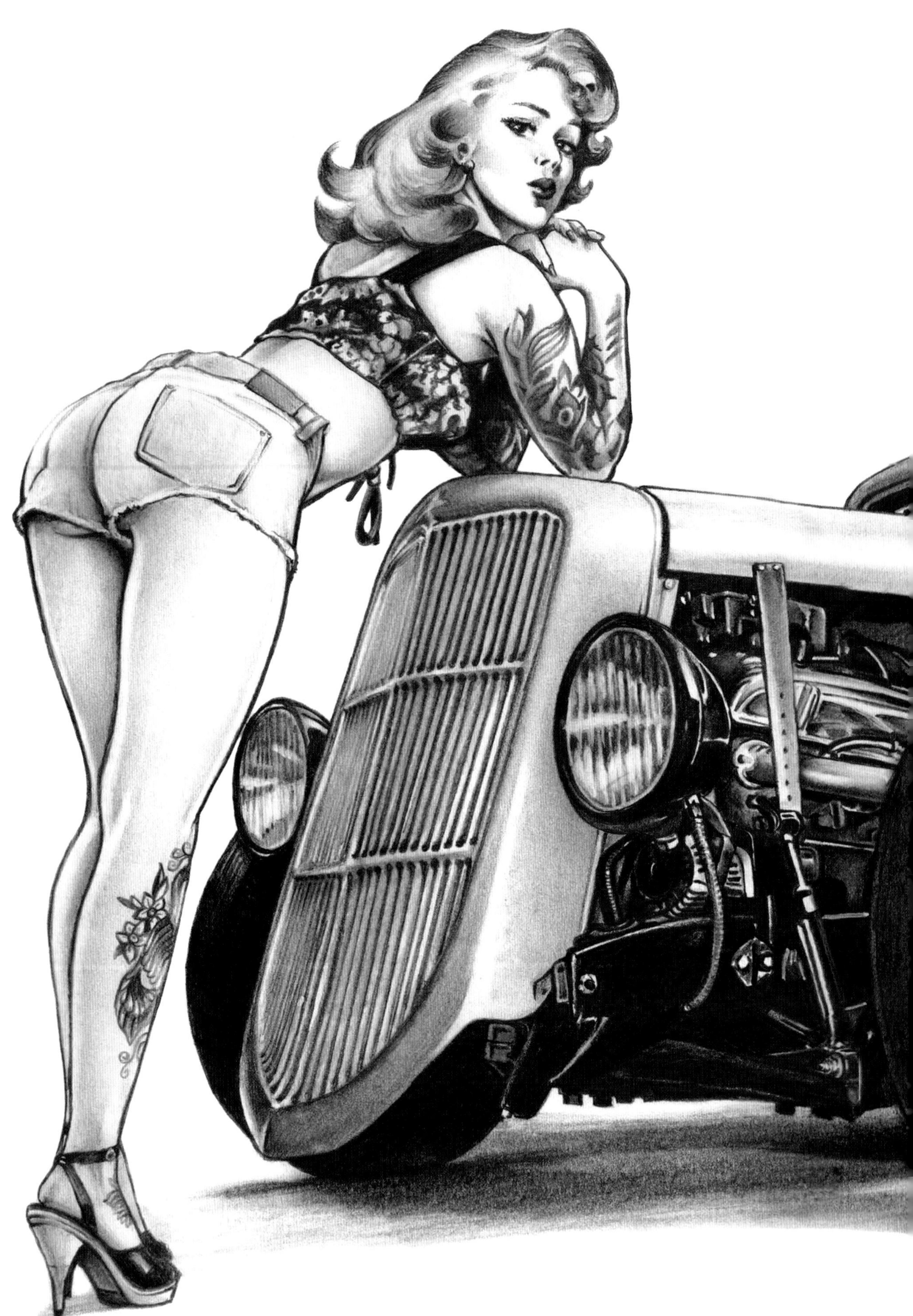

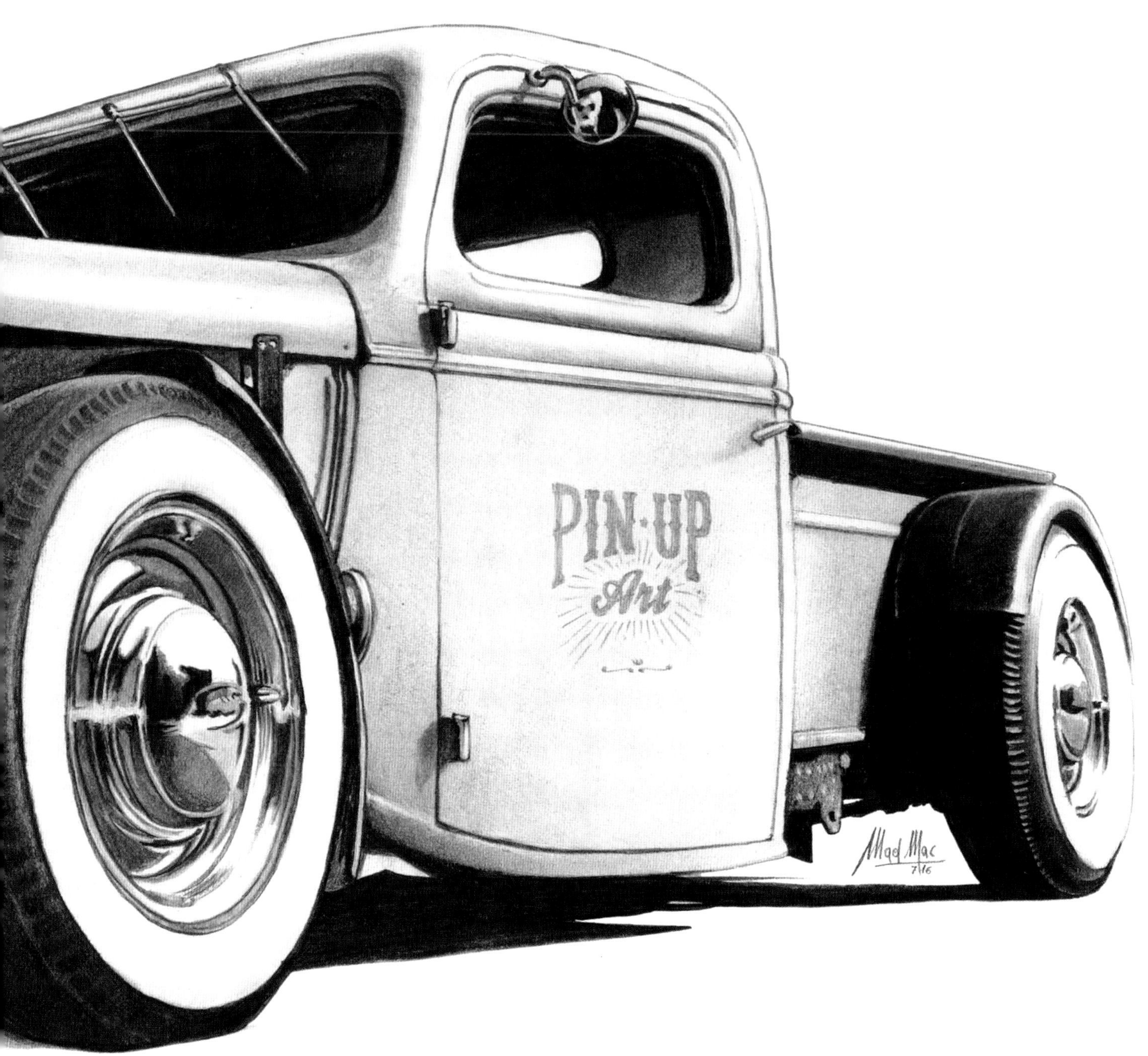
PIN-UP
Art
Mad Mac
7/16

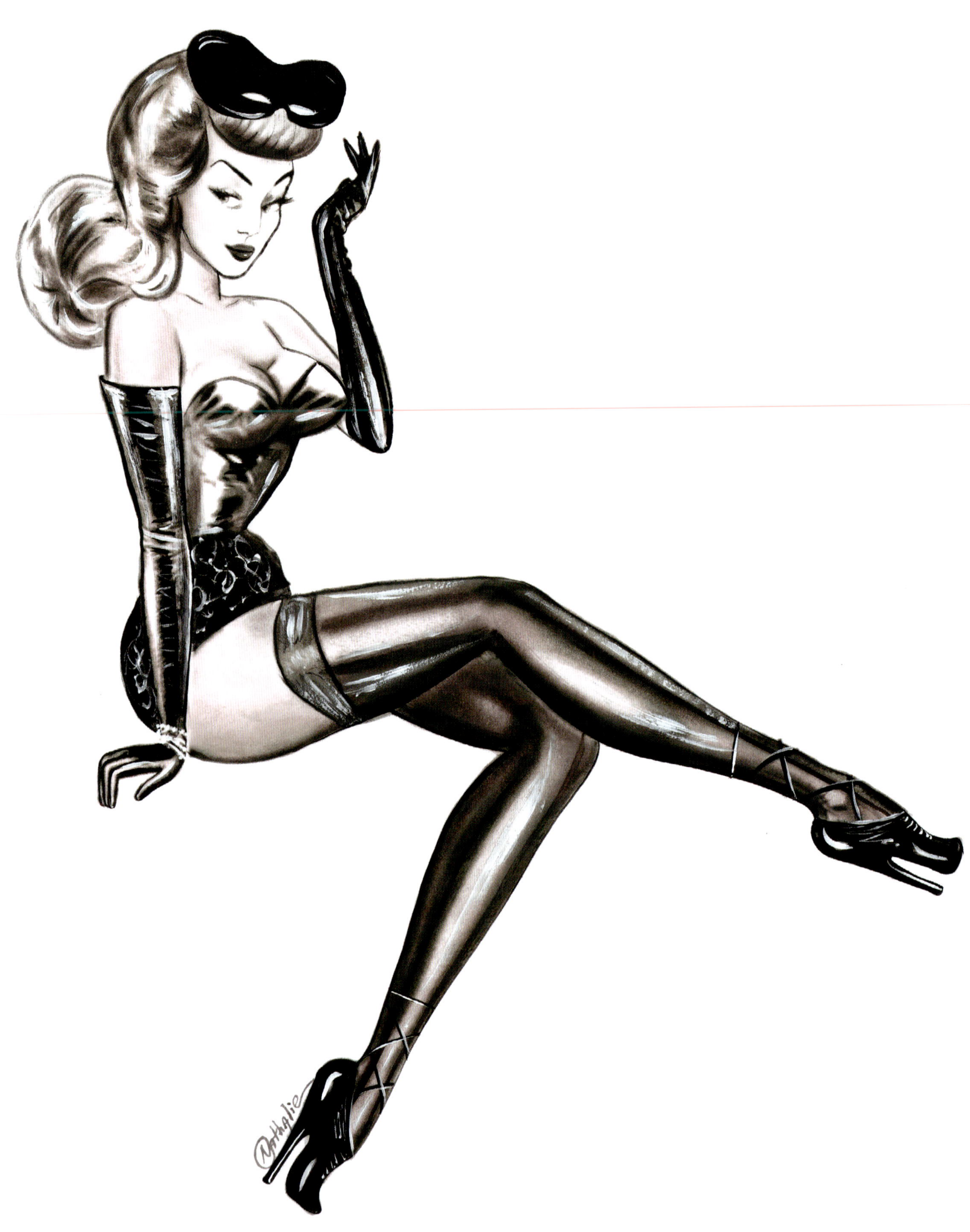
Nathalie

Seduction

When pinup art arose, strict rules governed what was appropriate and even legal to print. Artists used suggestion and the power of imagination to achieve the sexy quality so integral to the quintessential pinup, battling against the limitations of regulation and convention. This led to a burst of creativity and pinups which artfully and carefully straddled the line of conventional decency, public morality, and publication law, often one step ahead of their regulators.

The pinup served as the introduction to a more liberal sexuality for many, walking a careful path between converts of the new open minded era and those still bound by the chains of sexual repression. This seduction of those on either side of the divide may have been the pinups greatest achievement, dissolving barriers and opening minds.

The free-thinking movement of the 1960s saw an end to this censorship and these erotic images, already bubbling over in barely contained regulation exploded joyfully into modern culture. The soaring popularity of magazines such as Playboy and Modern Man galvanized overseas competitors, with the French Oui and British Penthouse and Mayfair set up as competitors and peers. Here was born the centerfold - the overtly sexual, ripely feminine figure who became an avatar for the era.

Yet even with this new and transgressive vanguard of artists blazing a trail for sexuality and cleaving the chains from depictions of the feminine, there was something older, more elemental being rediscovered and repositioned. This was the seductive, earthy depiction of the female form and soul, which had continued to exist as a rich and vital force hidden by the veil of a prudish society. When she was unleashed, she was as destructive and compelling as anyone could imagine, sweeping aside the staid and tired for the beautiful and timeless in a blaze of sensuality.

What lies at the core of the feminine, its warmth, soul, and passion, found a new home at the heart of the pinup artist's talents. Depicting the contemporary as something essential but intriguing, new but fundamental, helped these lusciously formed beauties to go beyond the physical and embody the rich soul of the feminine. It is in this tradition that seduction speaks to the pinup audience, both through the eyes of its subject but also in reminding us of the elemental truths to human experience.

LEFT: ***Untitled***
Nathalie Rattner

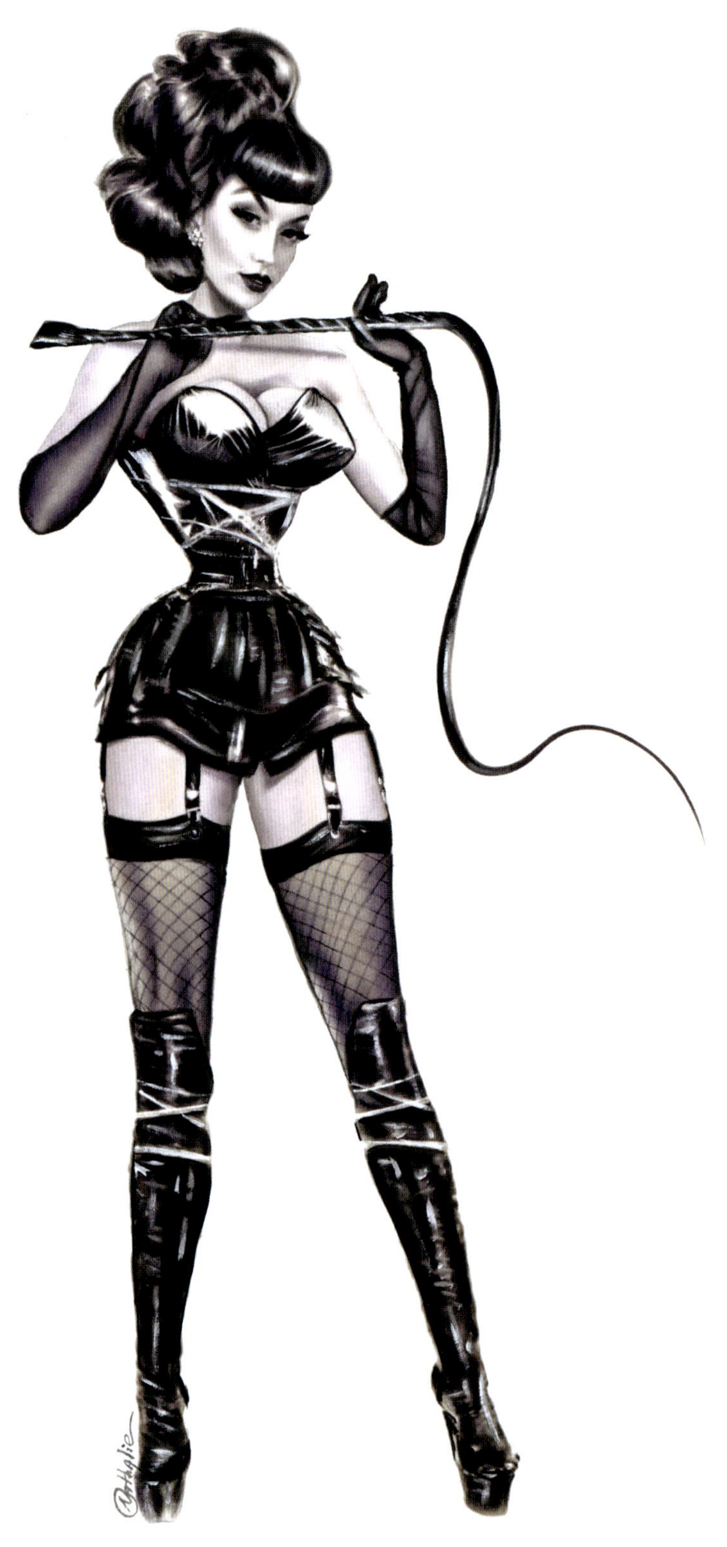

ABOVE: ***Bryona Ashly***
Nathalie Rattner

RIGHT: ***Bryona Ashly II***
Nathalie Rattner

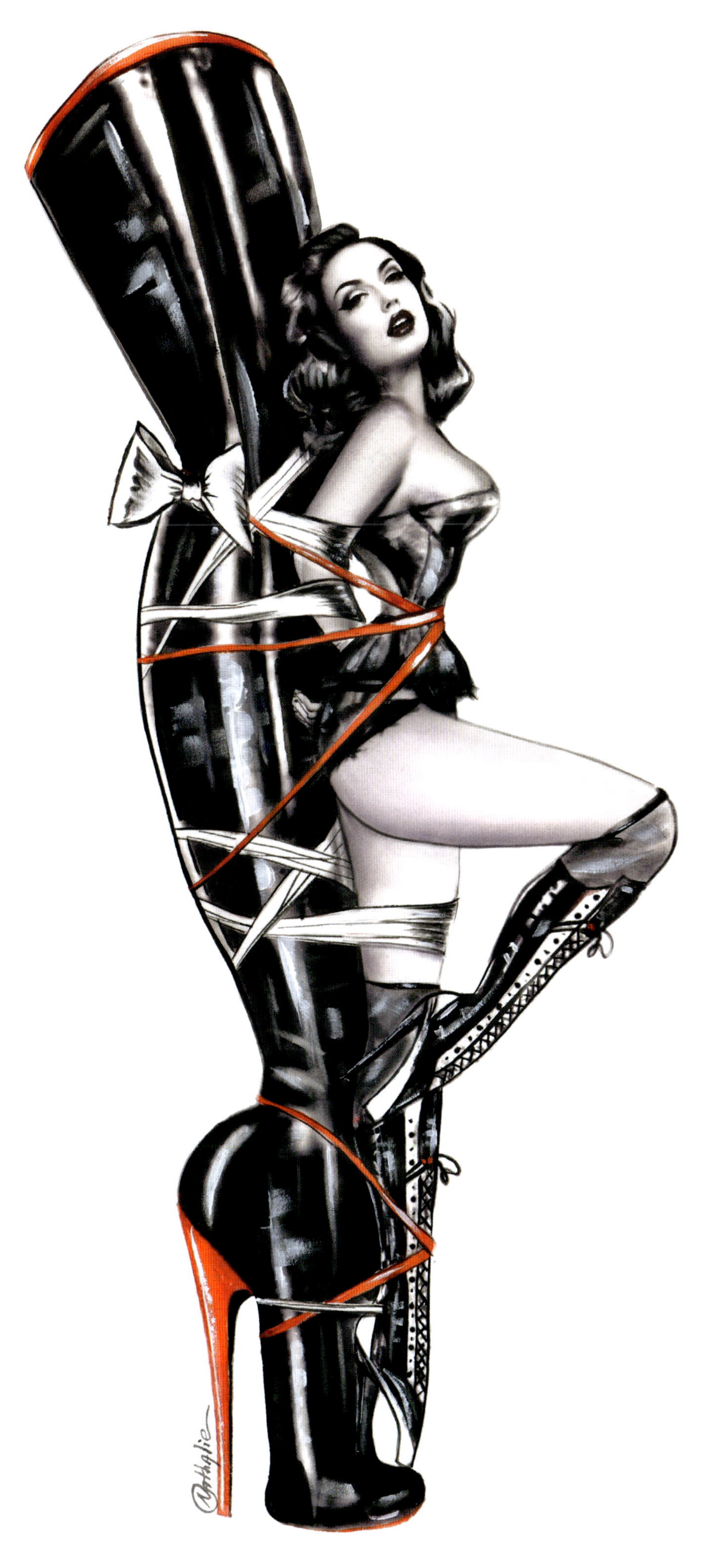

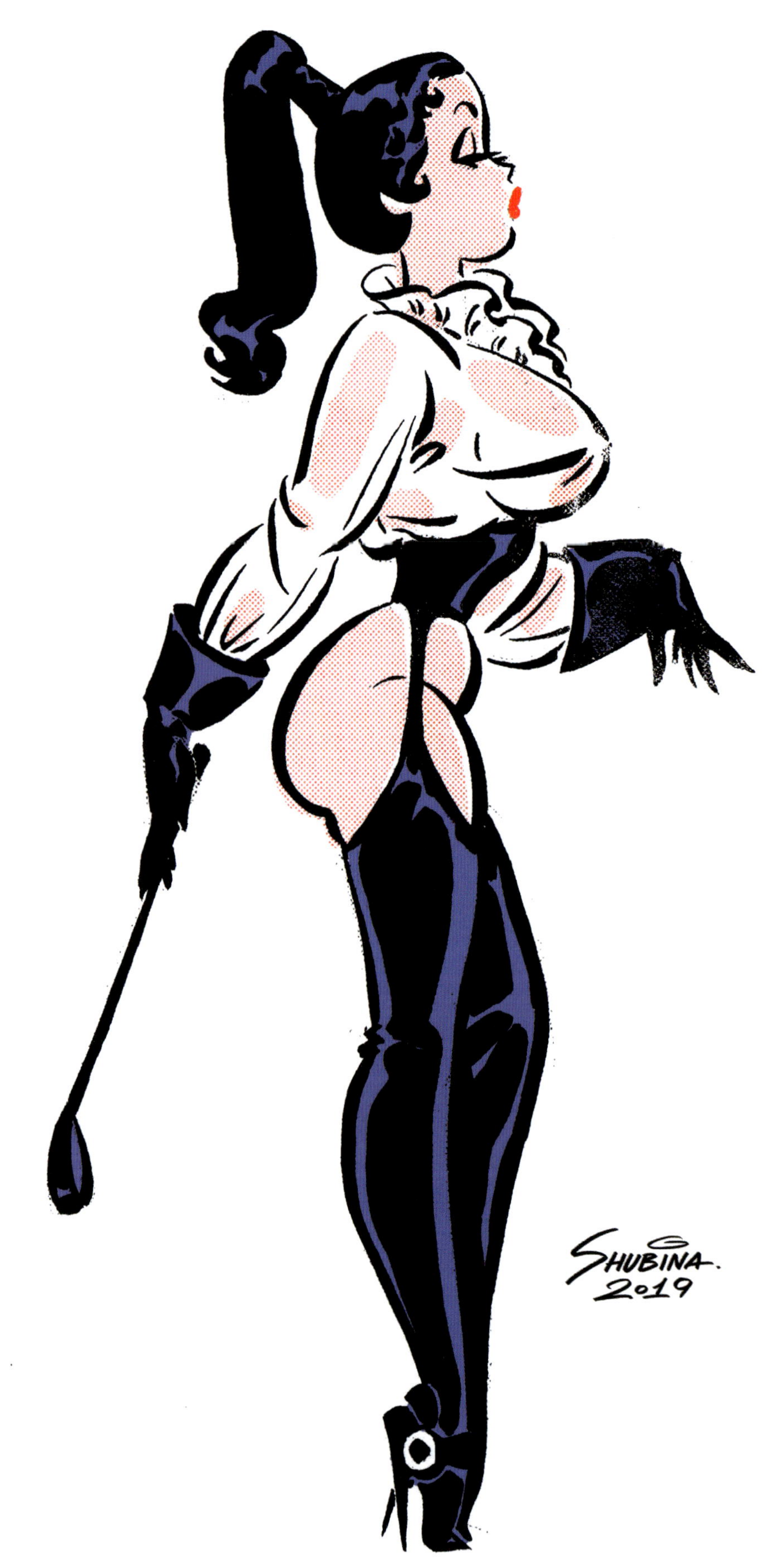
SHUBINA.
2019

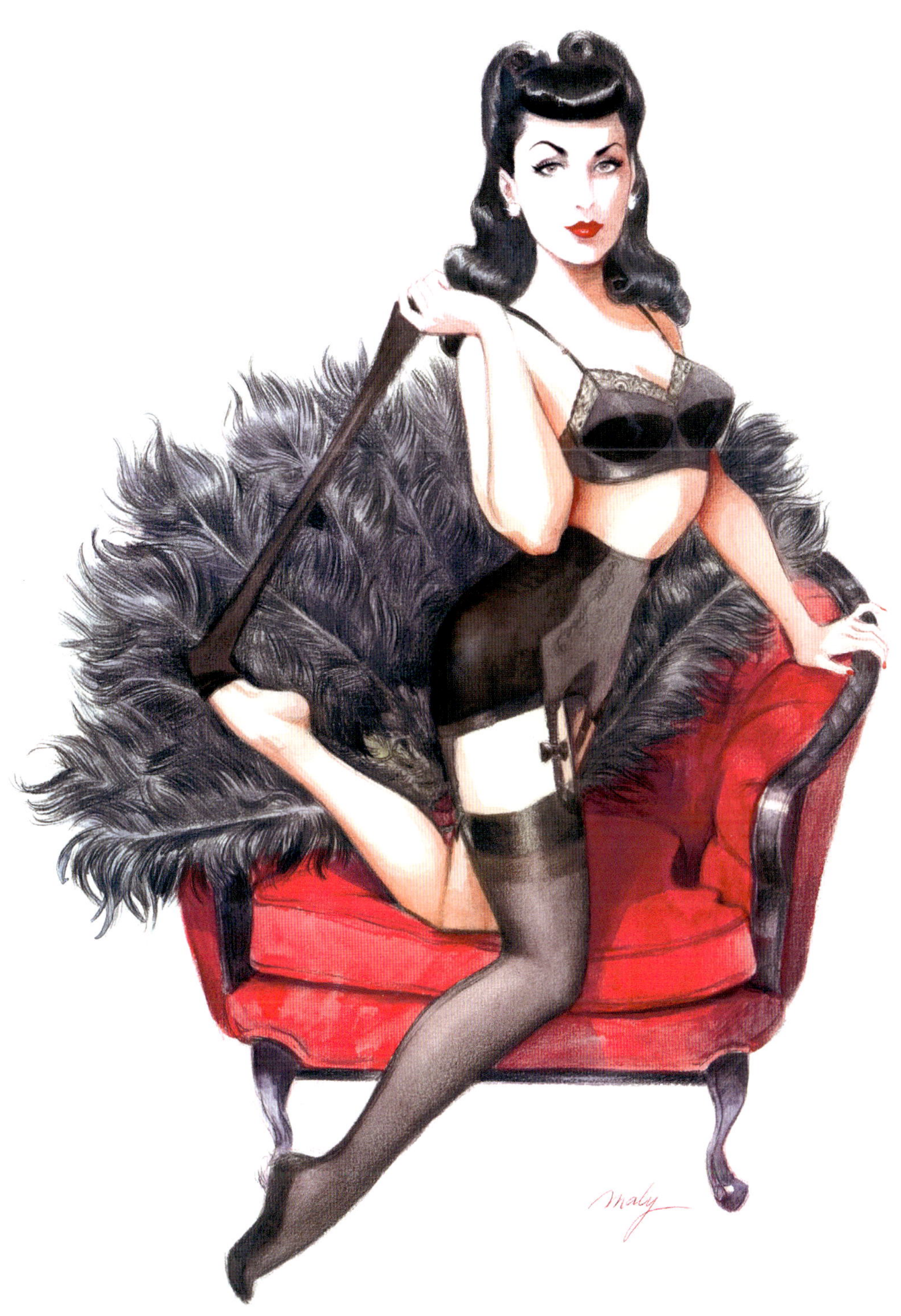

LEFT: ***Domin***
Sveta Shubina

ABOVE: ***Minsky Stockings***
Maly Siri

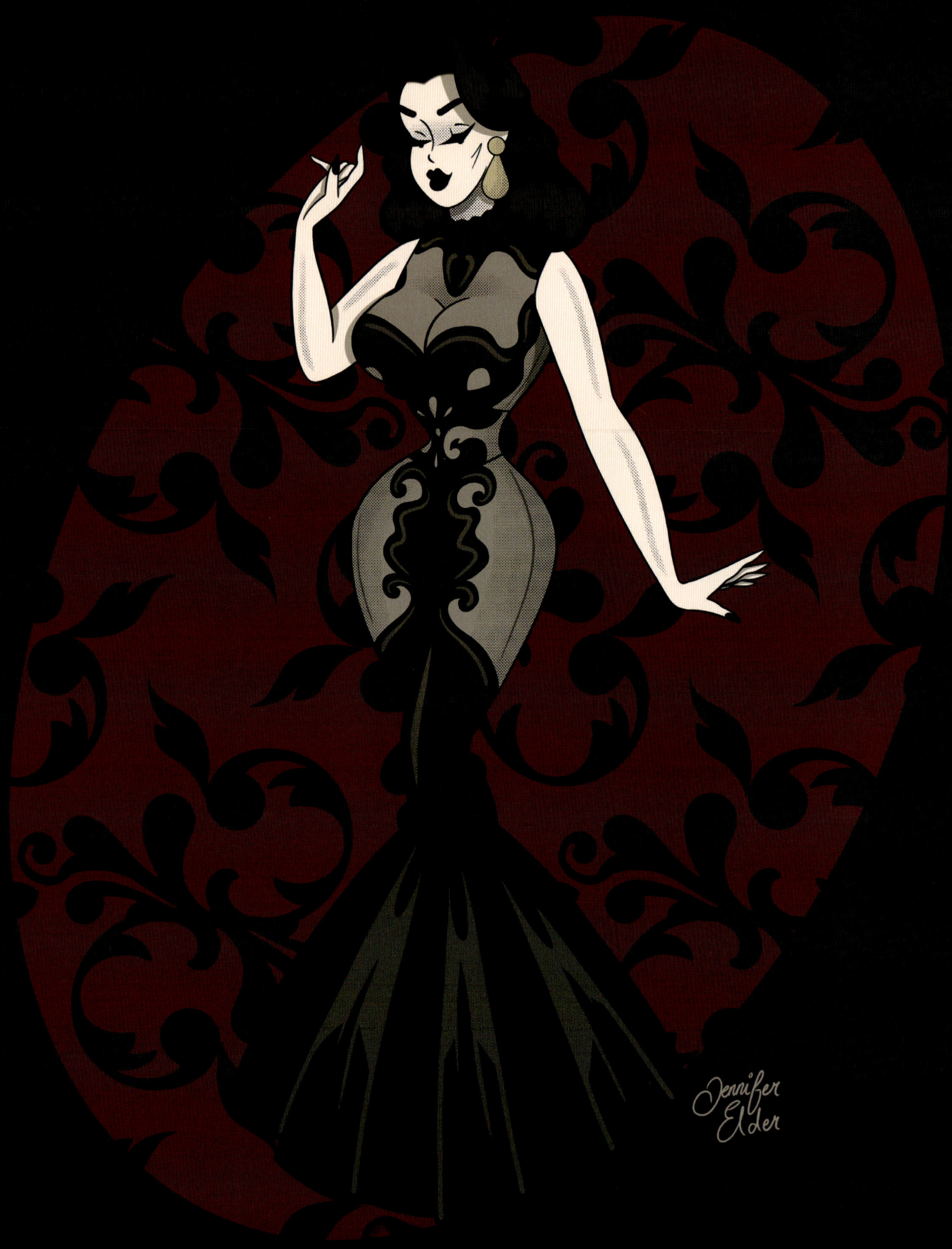
Jennifer Elder

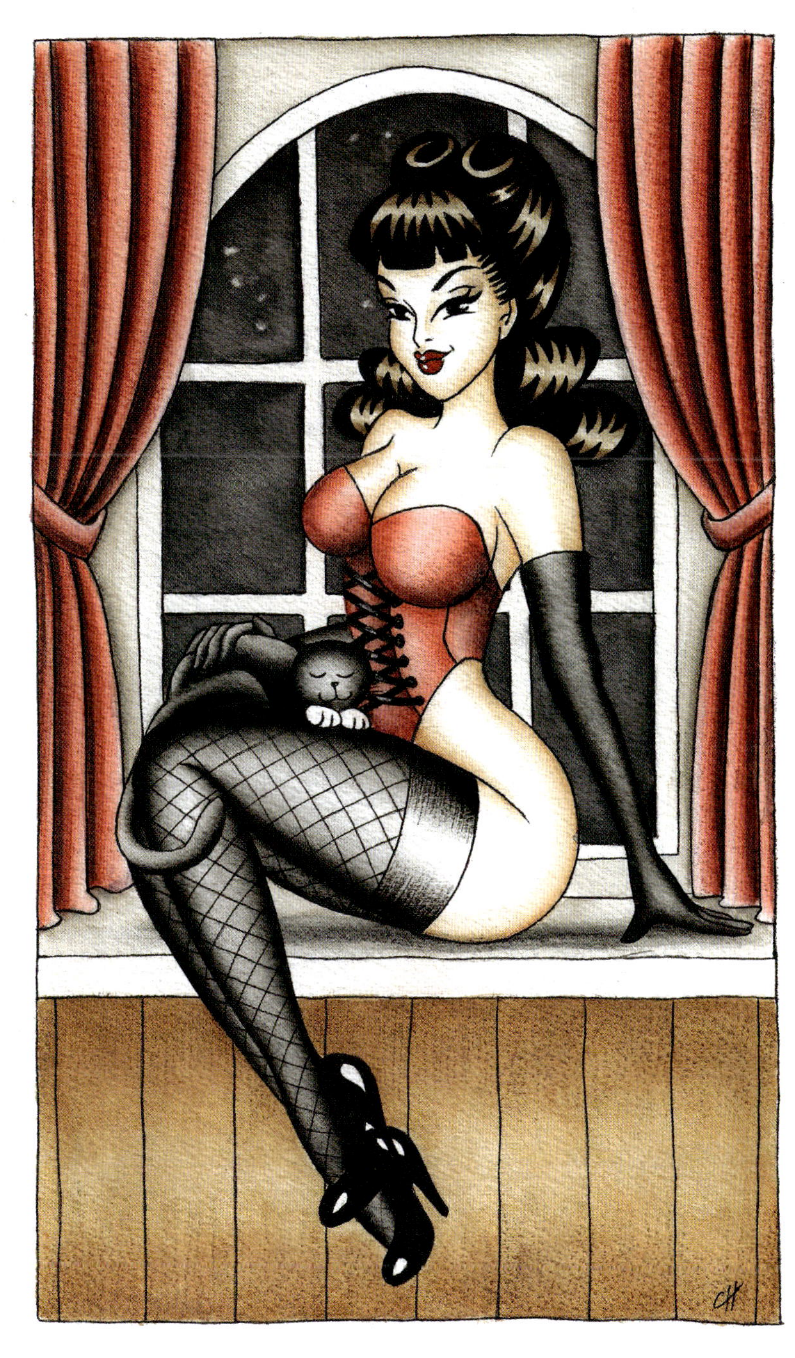

LEFT: ***Arielle Firecracker***
Jennifer Elder

ABOVE: ***Maggy***
Claudia Hek

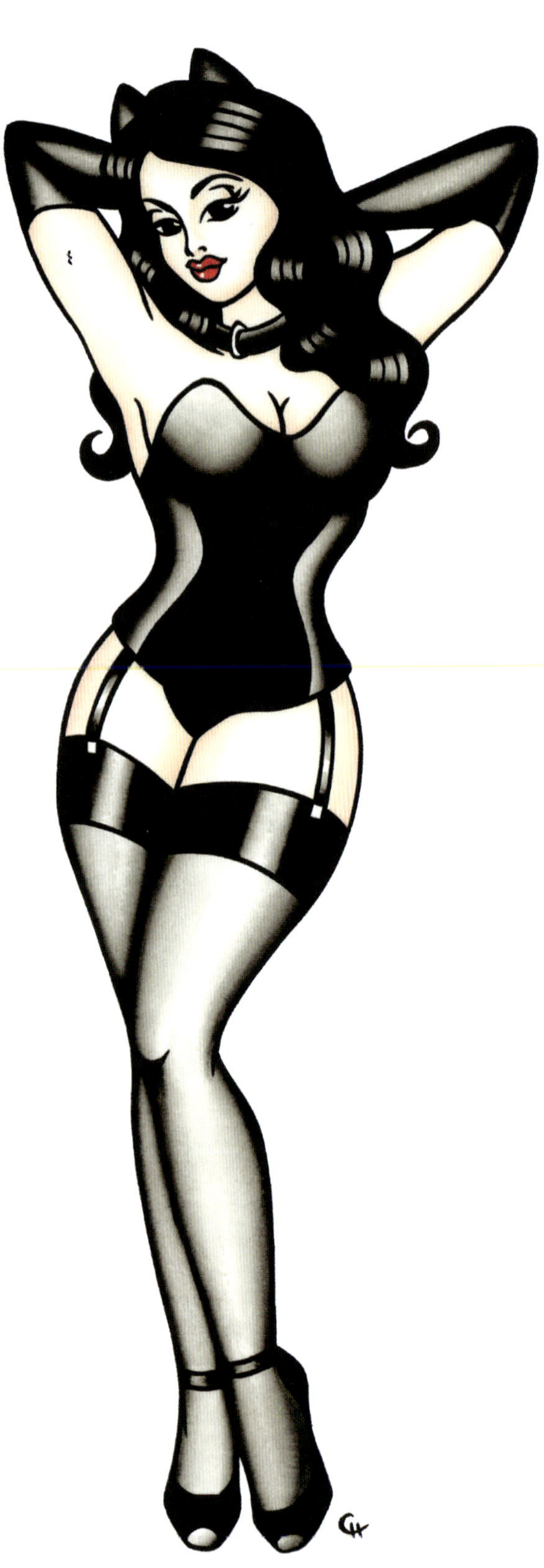

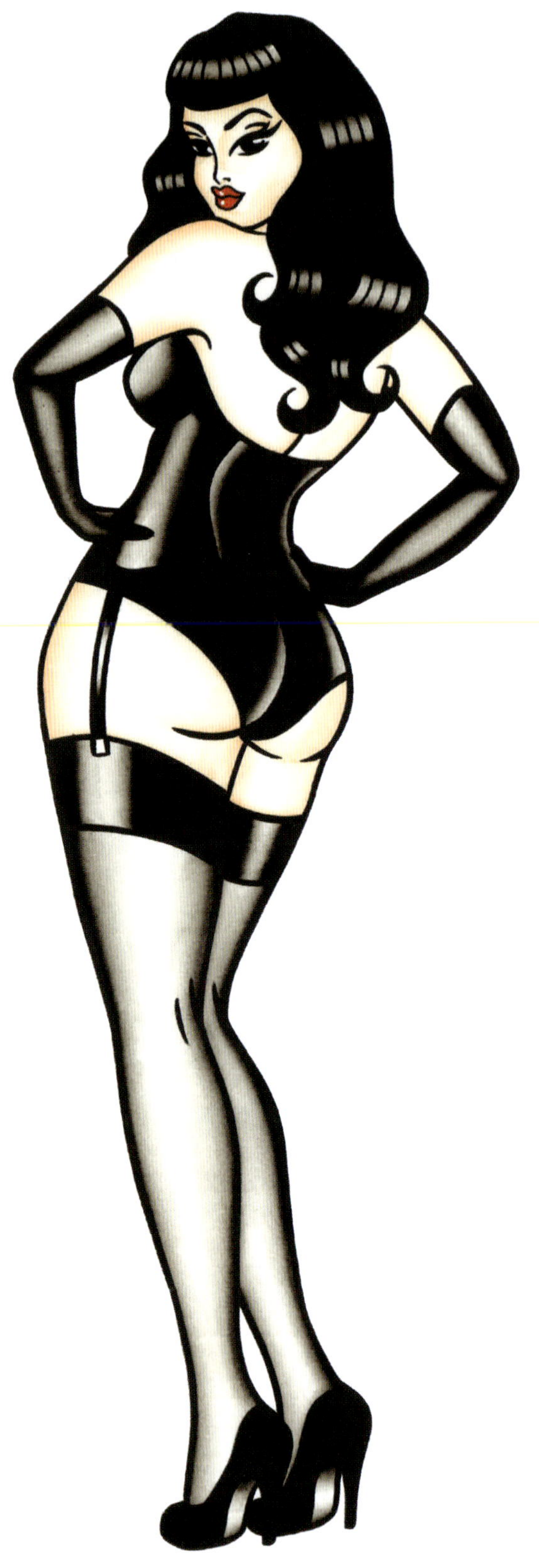

ABOVE LEFT: ***Kitty***
Claudia Hek

ABOVE RIGHT: ***Dorah***
Claudia Hek

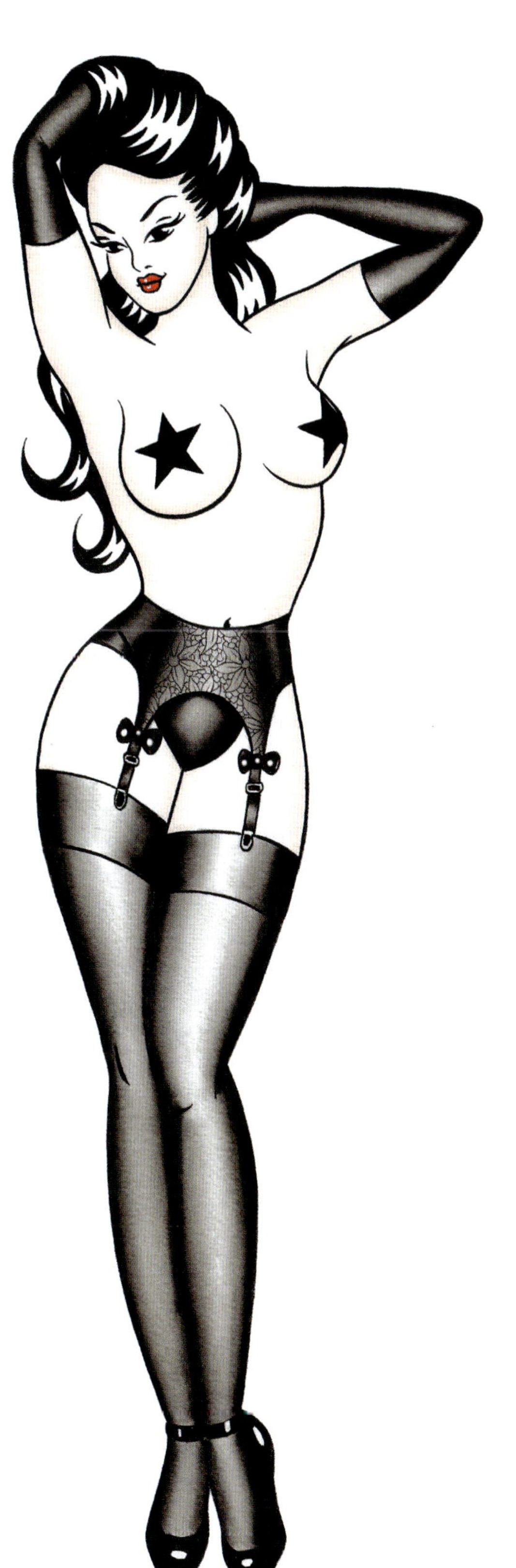

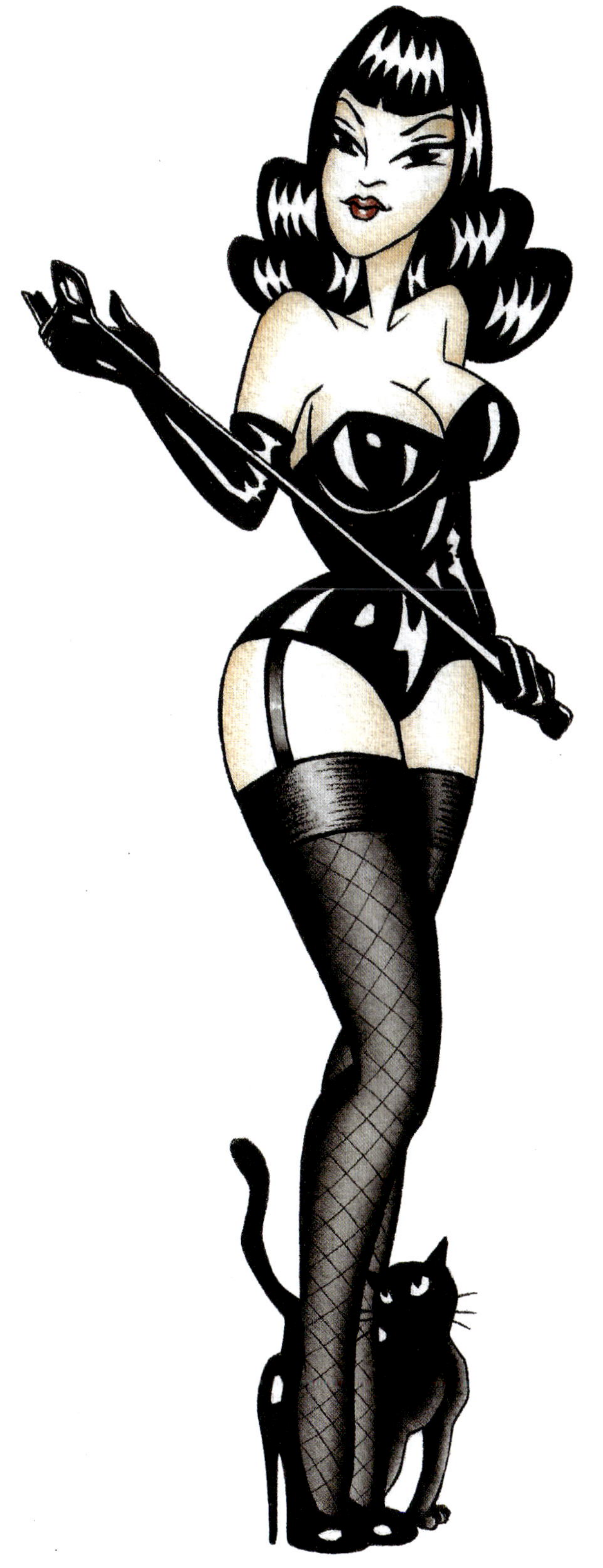

ABOVE LEFT: ***Donna***
Claudia Hek

ABOVE RIGHT: ***Marisa***
Claudia Hek

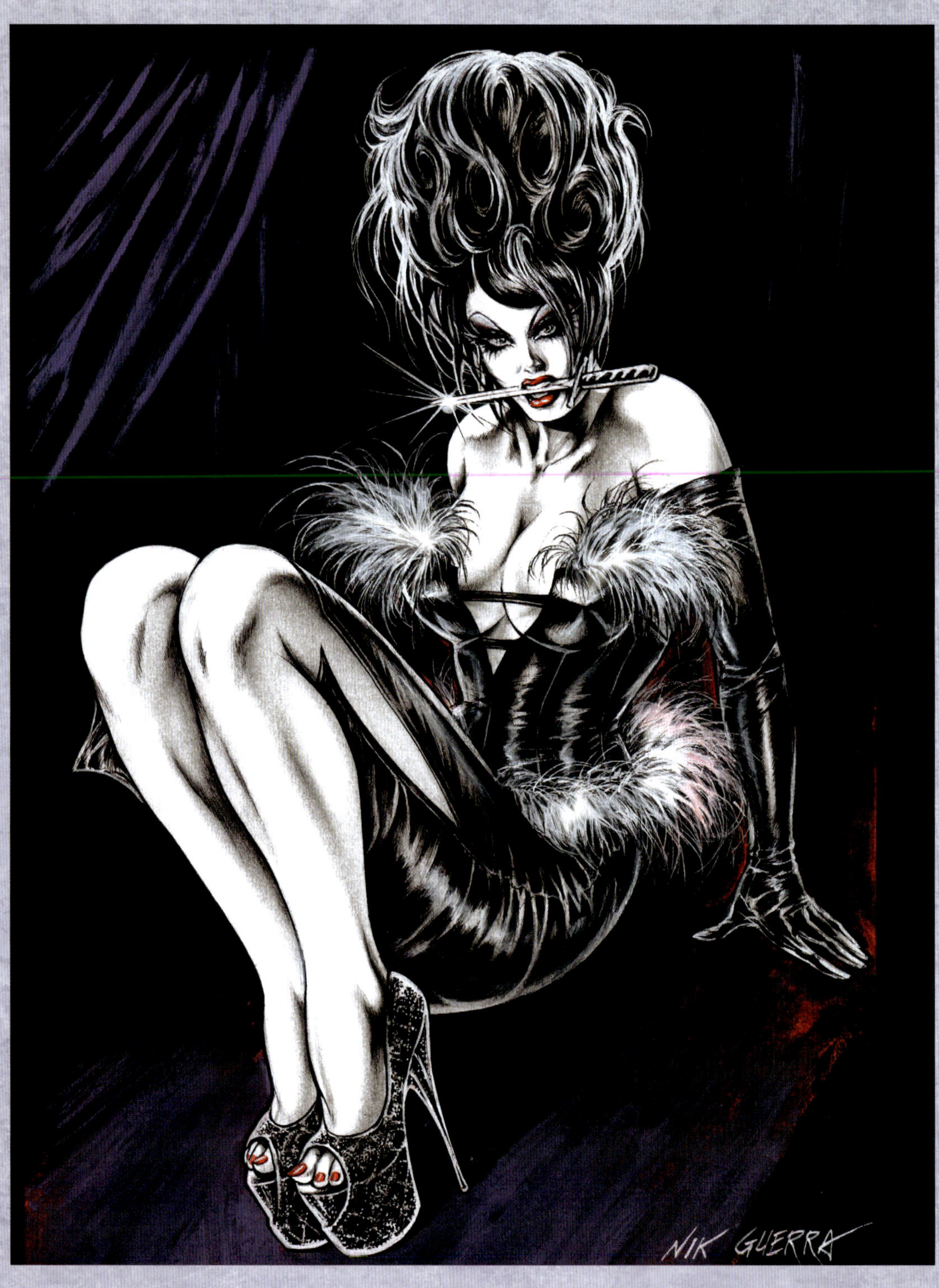

ABOVE: ***Magenta—In Tiro***
Nik Guerra

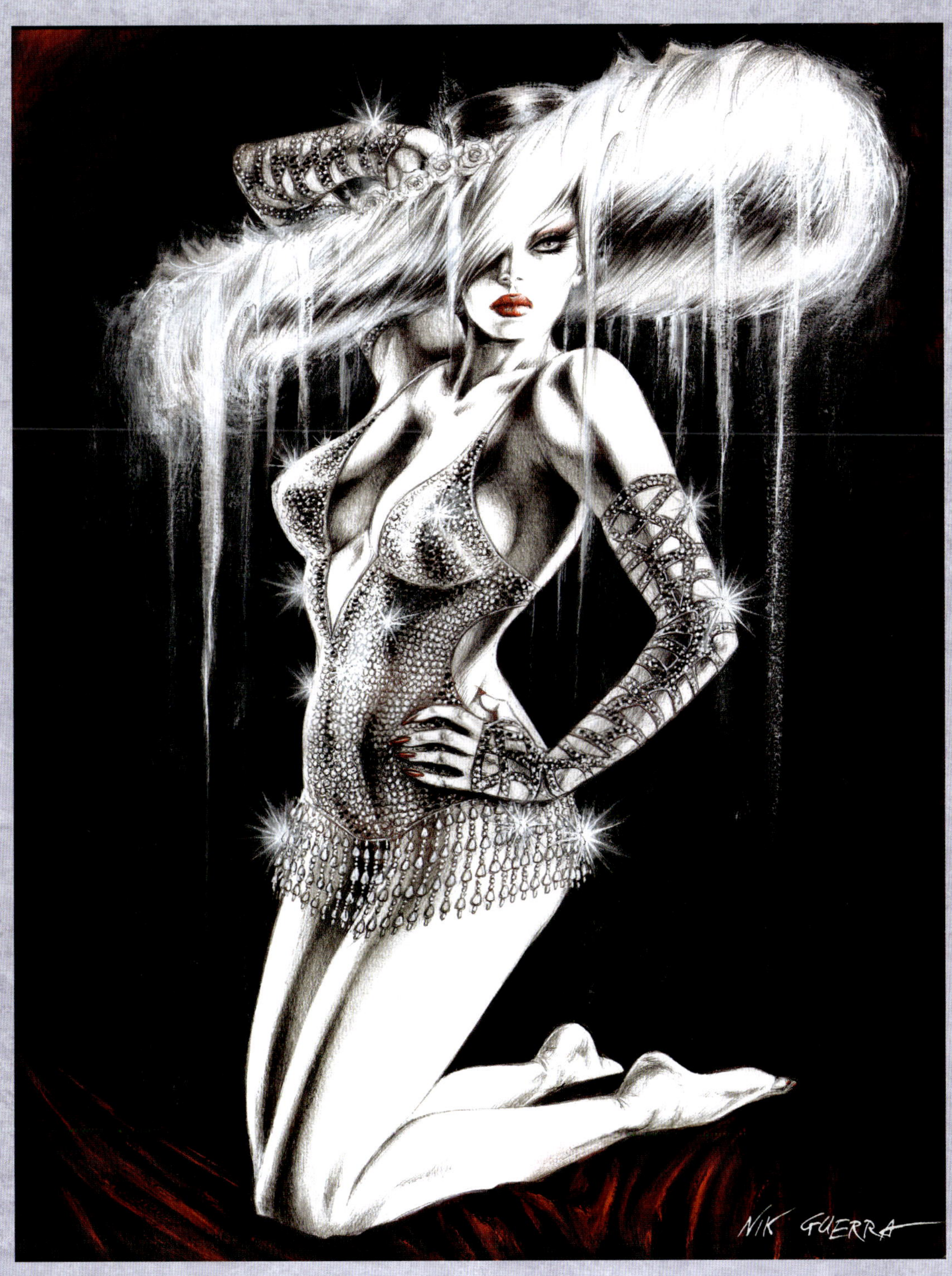

ABOVE: ***Coco–Night Sparkle***
Nik Guerra

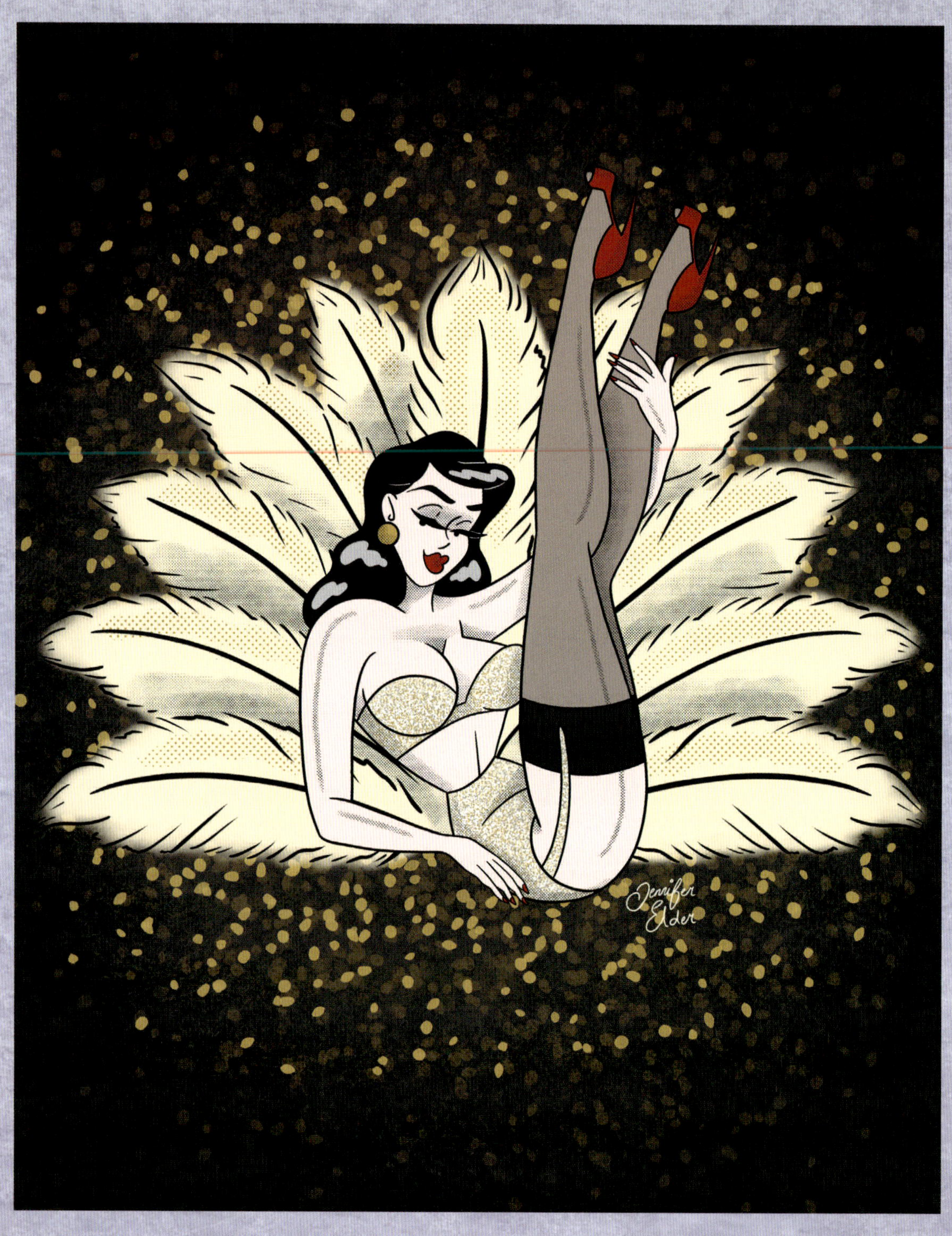

ABOVE: ***Fan Girl***
Jennifer Elder

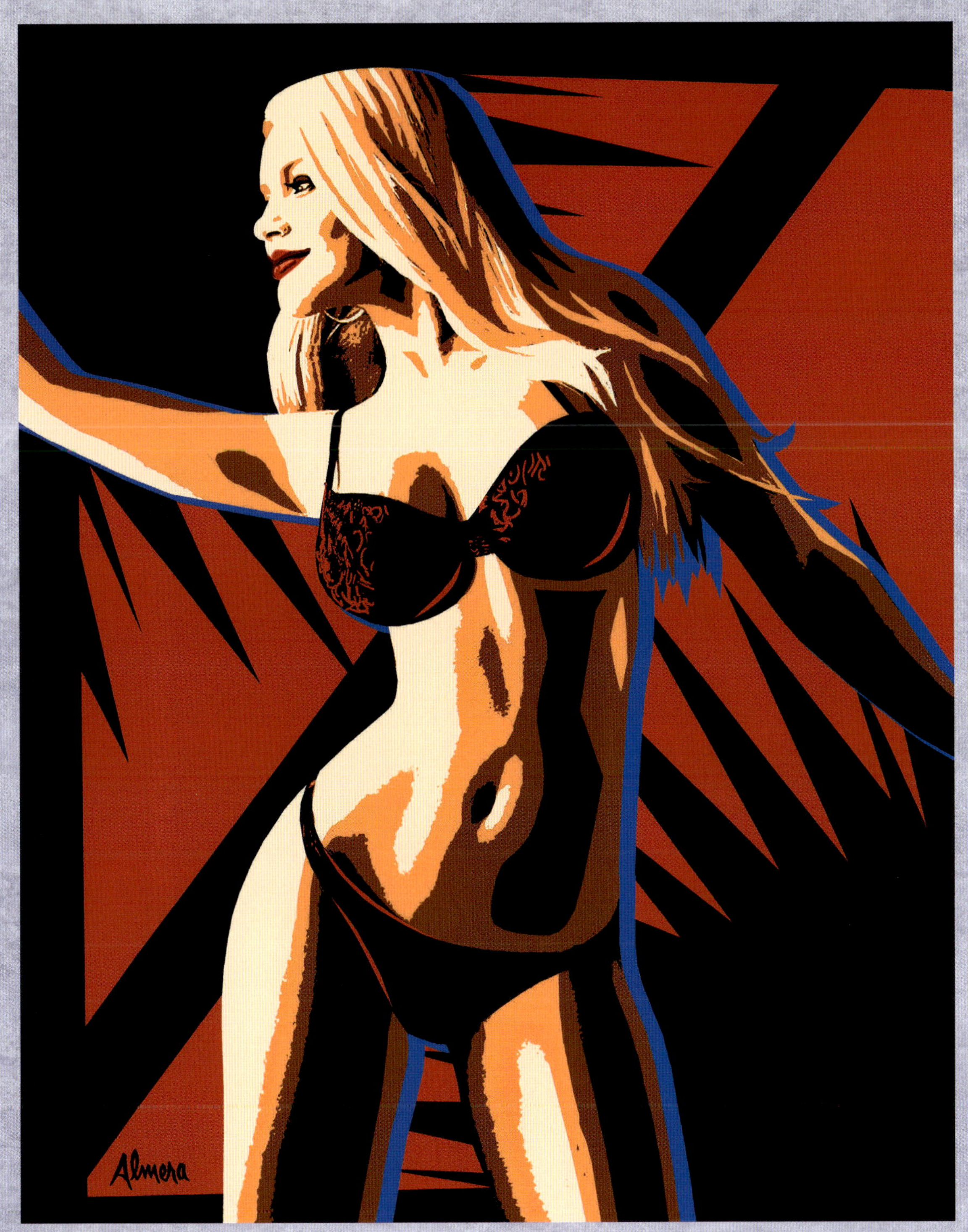

ABOVE: ***Shine***
Marco Almera

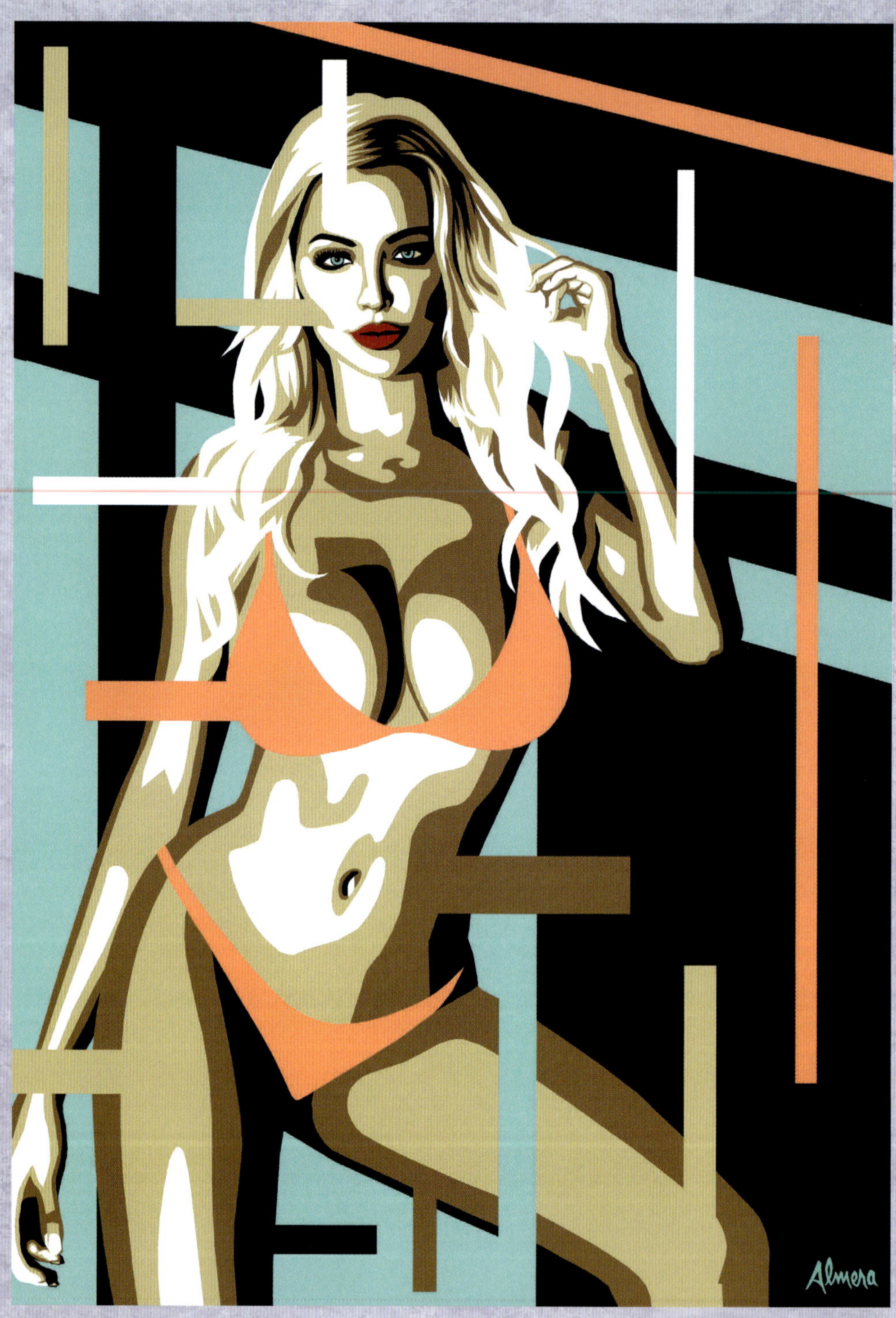

ABOVE: ***Fierce***
Marco Almera

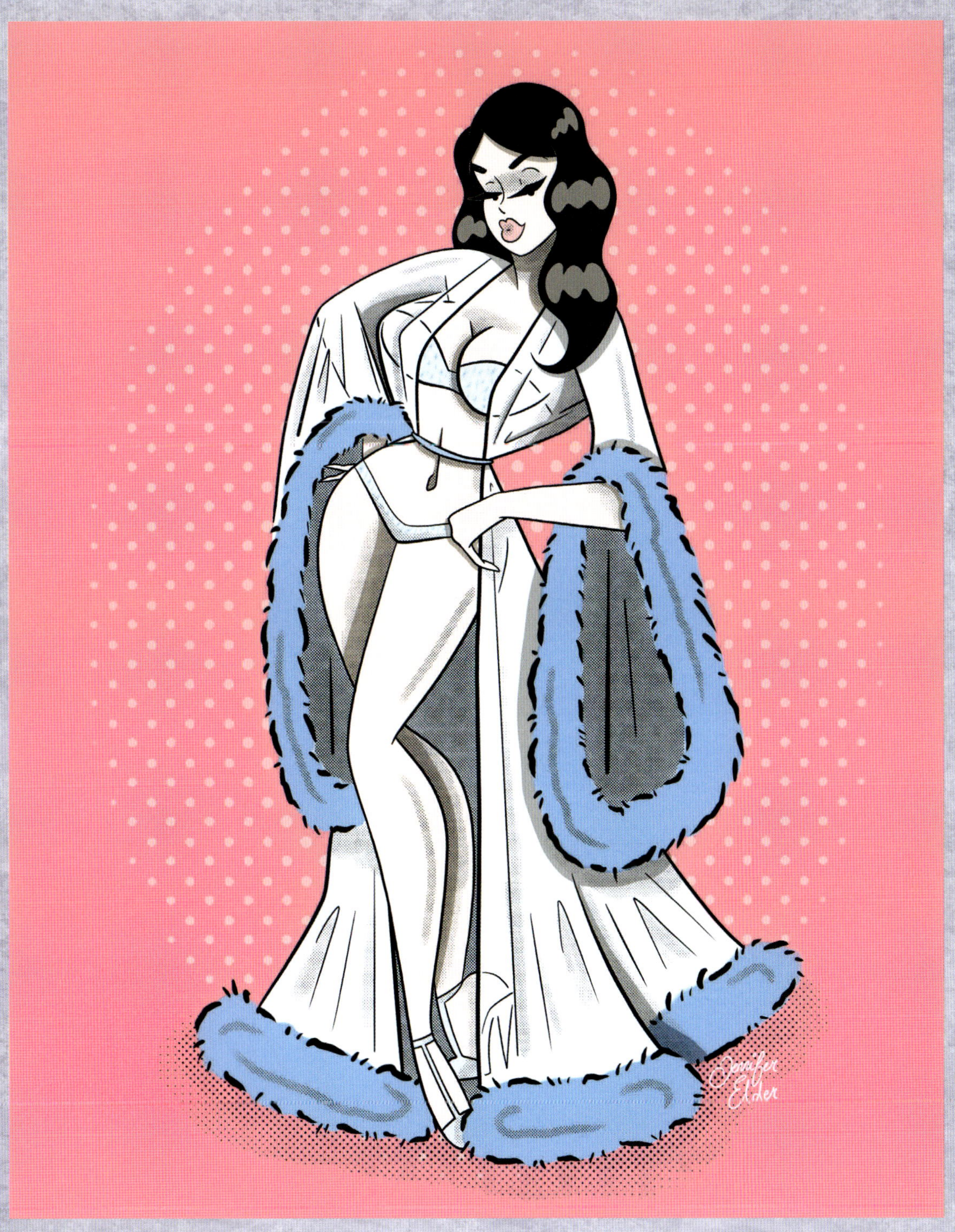

ABOVE: ***Kim Khaos***
Jennifer Elder

OVERLEAF: ***Floor Exercise***
Ben Tan

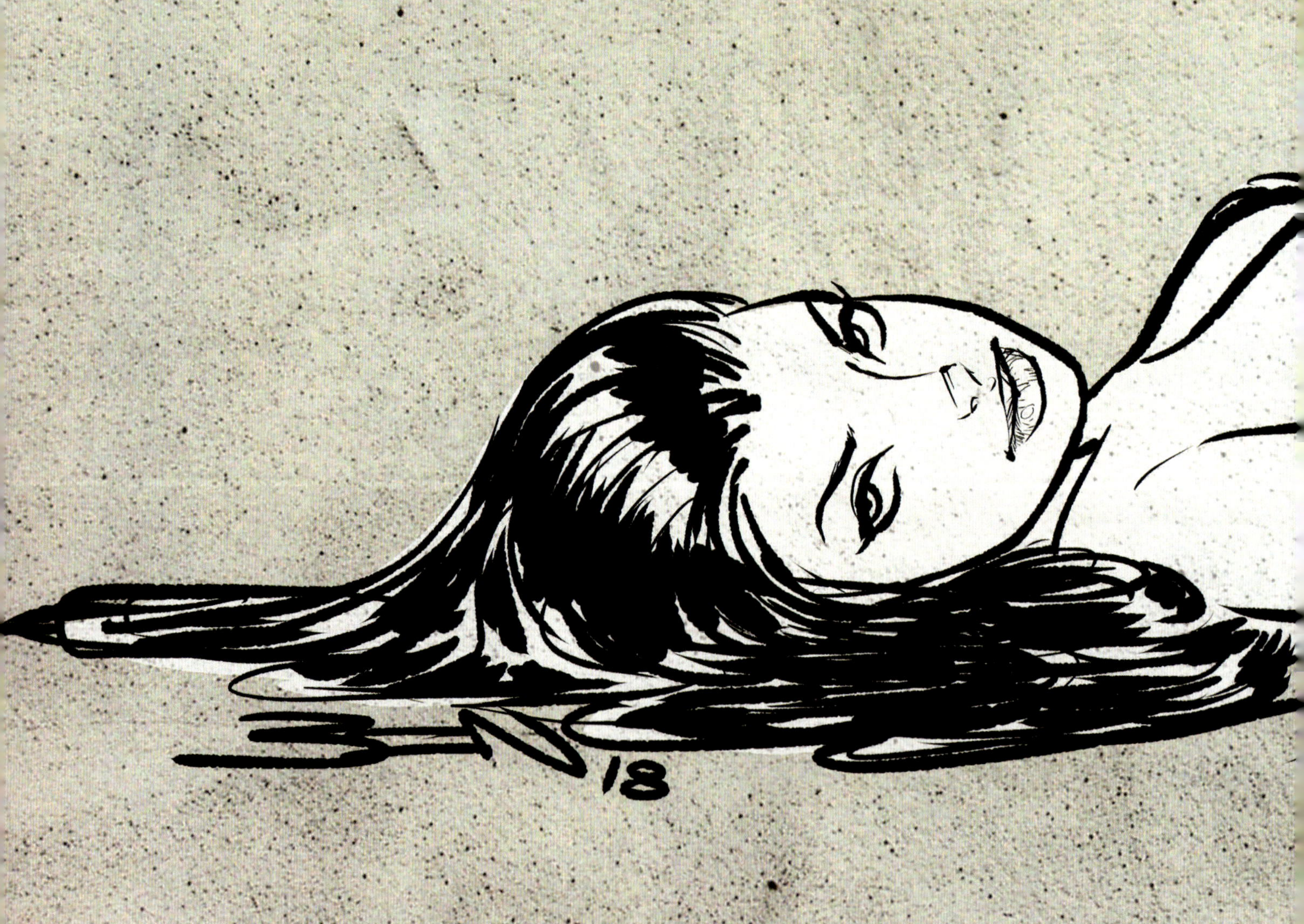

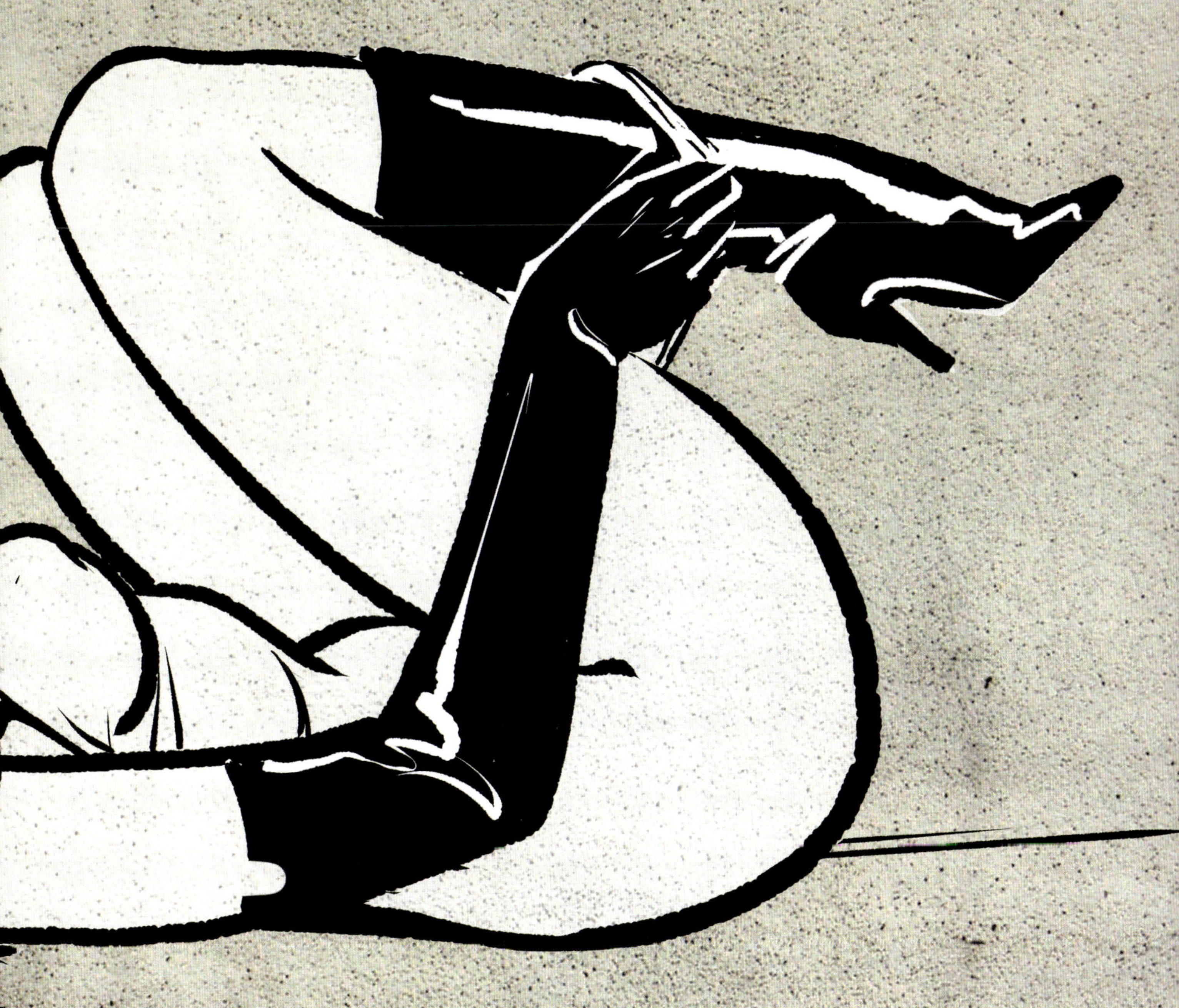

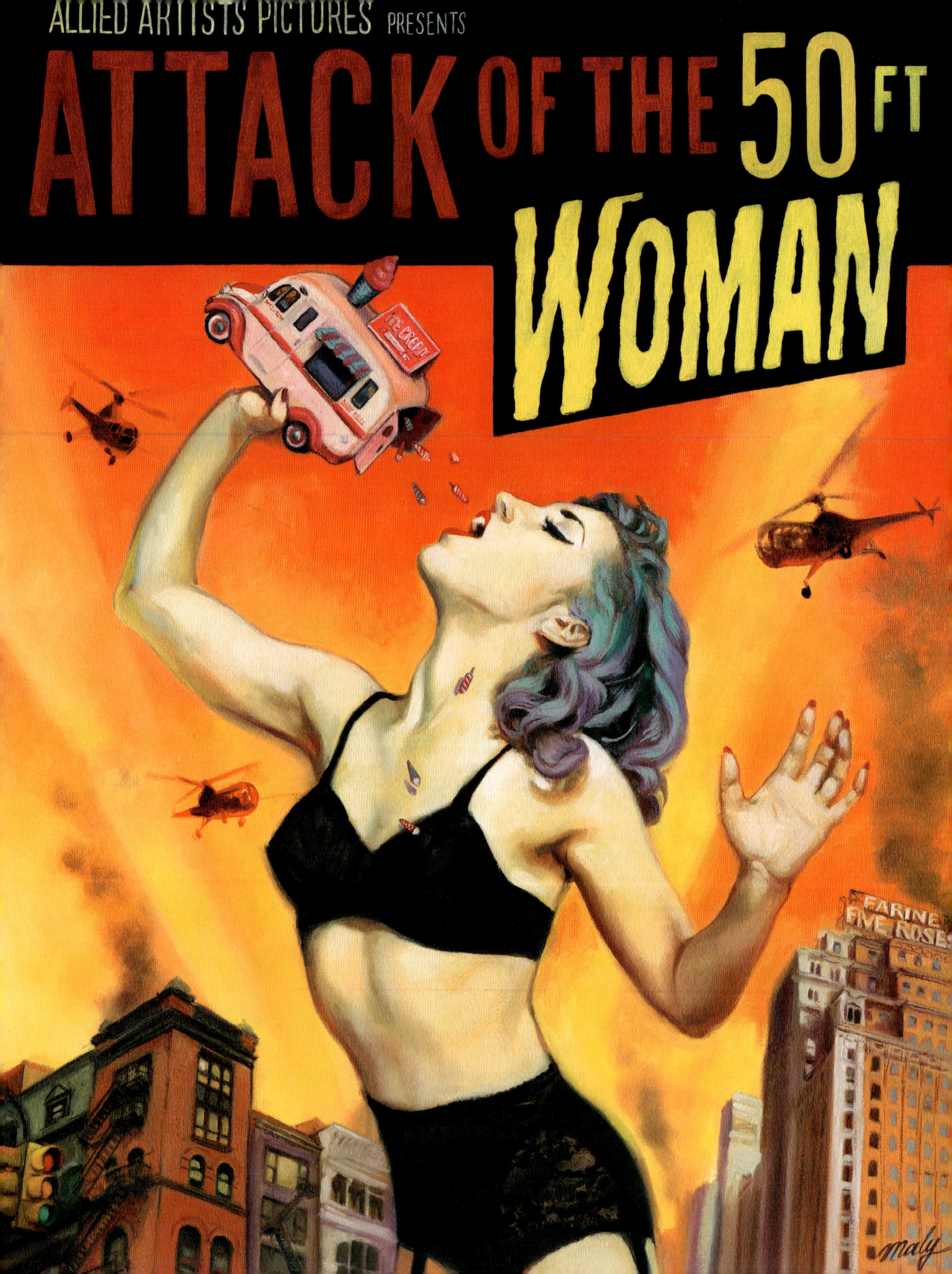
ALLIED ARTISTS PICTURES PRESENTS
ATTACK OF THE 50 FT WOMAN
ICE CREAM
FARINE
FIVE ROSES
maly

Sci-Fi, Fantasy, & Surreal

The sultry noir of pulp fiction, the high fantasy of myth and legend, a buccaneering space opera flirting with the boundaries of the possible and the acceptable; what could possibly be more appropriate for the transgressive realm of the pinup?

Rich lore from fantastic visions of a world drastically different to our own provide a primed canvas to the contemporary pinup artist, mining the wealthy seams of naughtiness inherent to exploring the outer limits of our galaxy or the nooks and crannies of the haunted forest.

The limitless possibilities of the magical, futuristic and surreal suggest the strange and intellectual pleasures of imagination while, pleasingly, we are reminded of the warm physical realities of sensuality and form in the shapes of these familiar feminine figures. Spaceships may whizz by overhead, a horde of orcish foes may gather, and clocks may melt into the floor, but the eternally female shape remains as provocative and mysterious as ever.

These visions play off our shared tropes of the future and our well-worn visions of the past, reminding us of outdated visions of times gone by and toying with that collective understanding. Reforming pop culture creations into transgressive outliers walks a delicate line between confrontation and supplication—ideal for the pinup. Whether battling her robot captor (no supine damsel in distress here) or cleaning the dwarves' Lilliputian proportioned dwelling, oblivious to their admiring looks, these are confident, sensual figures aware of their own power. A laser pistol propped on the swell of a hip, or a bloody spear thrust aloft, are as much a part of the fantasy as any form fitting, latex, super suit or cavewoman's loin-cloth.

Celebrating the visions of a hopeful future and a romantic past is important to our pinups but even more so is the triumph of the mysterious, evocative, and ageless feminine mystique: the essential ingredient to make a strange and alien universe just that little bit more inviting.

LEFT: ***Attack of the 50ft Woman***
Maly Siri

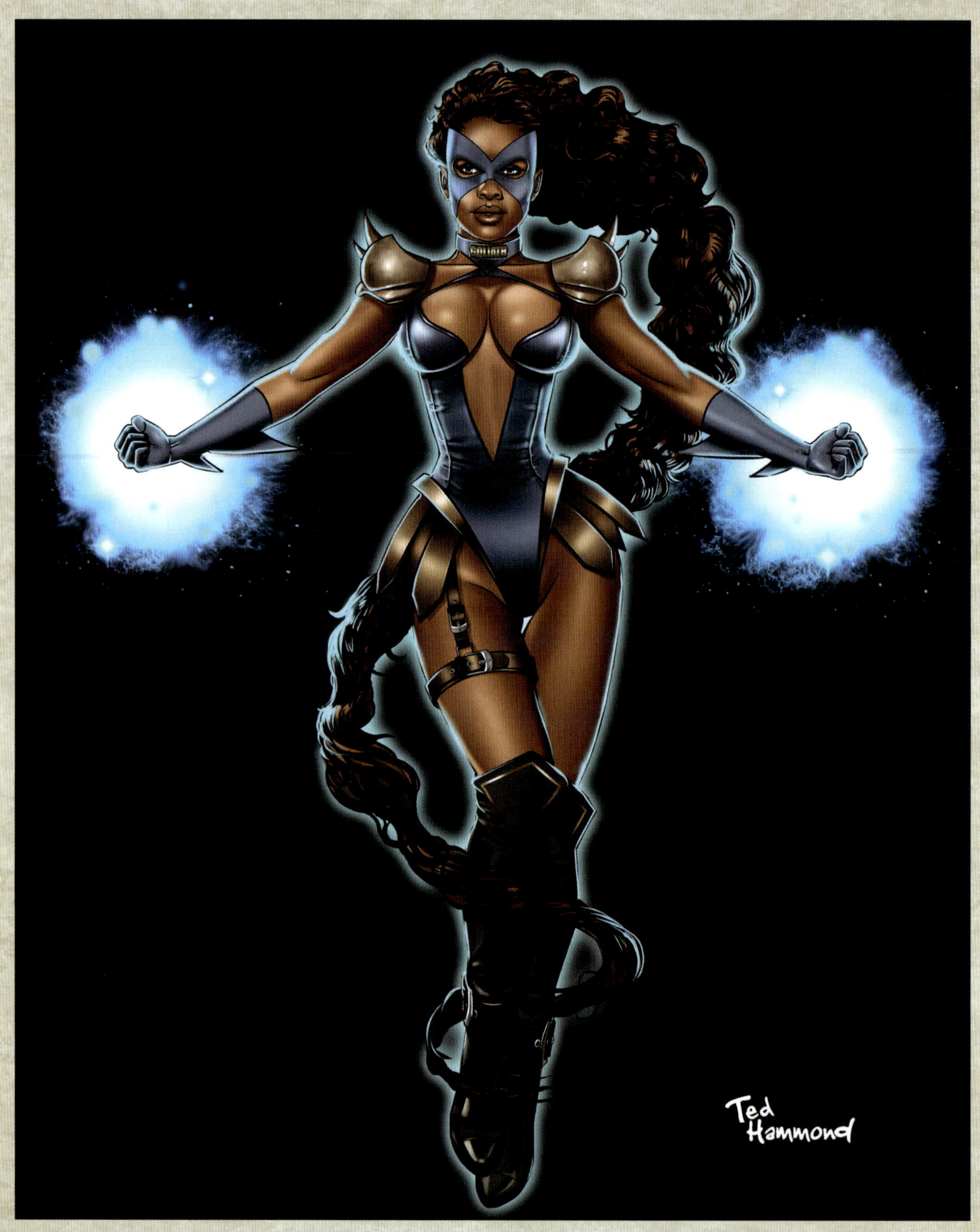

ABOVE: ***Goliath***
Ted Hammond

RIGHT: ***Armorous Orbit***
Fiona Stephenson

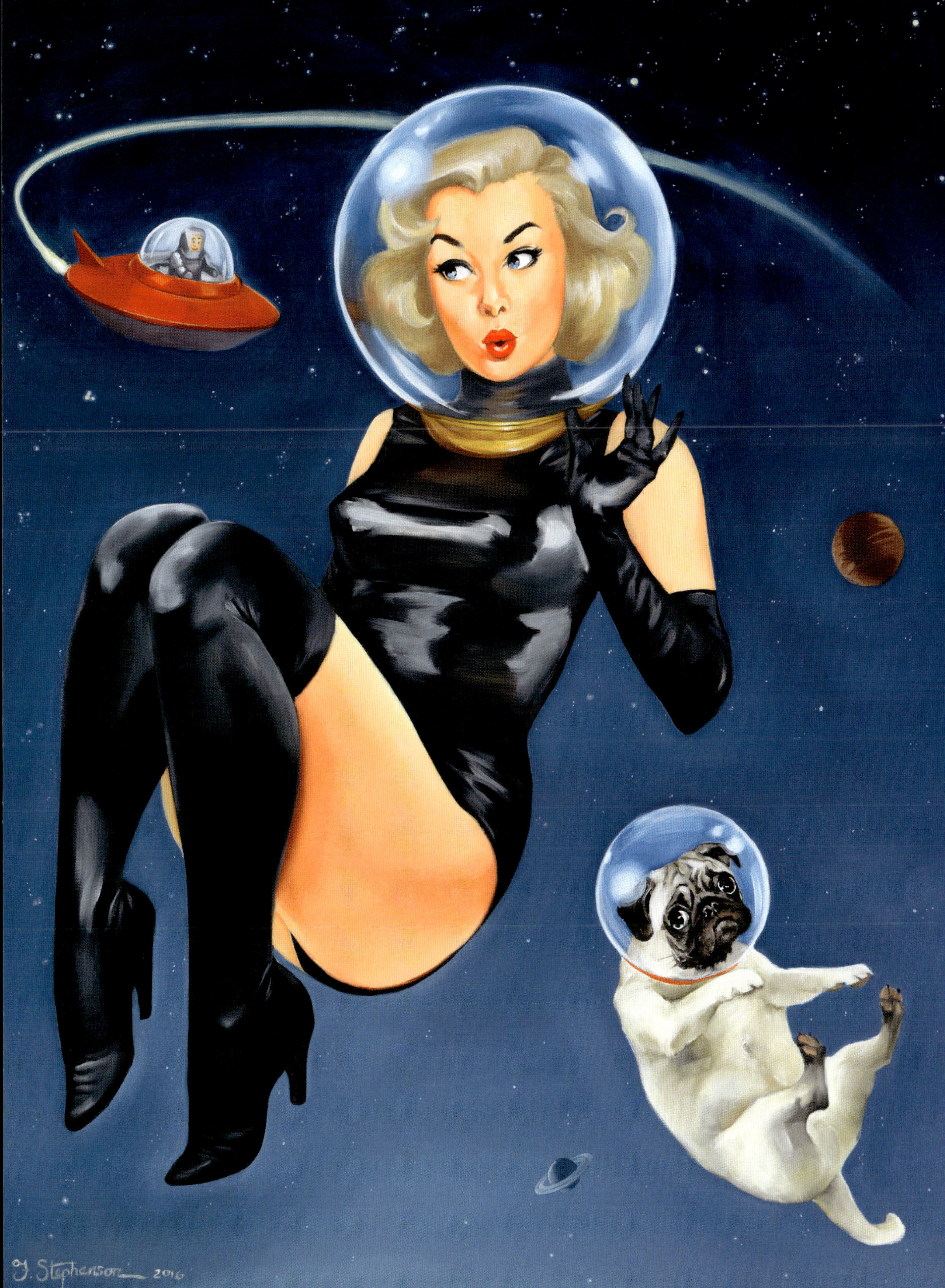
J. Stephenson 2016

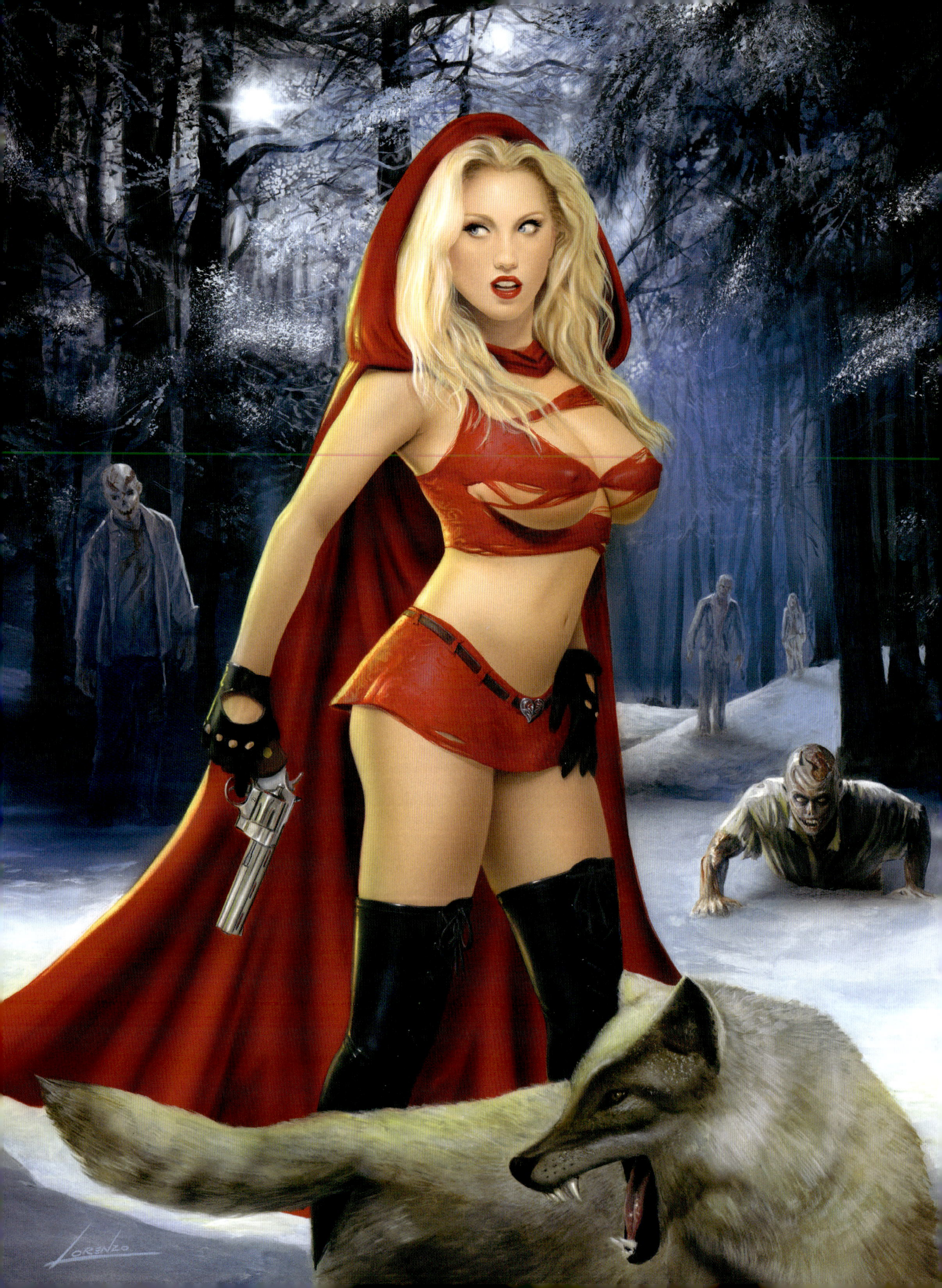
LORENZO

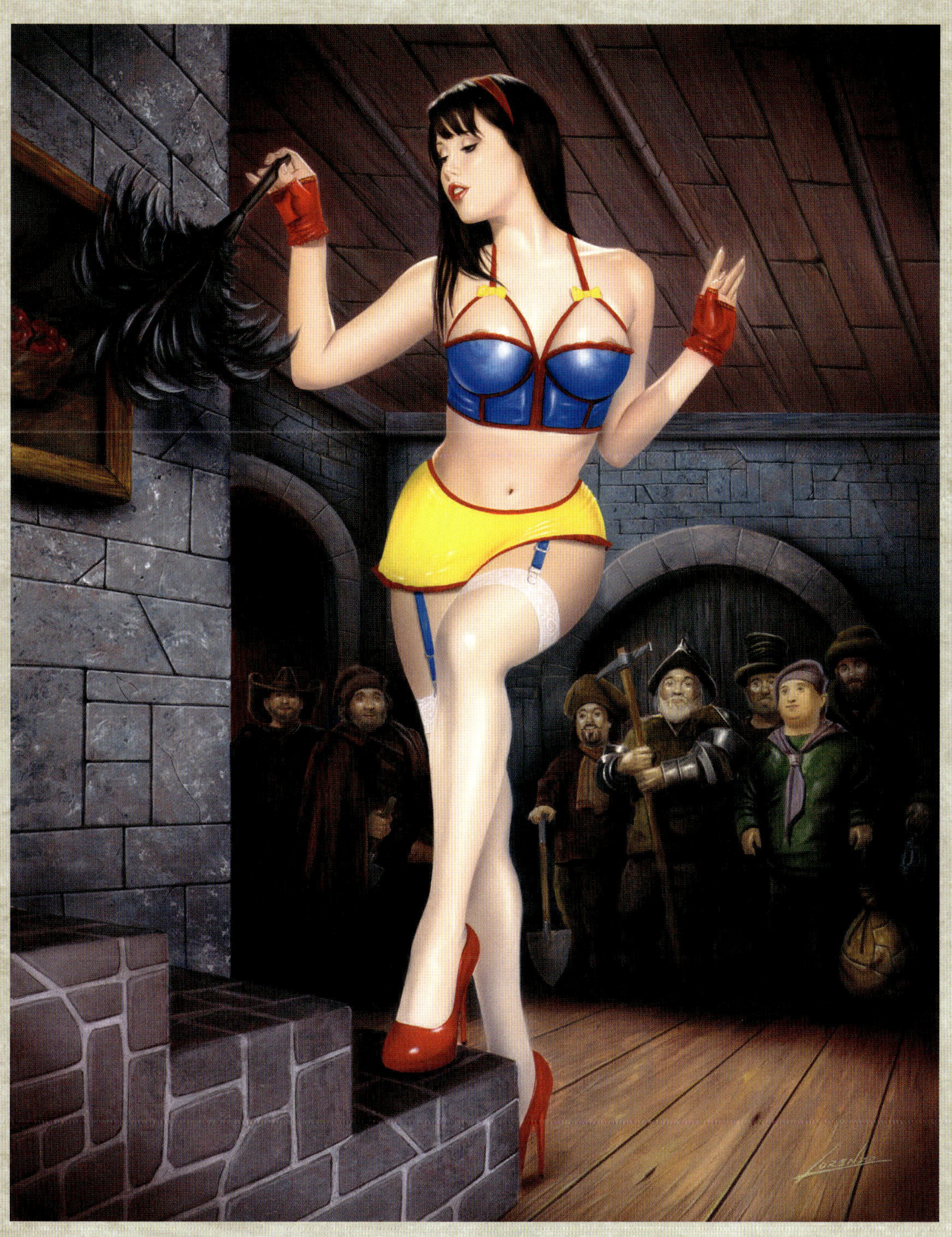

LEFT: ***Red in the Woods***
Lorenzo Sperlonga

ABOVE: ***Snow White***
Lorenzo Sperlonga

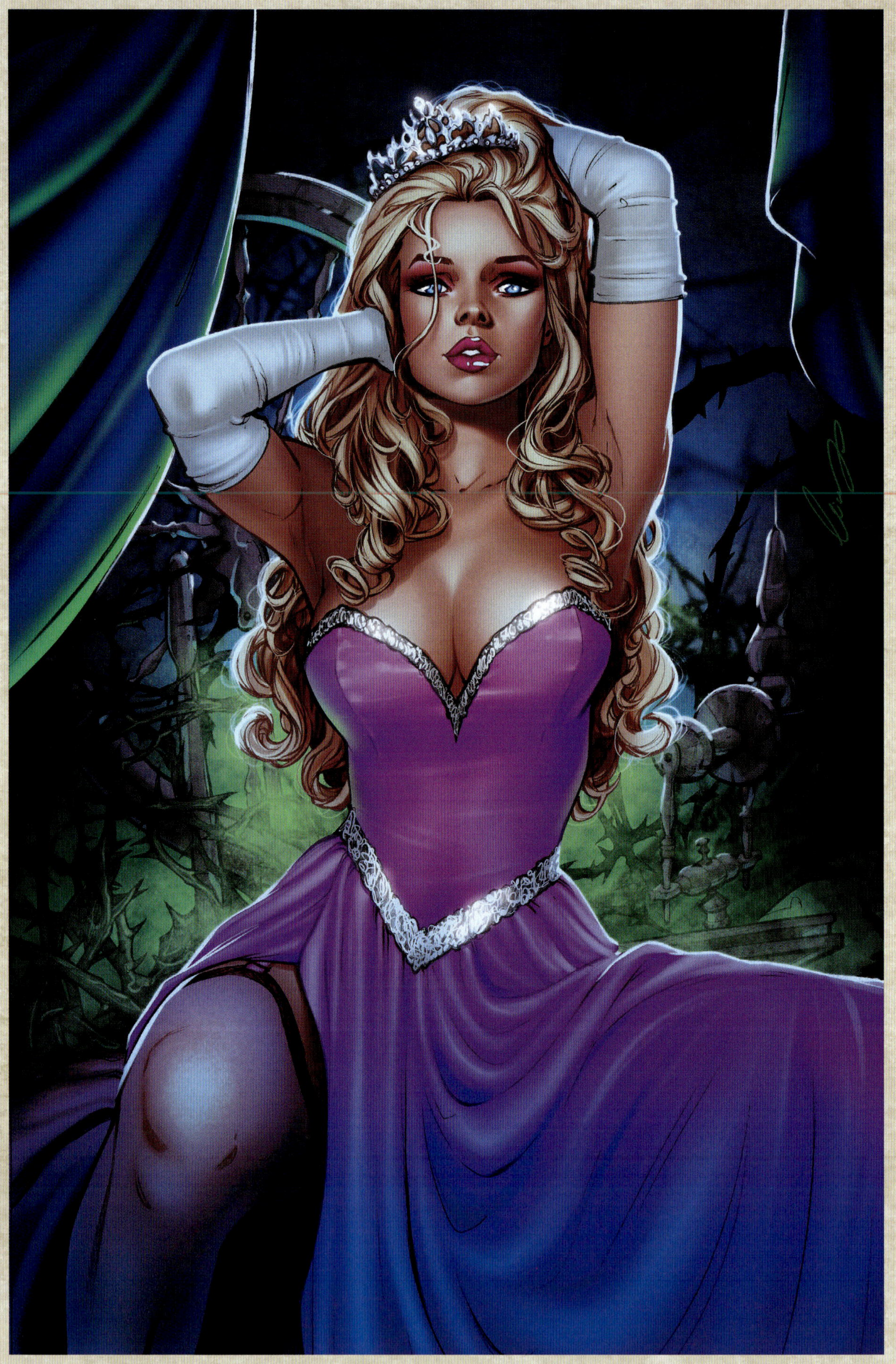

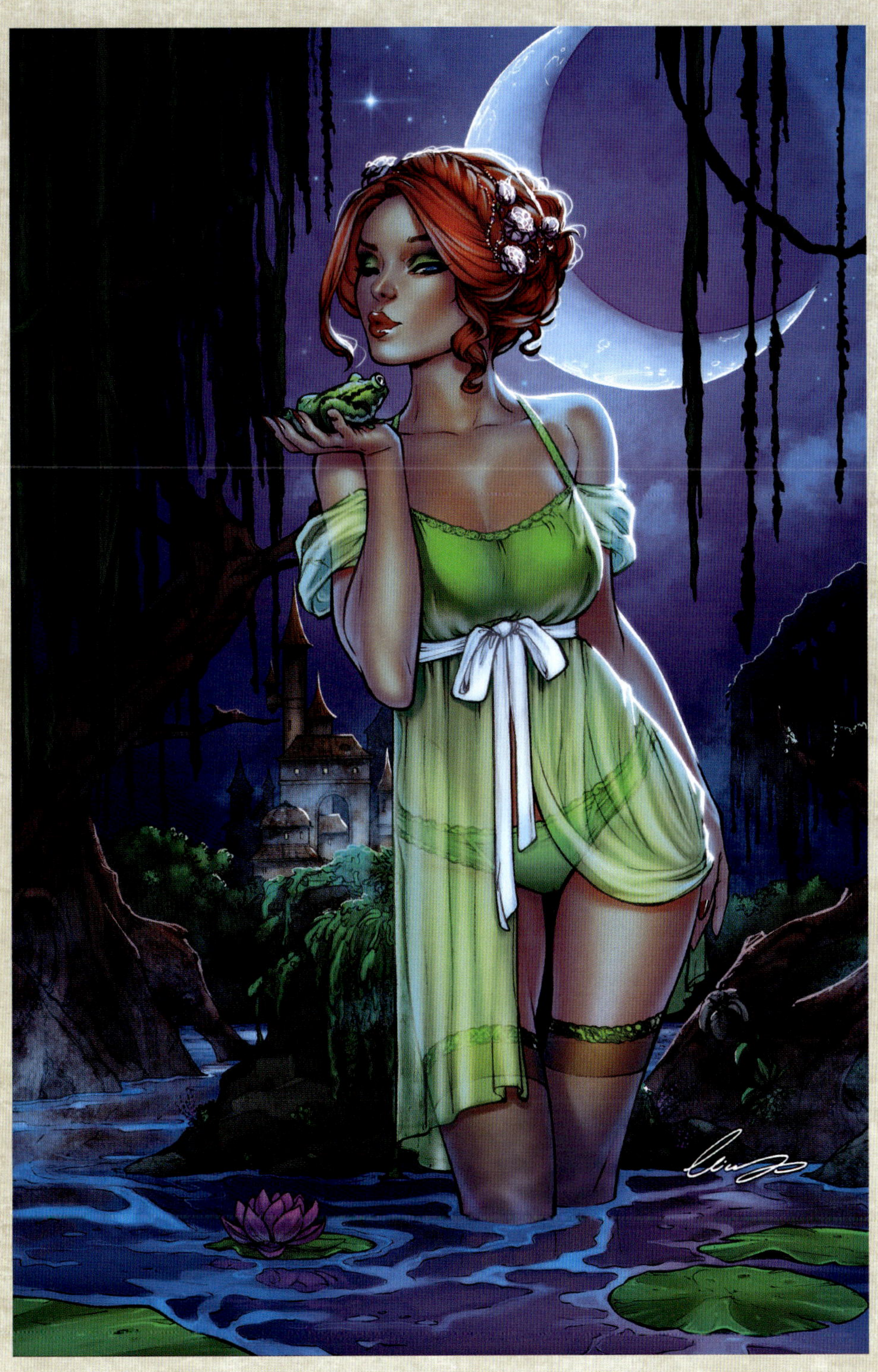

LEFT: *Aurora*
Elias Chatzoudis

ABOVE: *Princess & the Frog*
Elias Chatzoudis

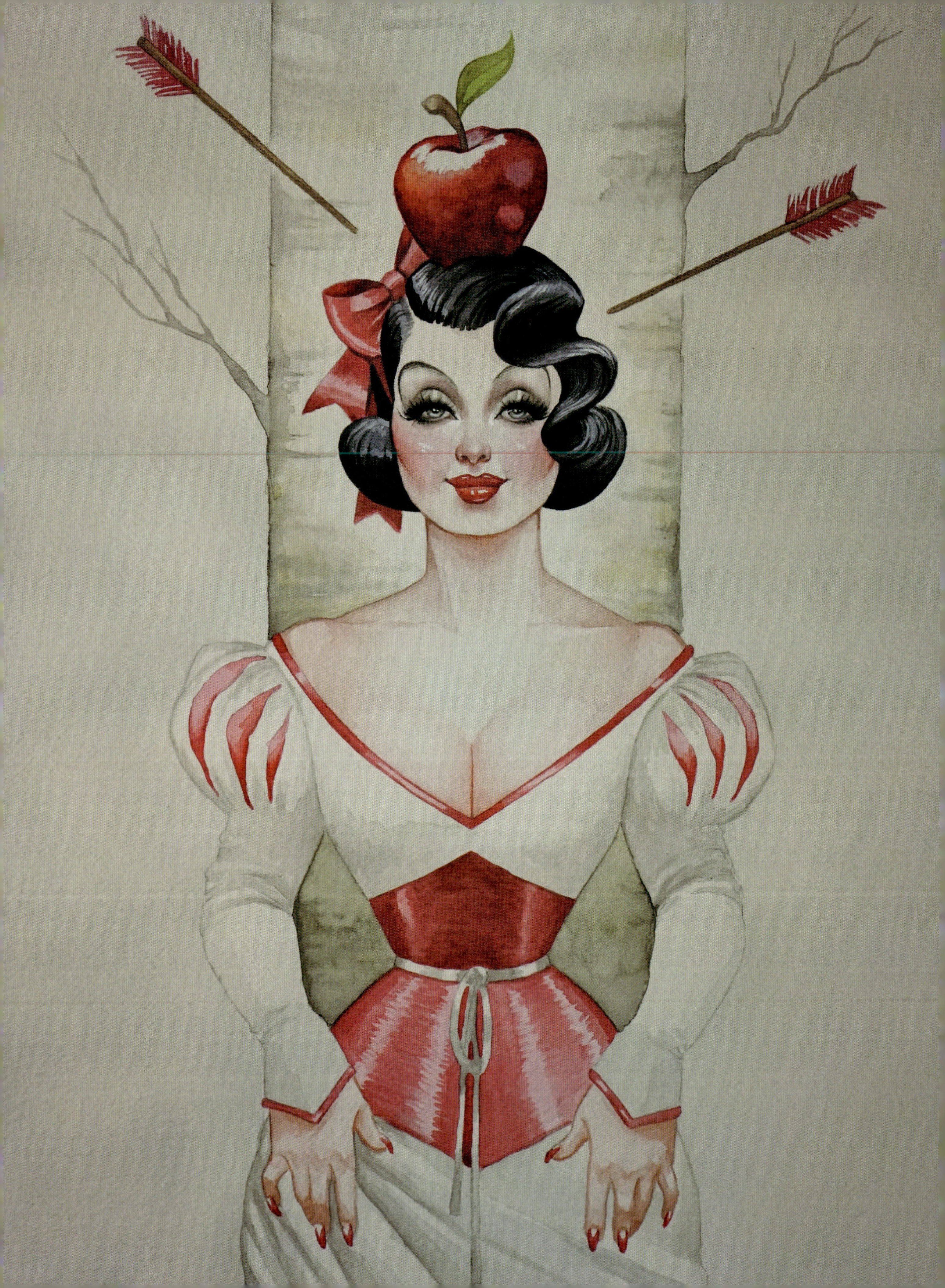

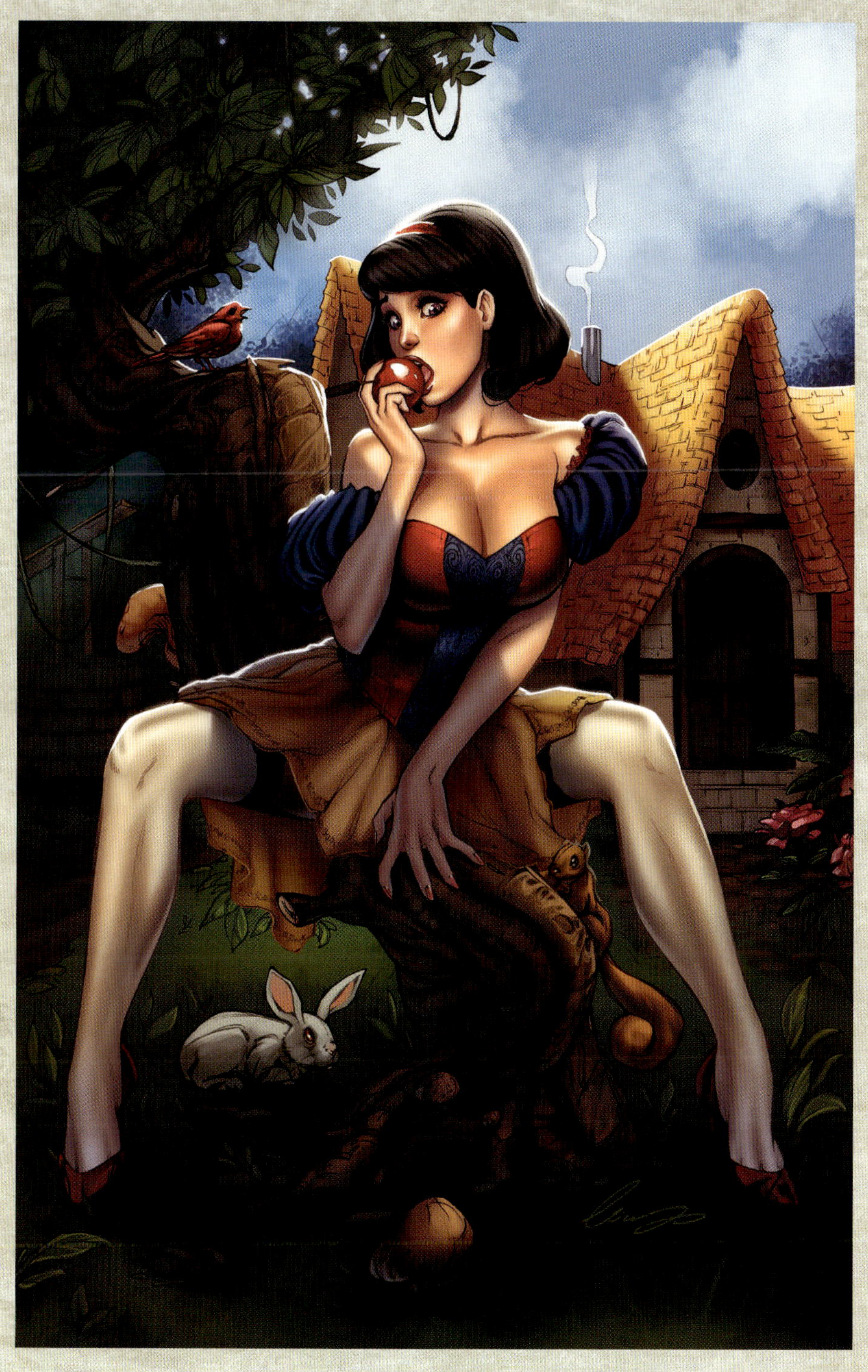

LEFT: ***Snow White***
Linda Vieweg Jackson

ABOVE: ***Snow White***
Elias Chatzoudis

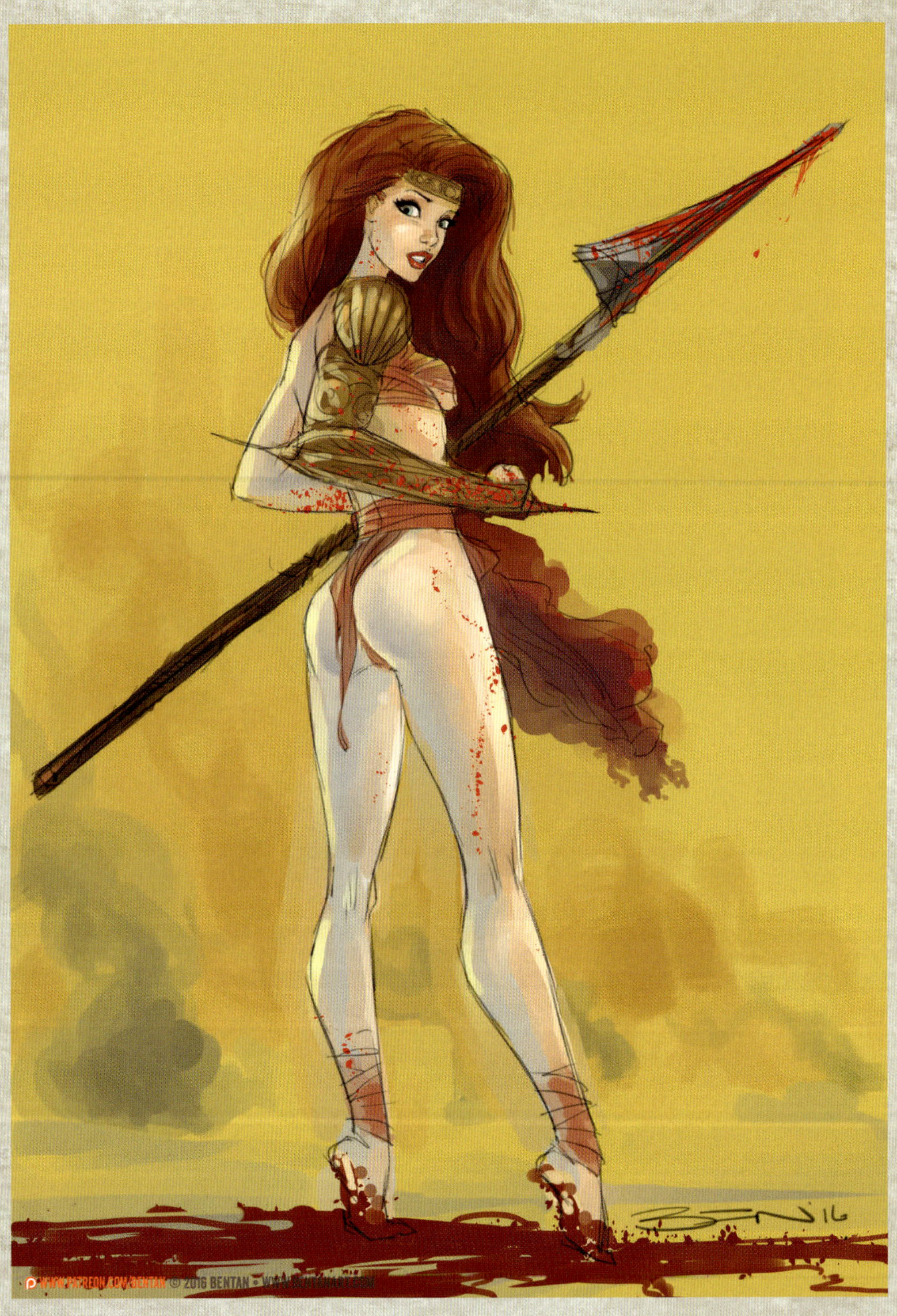

ABOVE: ***Warrior***
Ben Tan

RIGHT: ***Bettie Robbie***
Maly Siri

SAUCY ADVENTURE STORIES

MAY
25¢

!!

ROMANCE in a MAD UNIVERSE

an astonishing novel
By CYRIL MEYNIER

May

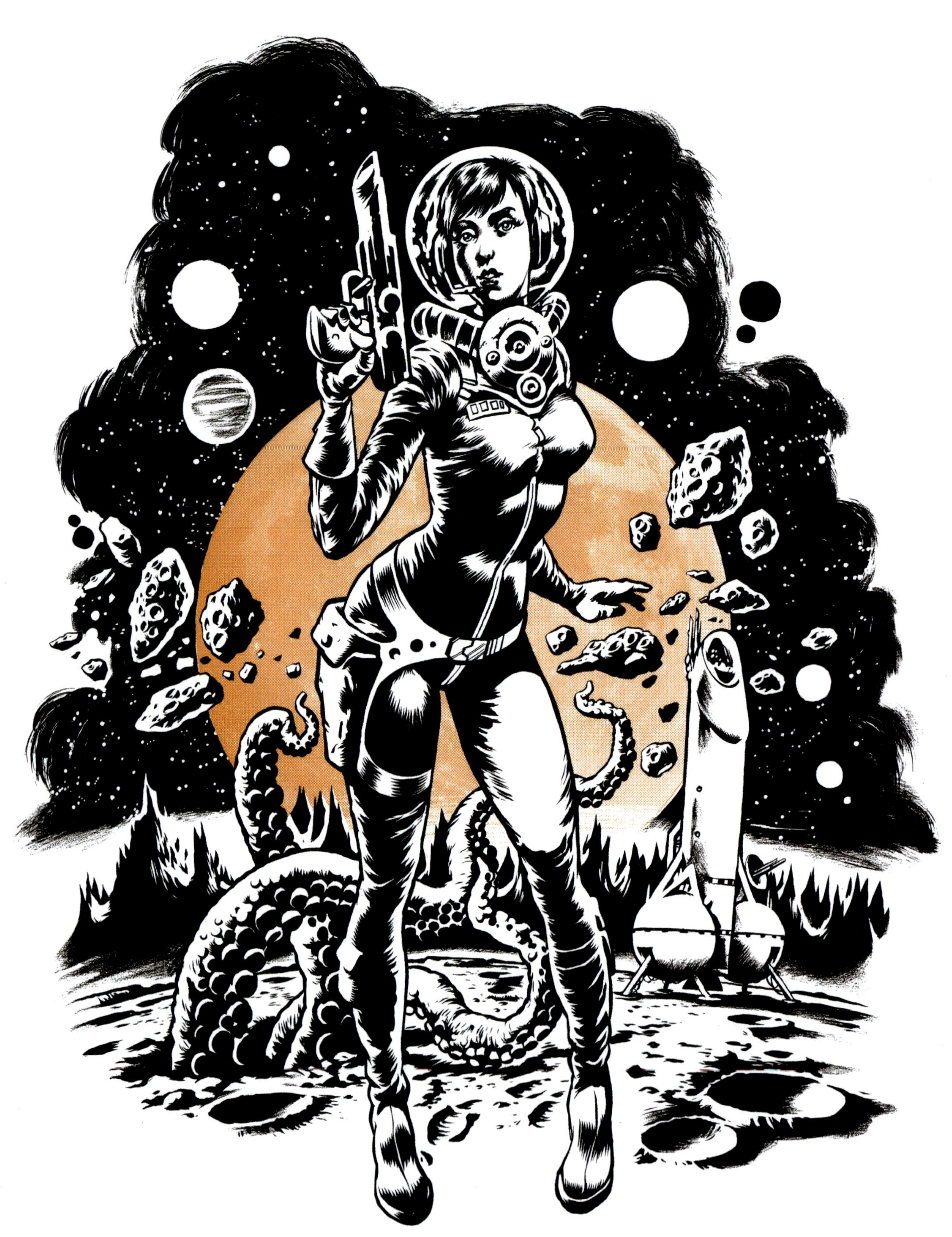

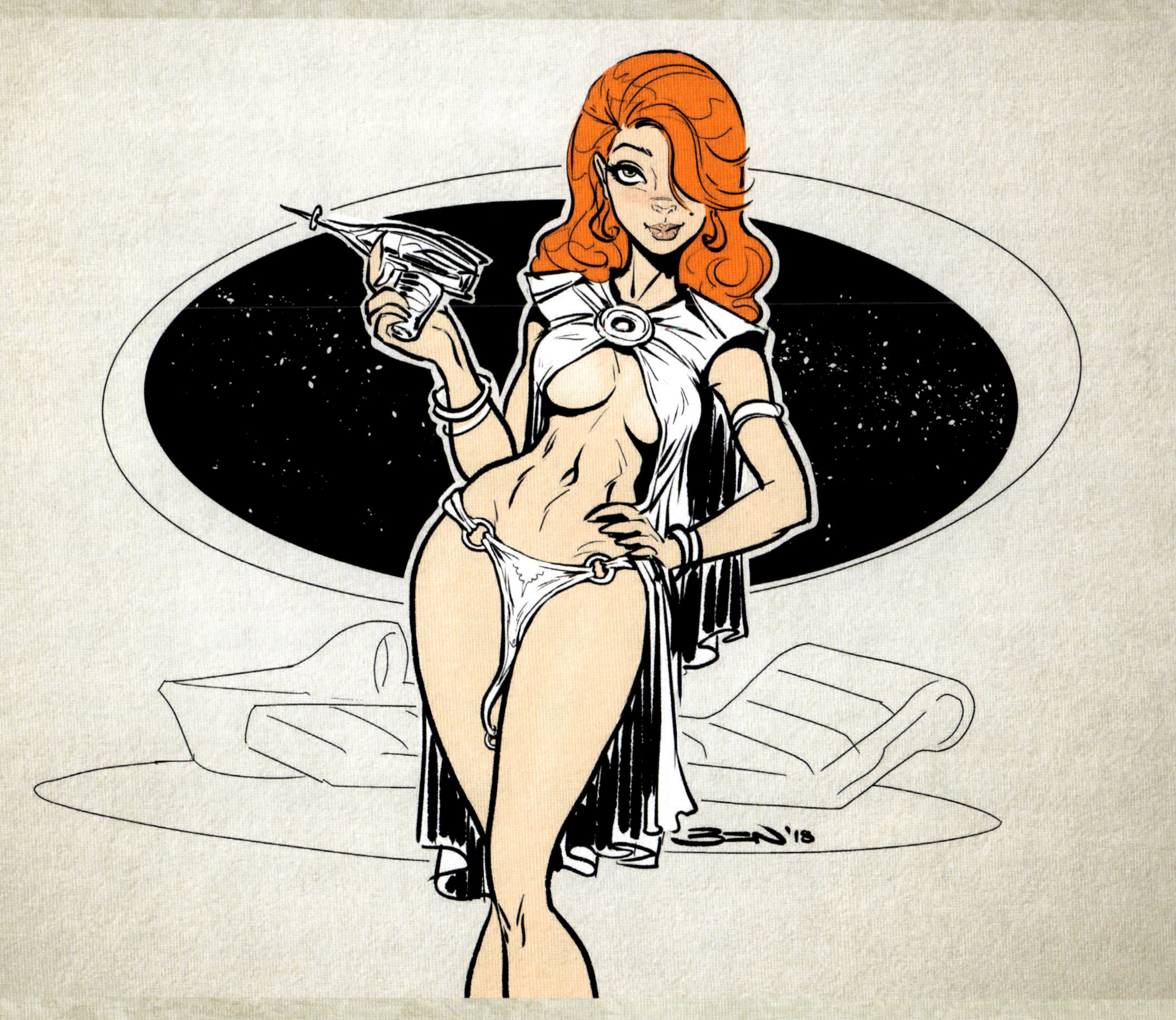

LEFT: ***Space Girl Kleur***
Erik Kriek

ABOVE: ***Space Vixen***
Ben Tan

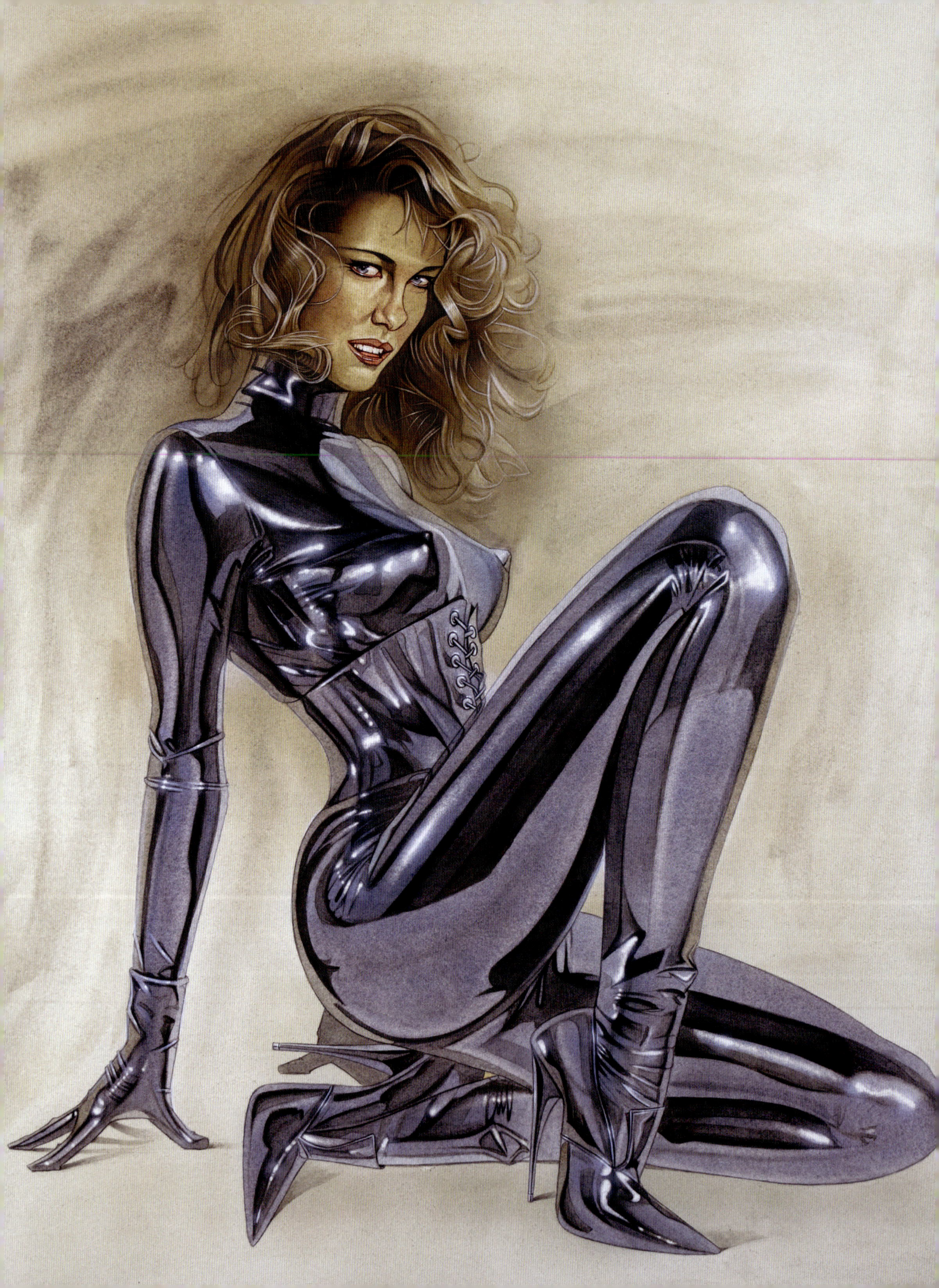

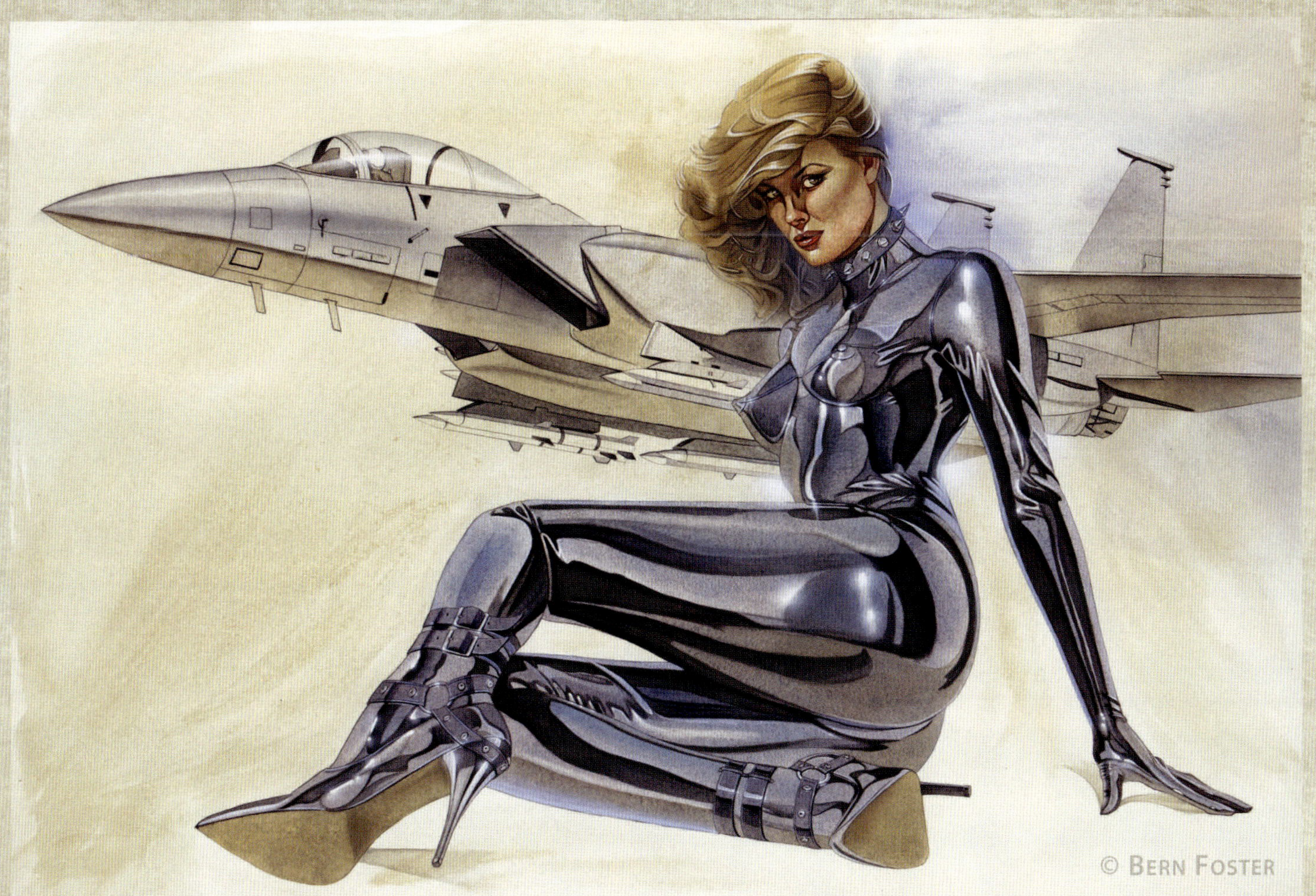

LEFT: ***Latex Girl***
Bern Foster

ABOVE: ***F15 Femme Fatale***
Bern Foster

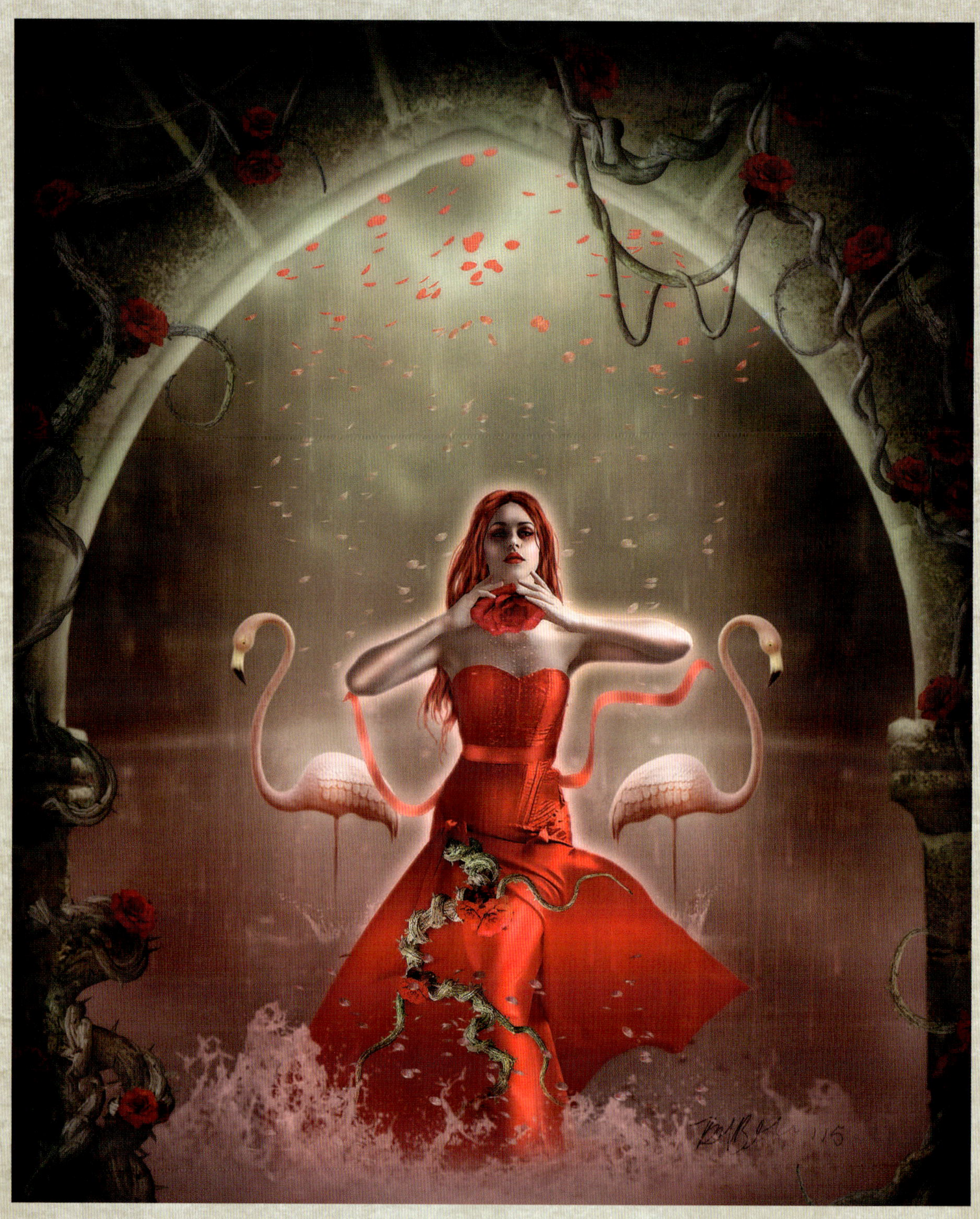

ABOVE: **Rose Water**
Bethany Spencer

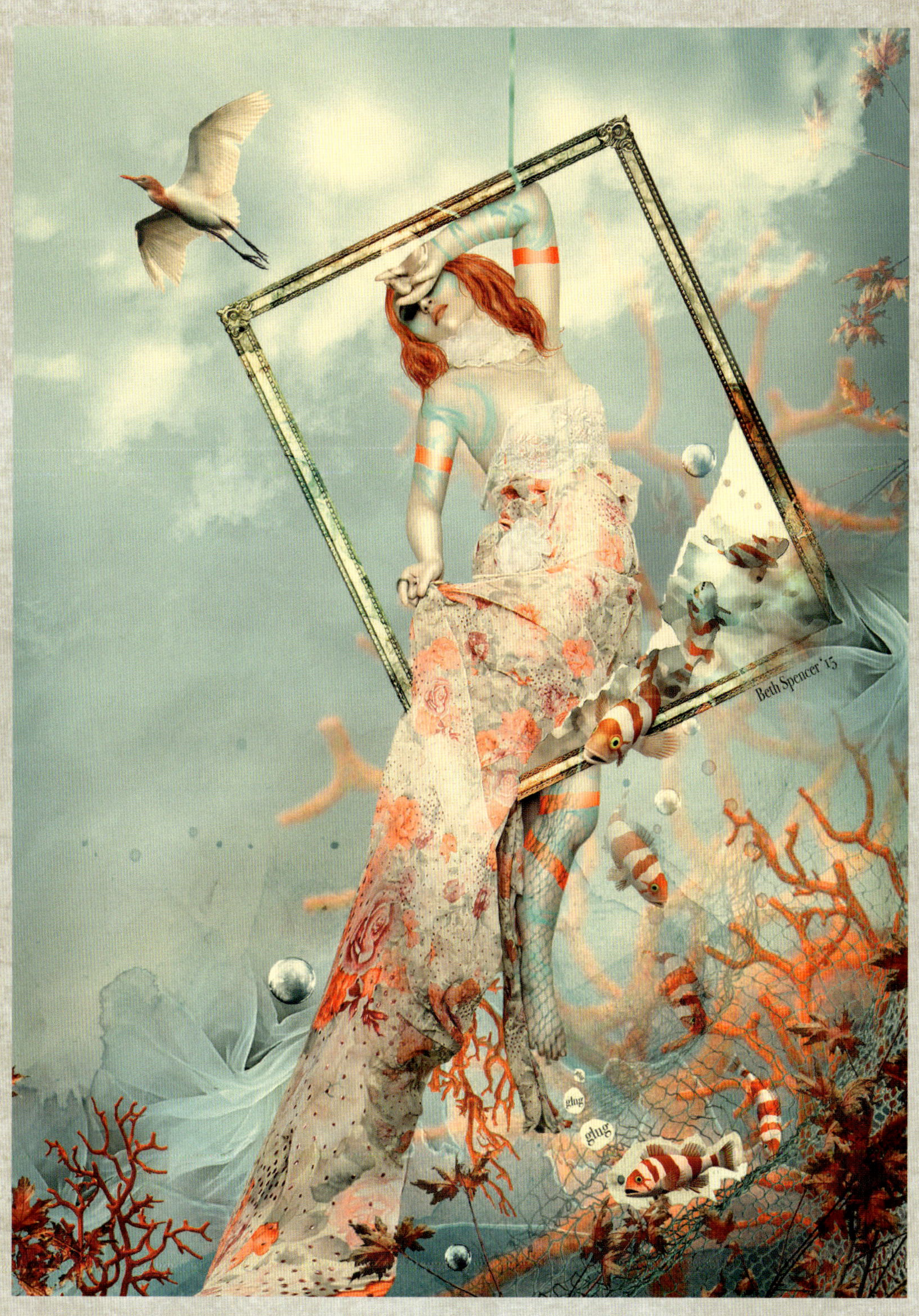

ABOVE: ***Water Colours***
Bethany Spencer

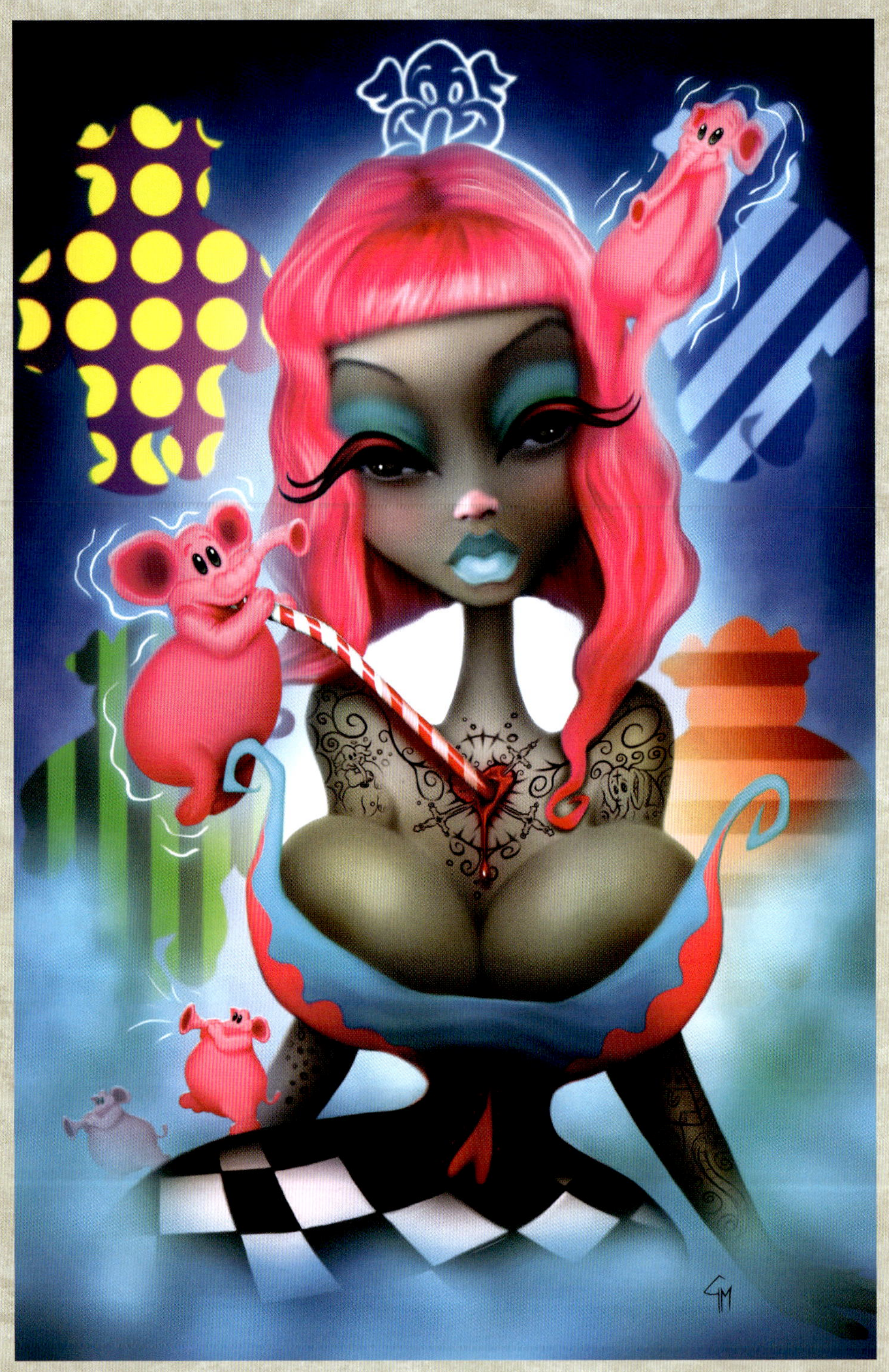

ABOVE: ***Pinktrip***
Gianluca Mattia

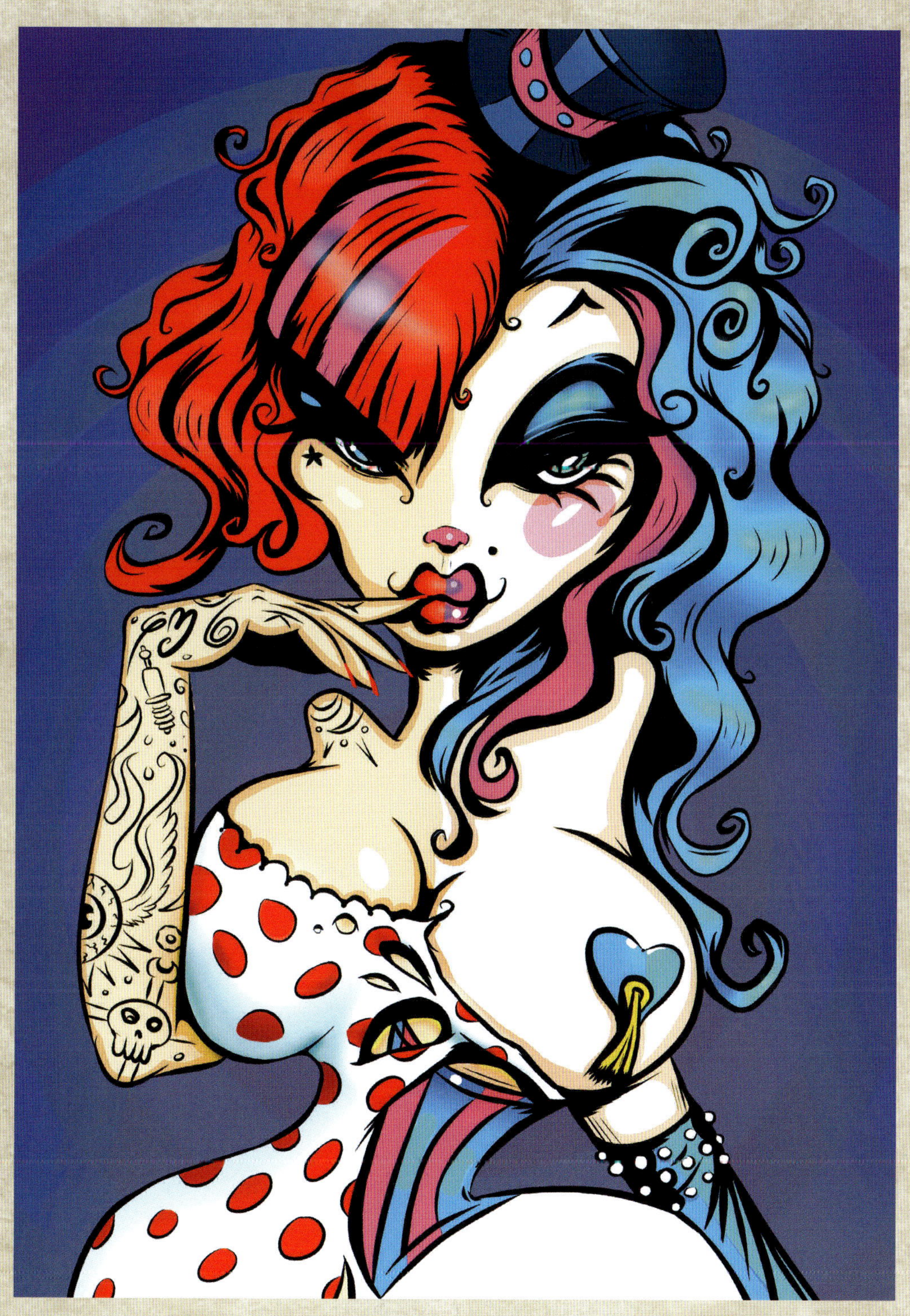

ABOVE: ***PinUp***
Gianluca Mattia

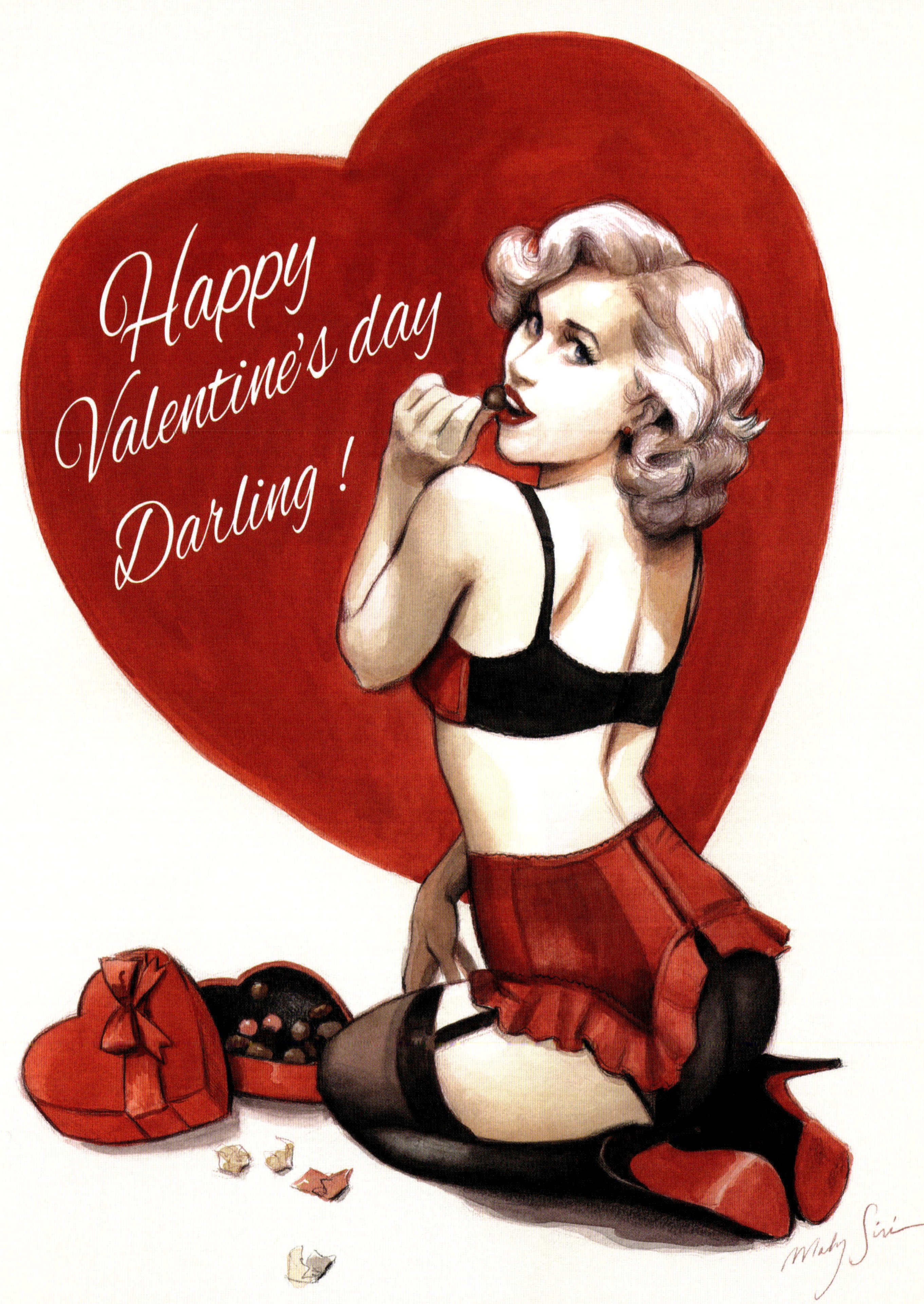
Happy
Valentine's day
Darling !

Holiday & Halloween

Christmas, Easter, Valentine's Day and Thanksgiving have provided a rich scenery for the pinup since the early cheesecake days. Opportunities for dress up, wholesome fun and of course domestic disaster are rife. Classic images of this genre are TN Thompson's *Snowman*, aghast at the skimpy festive skirt of a pinup, or Elvgren's *Valentine's Day* darling, covering her modesty with only a giant scarlet paper heart.

With the turn of the 20th century, the fear of the occult had waned and sexy met spooky; even adverts for cleaning products were adorned with images of racy witches. Every October, the United States was suddenly awash with the Halloween pinup emblazoned across illustrated postcards, playing cards, and party invitations. Hollywood got a handle on this and we were treated to publicity shots of starlets such as Ava Gardner in full witchy attire, or Judy Garland, clutching a ghost book in one hand and cuddling a black cat in the other.

These days, Halloween is a consistent favorite for pinup artists, with horror icons and supernatural characters being transformed into macabre minxes—the *Bride of Frankenstein* stares out of the page, all legs and lashes, never mind the green hue to her skin. Robert Bloch's *Psycho* is reimagined as Norma Bates and appears as a mini-dress adorned, blood spattered cutie. Tempting, but don't get too close!

LEFT: ***Valentine***
Maly Siri

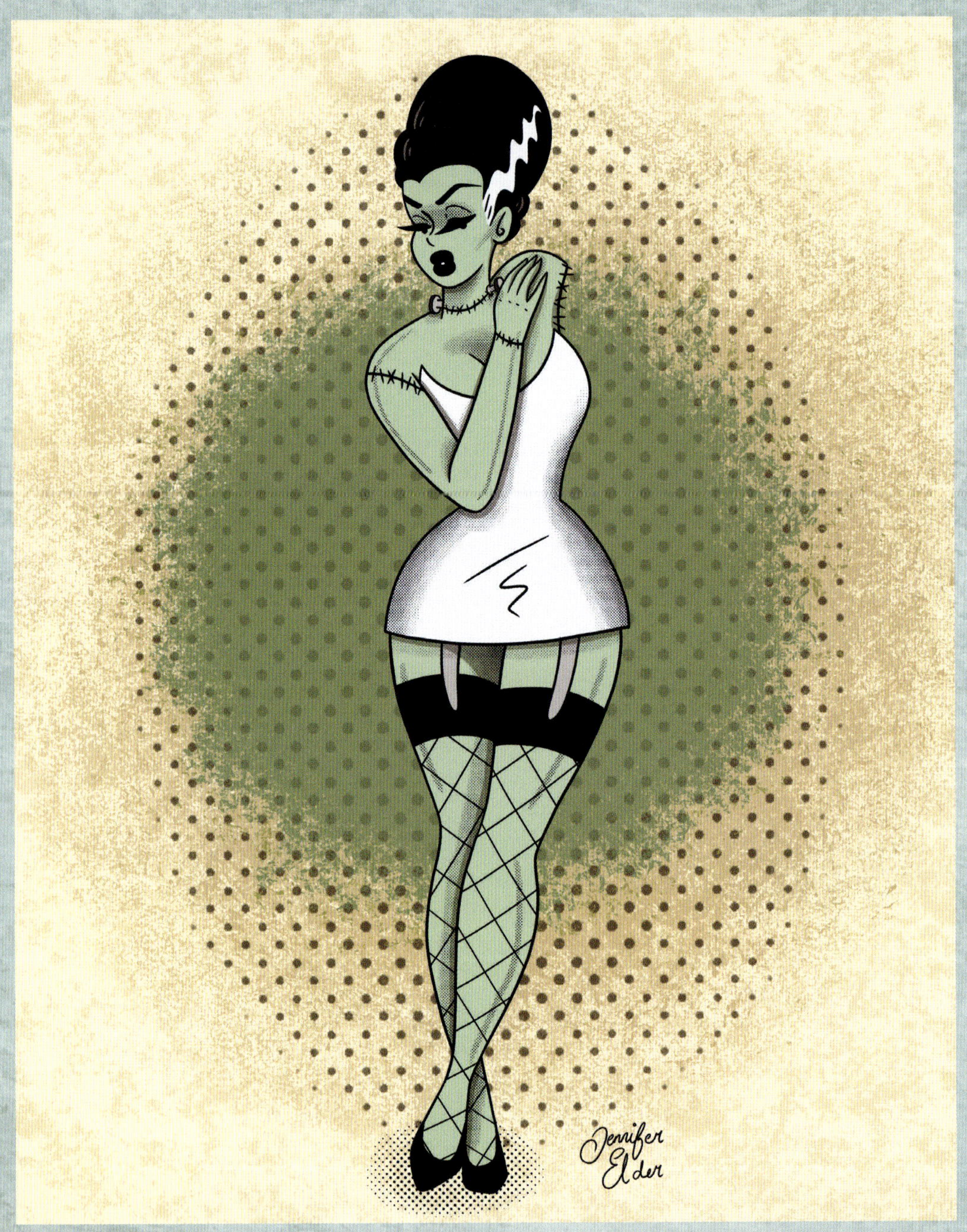

ABOVE: **Bride of Frankenstein**
Jennifer Elder

RIGHT: **Bettie and Skulls**
Ivan Valle

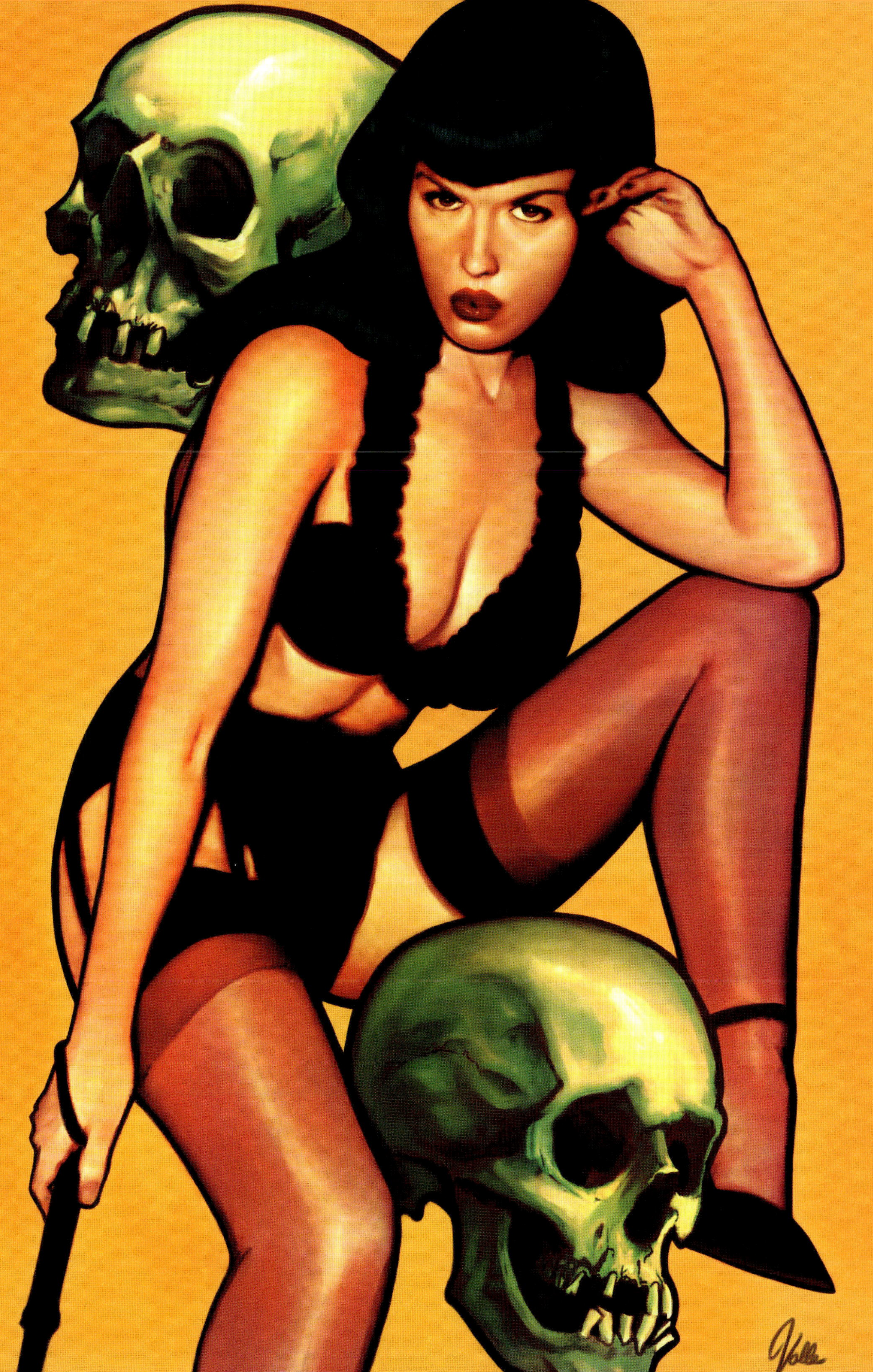

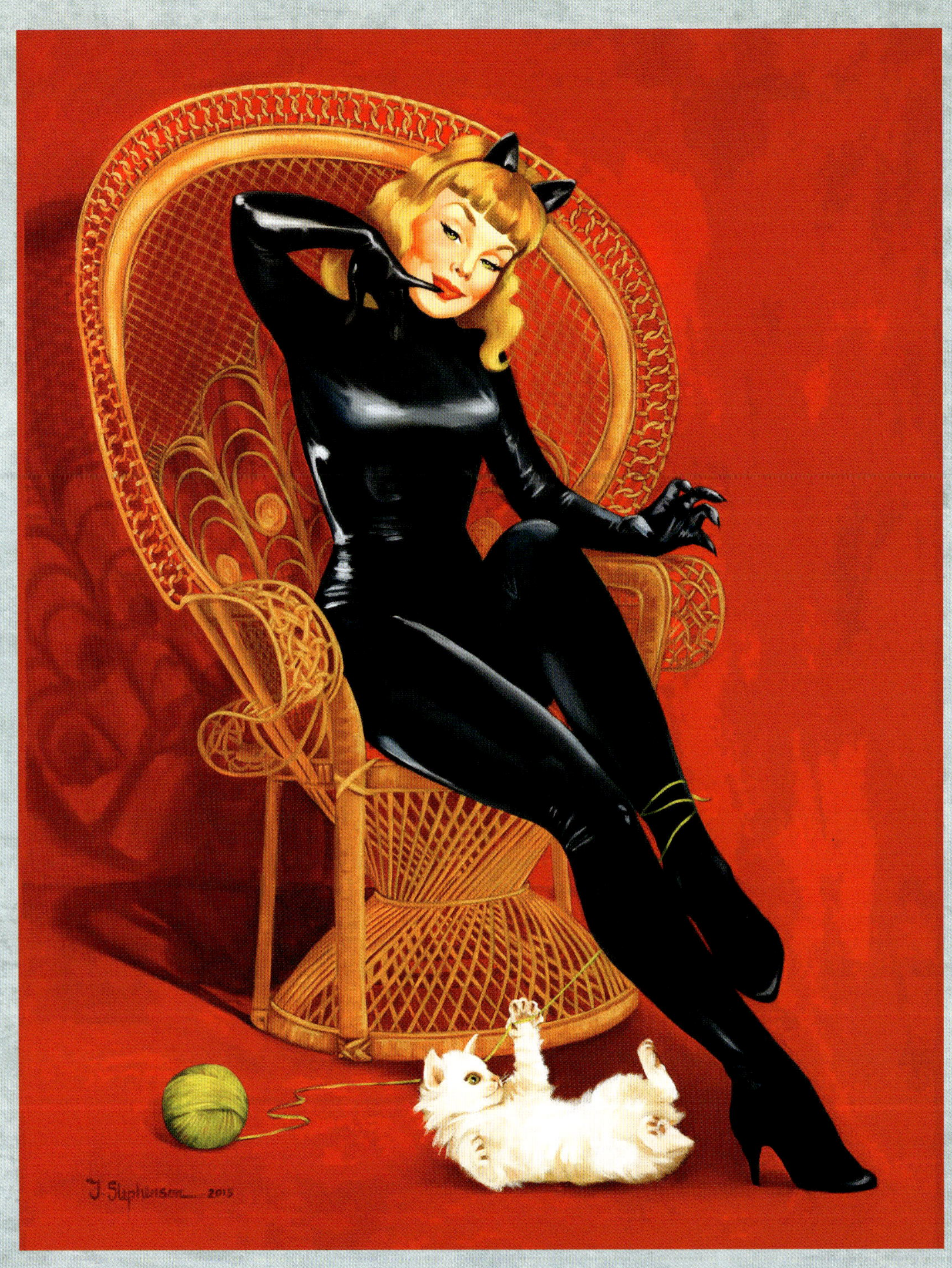

ABOVE: ***Feline Good***
Fiona Stephenson

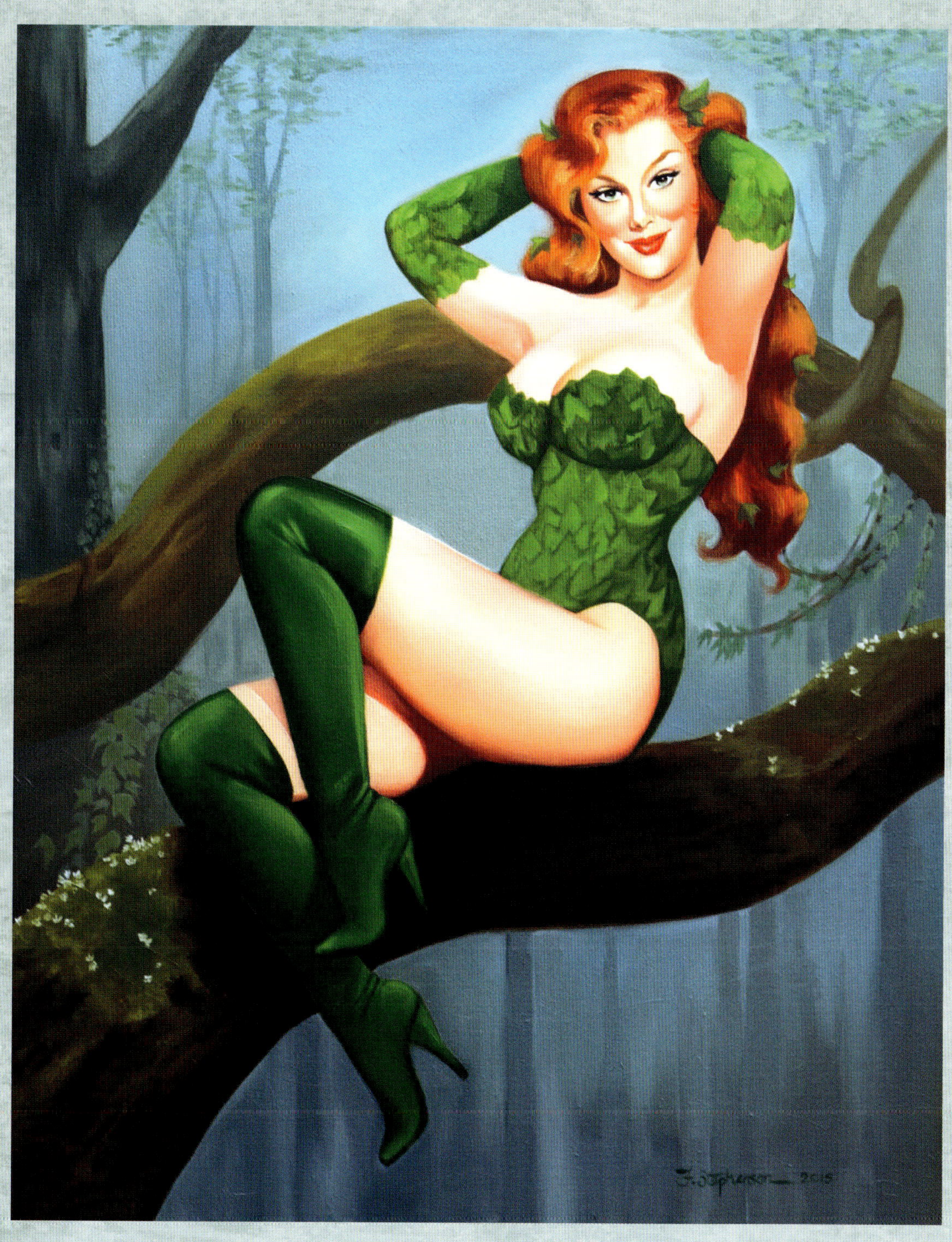

ABOVE: ***Splendid View***
Fiona Stephenson

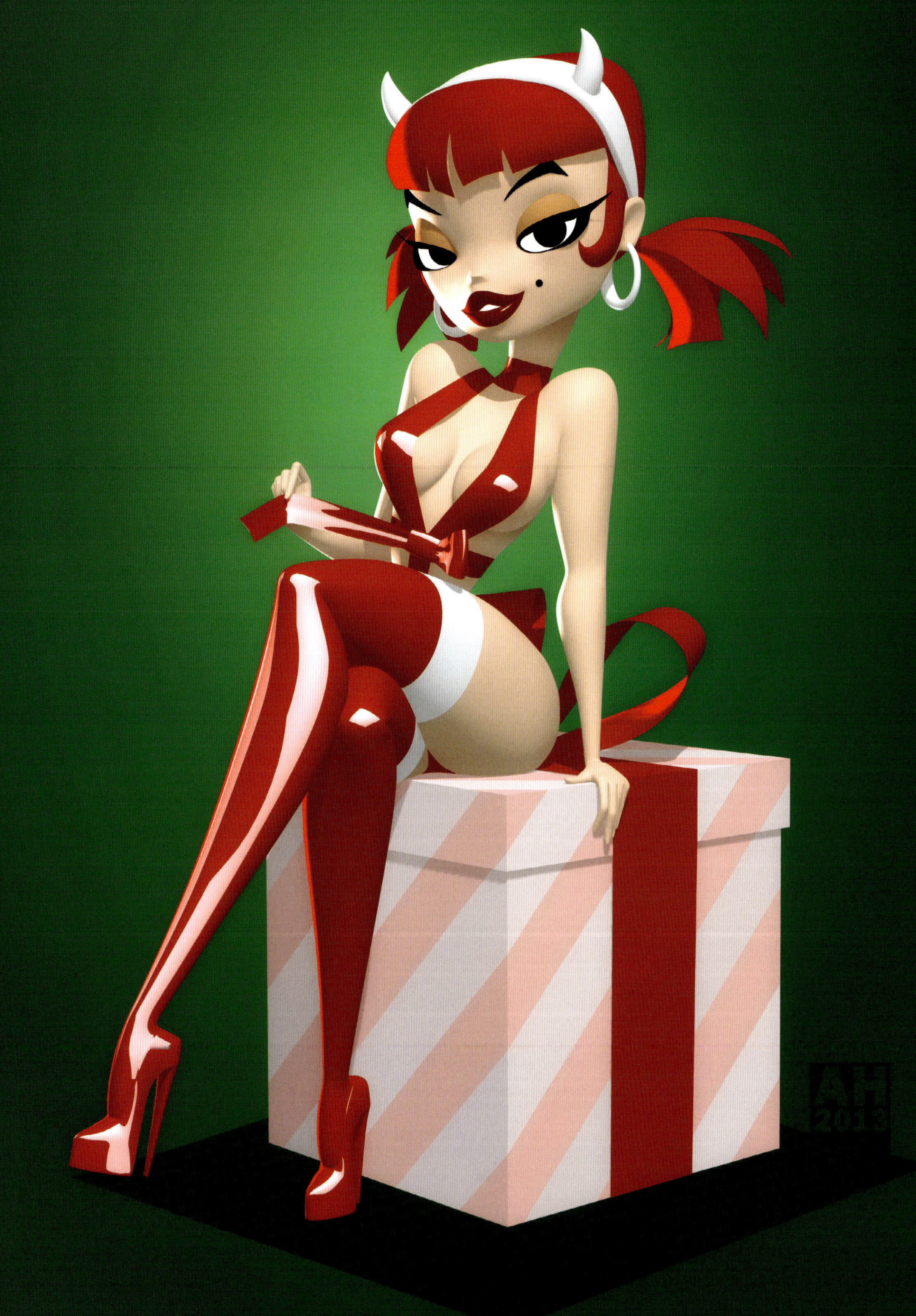
AH
2013

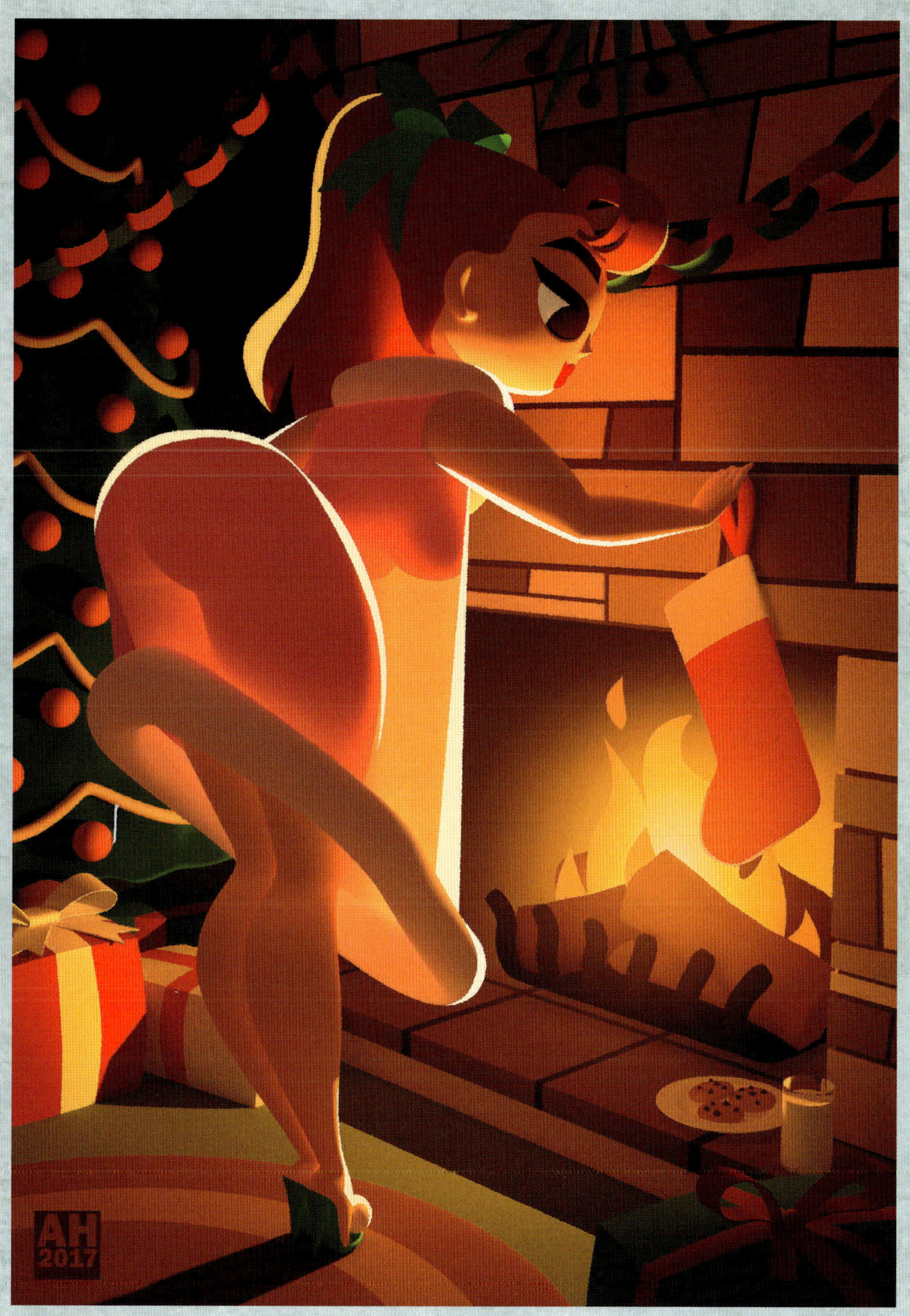

LEFT: ***Merry Trixmas***
Andrew Hickinbottom

ABOVE: ***Doris Decorating***
Andrew Hickinbottom

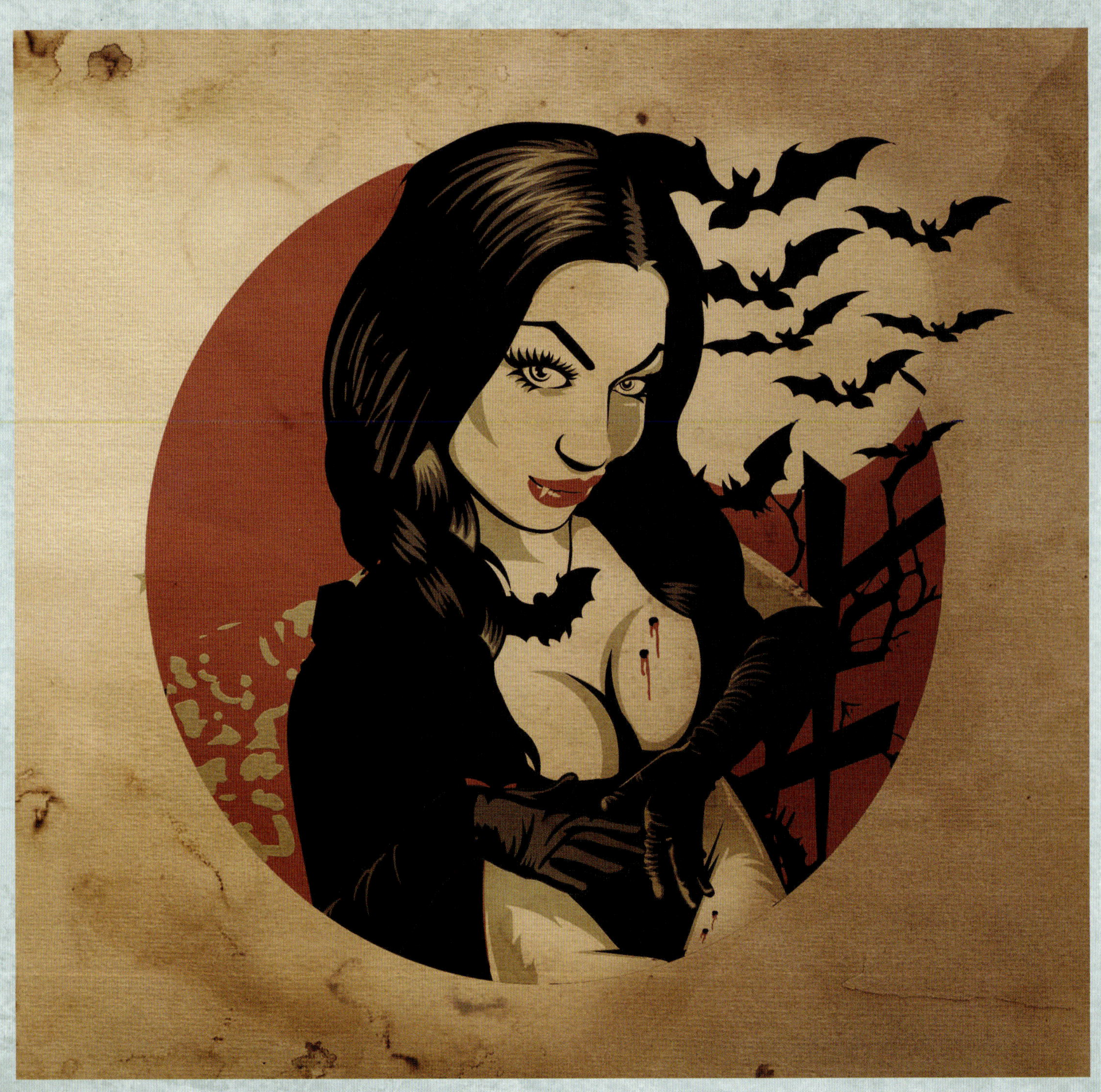

ABOVE: ***Vamp***
Leviathan

RIGHT: ***Lucy***
Claudia Hek

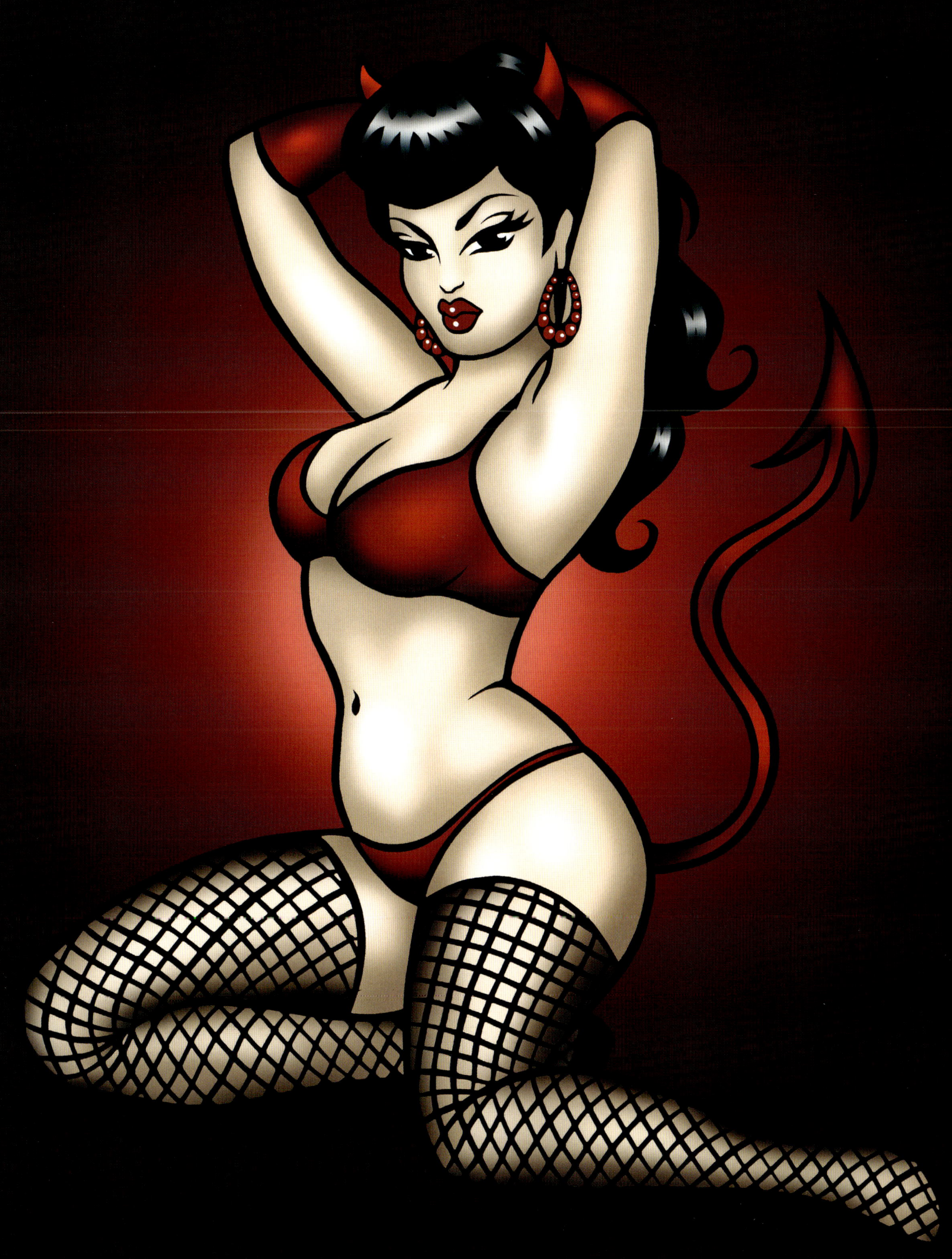

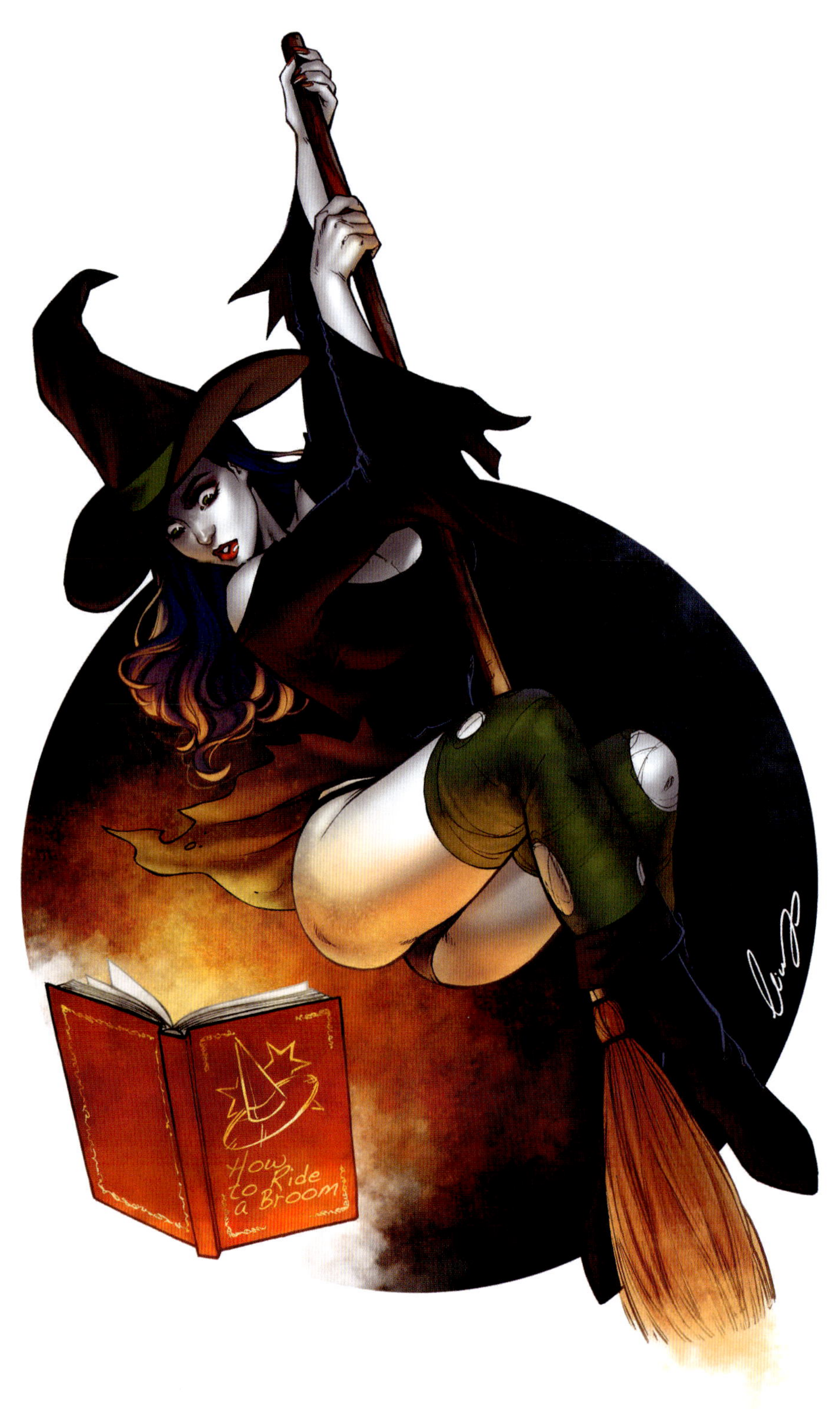

ABOVE: ***Witch Broom***
Elias Chatzoudis

RIGHT: ***Halloqueen***
Elias Chatzoudis

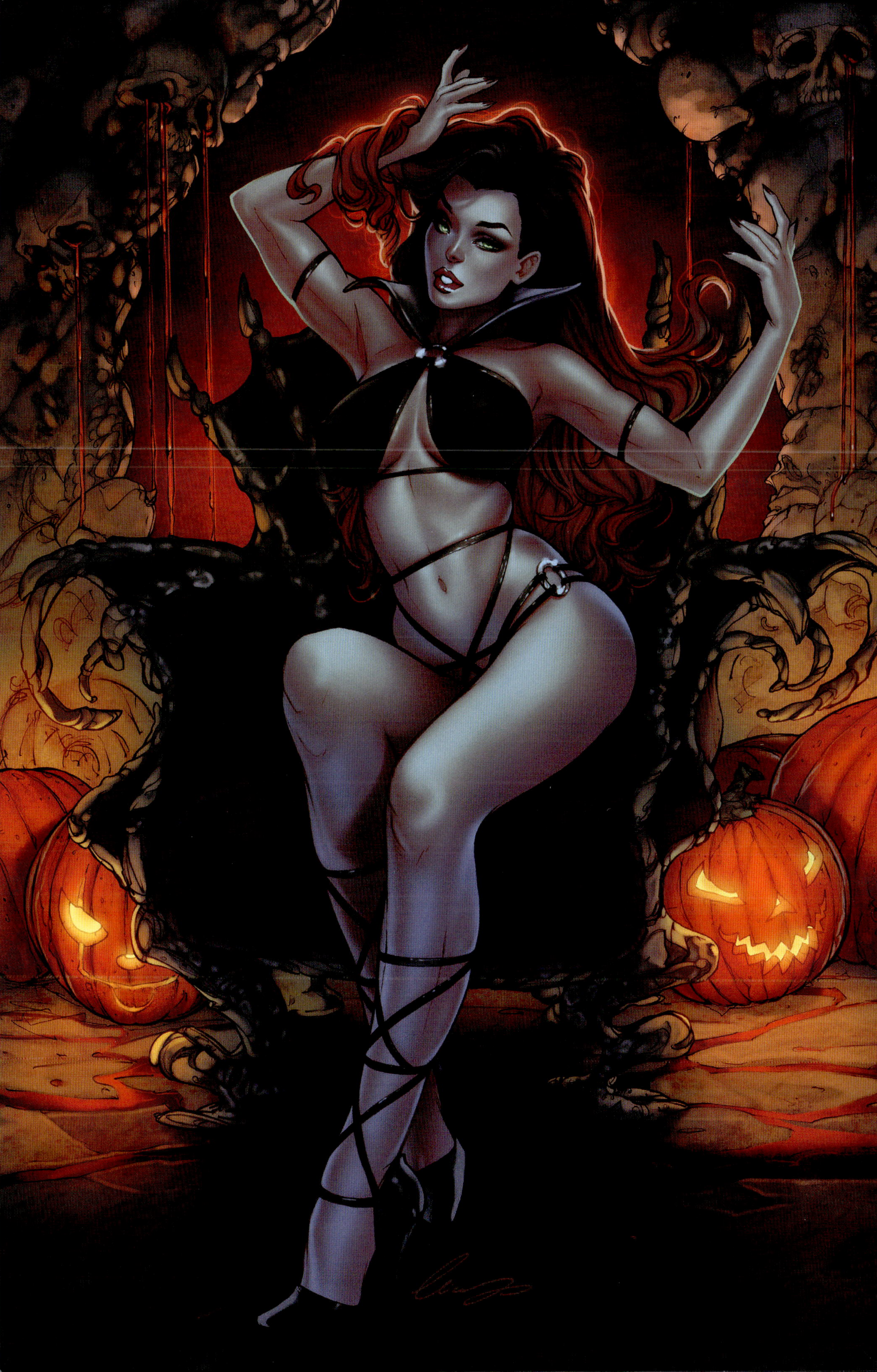

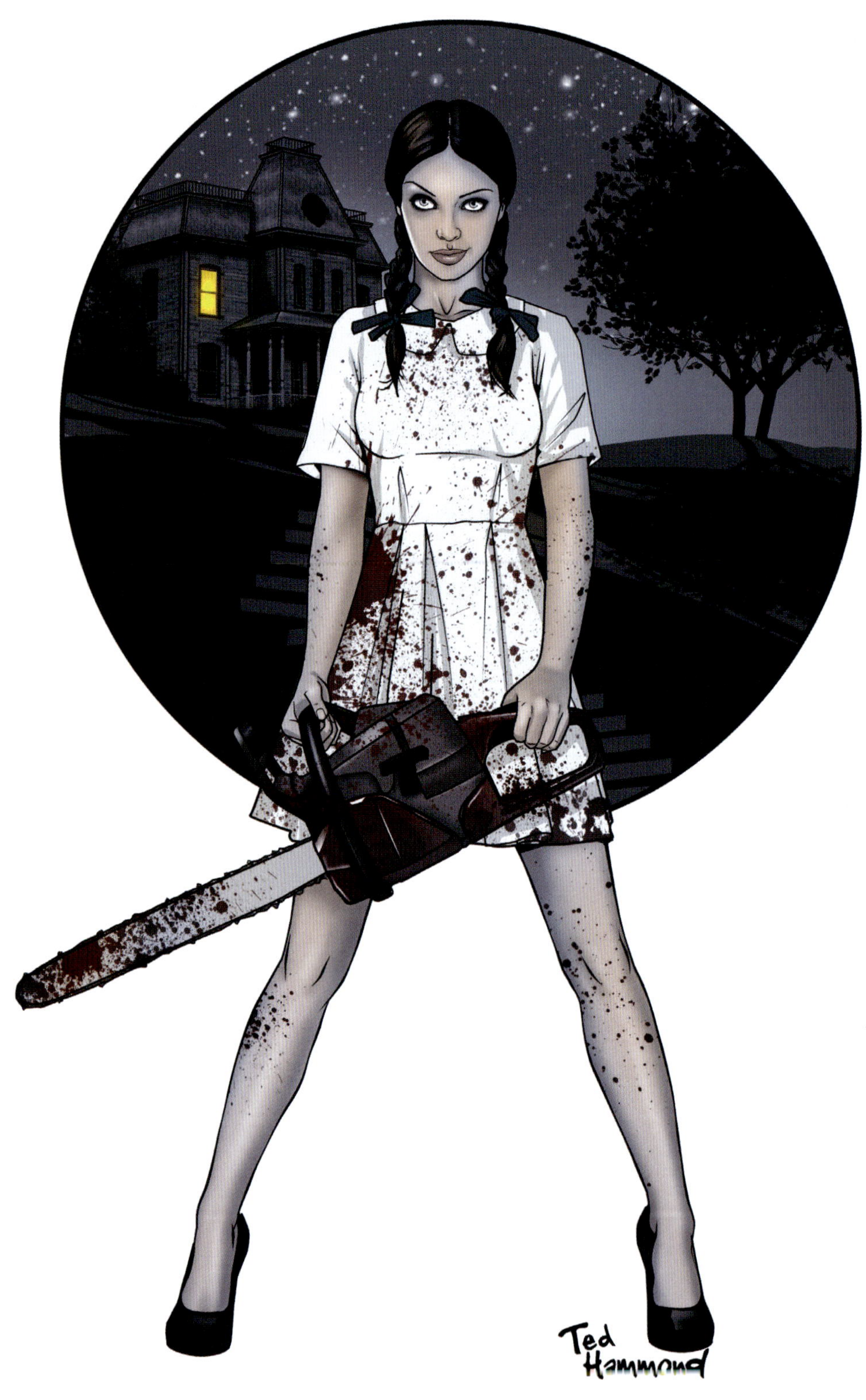

ABOVE: ***Norma Bates***
Ted Hammond

RIGHT: ***Bride of Frankenstein***
Linda Vieweg Jackson

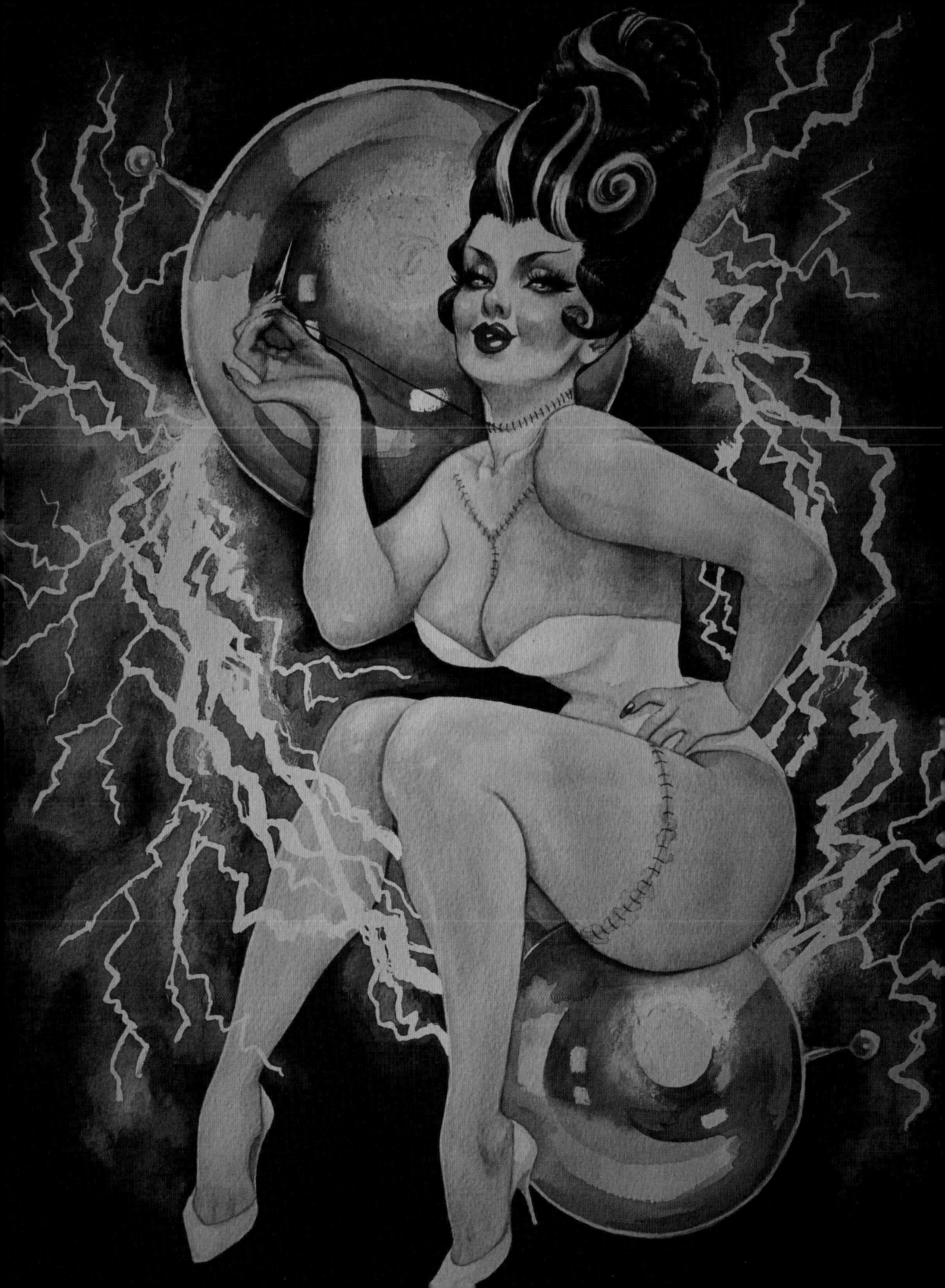

Artist Contact Details

All artworks are the copyright of the artists, unless indicated otherwise.

Marco Almera
California, USA
www.marcoalmera.com

Matthew Britton
Wales, UK
www.matthew-britton.com

Elias Chatzoudis
Athens, Greece
www.eliaschatzoudis.com

Jennifer Elder
Scotland, UK
www.jenniferelderart.bigcartel.com

Bern Foster
Cadiz, Andalusia, Spain
www.bernfoster.com

Nik Guerra
Tuscany, Italy
www.nikguerra.it

Ted Hammond
Mississauga, Ontario, Canada
www.tedhammond.com

Claudia Hek
Amsterdam, The Netherlands
www.claudiahek.com

Andrew Hickinbottom
London, UK
www.andrewhickinbottom.com

Adam Isaac Jackson
Tacoma, Washington, USA
www.adamisaacjackson.com

Linda Vieweg Jackson aka DarlinDesign
London, UK / Sweden
www.freelanced.com/darlindesign

Erik Kriek
Amsterdam, The Netherlands
www.gutsmancomics.com

Leviathan aka Manel LaVey
Valencia, Spain
www.leviathan13.com

Mad Mac
Bari, Italy
www.pinupart.it

Gianluca Mattia
Bari, Italy
www.gianlucamattia.com

Guillaume Poux
Barcelona, Spain
www.elgunto.com

Nathalie Rattner
Calgary, Canada
www.nathalierattner,com

Dirk Richter
Hanover, Germany
www.dirkrichter.art

Erica Lynn Shaw
Southern California, USA
www.erilynns.com

Sveta Shubina
Rostov-on-Don, Russia
www.etsy.com/shop/SvetaShubinaGallery

Maly Siri
Montreal, Canada
www.pinup-doodles.blogspot.com

Lorenzo Sperlonga
Los Angeles, California, USA
www.lorenzosperlonga.com

Bethany Spencer
North Dakota, USA
www.artbyvacuumslayer.com/

Fiona Stephenson
Barnsley, South Yorkshire, UK
www.fionastephenson.com

Ben Tan
Bay Area, San Francisco, USA
www.bentanart.com
Ivan Valle
California, USA
www.instagram.com/ivan_vallena

David Vicente
Salles, France
www.dvicente-art.com

Acknowledgments

Front cover art:
David Vicente.

Back cover art:
Back cover images (clockwise from top left):
Sunshine Smile, Fiona Stephenson; *Geisha*, Lorenzo Sperlonga; *Usher*, Sveta Shubina; *Hawaii*, Mad Mac; *Wilco*, Leviathan.

Acknowledgments

The Publisher would like to thank all the artists included in this book. Their brilliant, and very different, takes on pinup show what good health this art form is in, and also keeps the traditions of the form alive by providing inspiration for a new generation of artists.

If you have enjoyed the images in this book, we would encourage you to go and visit the sites of your favourite artists and to buy a print, or even better, commission an original work. It's a a very satisfying thing to do and will give you or a loved one hours of pleasure into the future.

In our increasingly digitised and automated world it is the work of original artists, and their creative spark, that remind us that we are humans who love individuality outside the frame of Facebook, Instagram and Whatsapp. You'll be amazed how great it is to look at something which isn't on a screen!

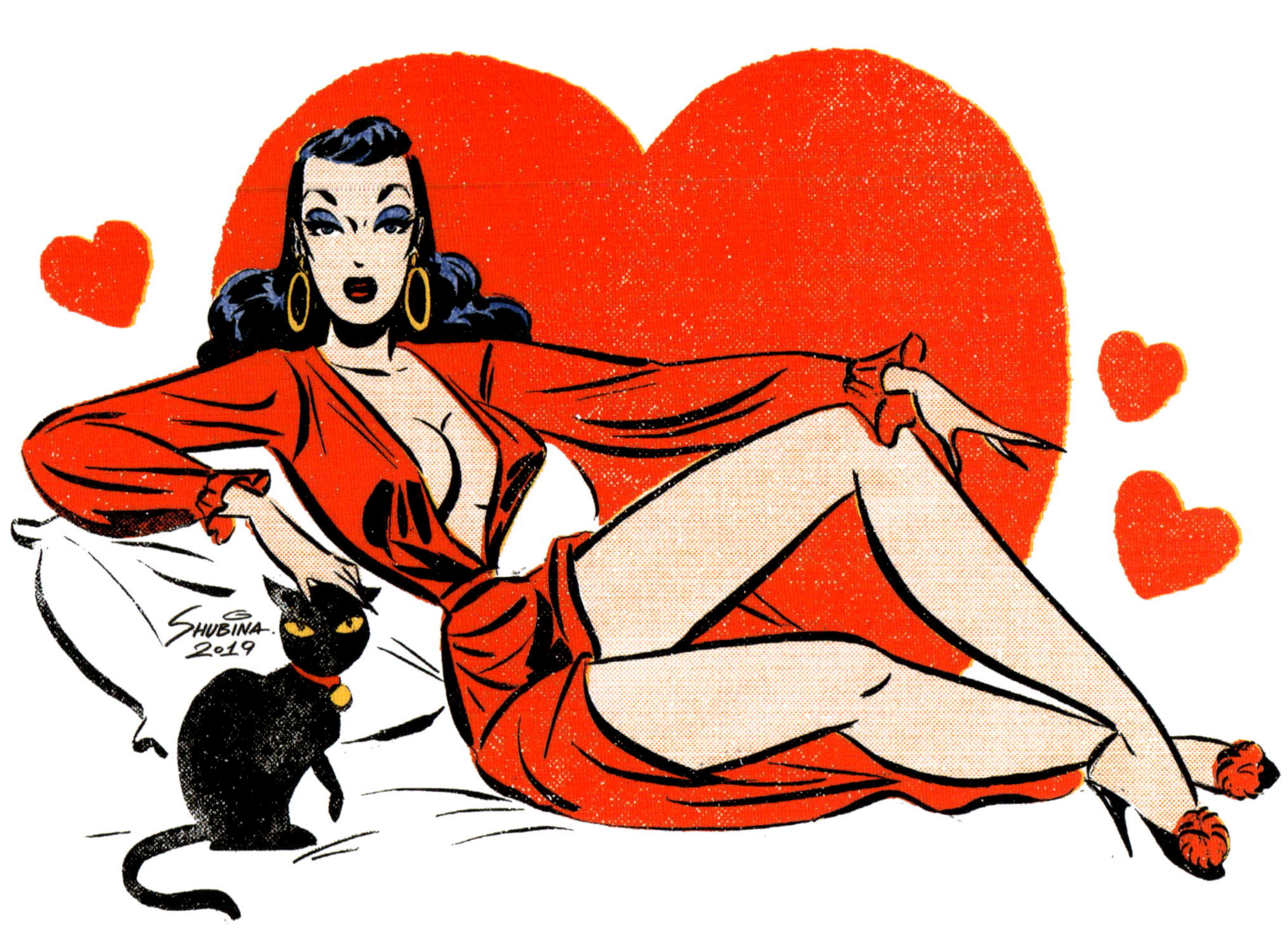

ABOVE: **Cattie**
Sveta Shubina